THE QUEST FOR QUEEN MARY

First published in 2018
By Zuleika
89G Lexham Gardens, London, W8 6JN

Printed in England
Designed by Euan Monaghan

A CIP record for this book
is available from the British Library

ISBN 978-1-9997770-3-6

Princess Victoria Mary of Teck

THE QUEST FOR QUEEN MARY

JAMES POPE-HENNESSY

Edited by Hugo Vickers

ZULEIKA

CONTENTS

PART ONE: THE COMMISSION

By Hugo Vickers

INTRODUCTION

Q ueen Mary, the widow of George V, and grandmother of the Queen, died at
Marlborough House on 24 March 1953, a few months before the Coronation.
She was eighty-five years old. Unusually for a Queen consort, an official biography
was commissioned. The last such exercise was the life of the Prince Consort, commissioned by Queen Victoria. The task was entrusted to James Pope-Hennessy.

Pope-Hennessy was a writer of considerable distinction, but he was young
to be chosen – thirty-eight years of age. Born in 1916, he came from an intellec-
tual Catholic family. His mother, Dame Una Pope-Hennessy, was herself a well-
known writer, who produced books on Sir Walter Scott, Edgar Allan Poe, Charles
Dickens, Canon Charles Kingsley and many others. His brother, Sir John Pope-
Hennessy, was an art historian, who rose to be Director of the Victoria and Albert
Museum in London, then of the British Museum, and finally Chairman of the
Department of European Paintings at the Metropolitan Museum in New York.
While both brothers were still in the nursery they were given type-writers, and as
they grew up they were paid by their mother to type her manuscripts (though she
made deductions for mistakes).

James was educated at Downside and Balliol College, Oxford. From his earliest days he was destined to be a writer, and during his life he held few regular jobs.
He worked for a Catholic publishing firm; he served as private secretary to Sir
Hubert Young, Governor of Trinidad; he worked in military intelligence during
the war; and he was literary editor of the *Spectator* from 1947 to 1949. His first
book, *London Fabric* (1939), won the Hawthornden Prize.

His personal life was always somewhat chaotic. James Lees-Milne wrote: 'A
natural rebelliousness was accentuated by his unremitting homosexuality ...
Although physically attracted to his own sex he loved the companionship of
women to whom most of his enchanting correspondence was addressed. They
were fascinated by his understanding and sensitivity. All his life he was much
sought after by hostesses for his sparkling conversation.'[1] His friends were
amongst the most interesting artists, writers and muses of their generation

– Cecil Beaton, James Lees-Milne, Clarissa Churchill (now Countess of Avon), Joan Moore (Countess of Drogheda), Viscountess Rothermere (Ann Fleming), and others. His brother, John, described him thus:

> I had never known James really well. I had boundless admiration for his talent, but his life seemed secretive (more so to me than to other people, I suspect), and I looked upon his forays into low life and smart society with some reserve. Years later, a close friend, Maud Russell, described him to me as 'two characters lodged in one shell. The serious, hardworking, self critical (so far as his writing was concerned) workmanlike being, and that other self, wild, careless, unheeding. A person might easily have known only one half of him and not had a clue to the other half.'[2]

John Pope-Hennessy also addressed James as a writer:

> James regarded himself as an artist, in the rather old-fashioned way that writers in the 1920s and 1930s had been prone to do. He was unintellectual, not in the sense of being unintelligent (he was indeed extremely clever), but of being uninterested in criticism or in ideas. Most of my friends were my own contemporaries; most of his were much older or younger than himself. In the 1950s it worried me that his life seemed to be built around people he was likely to outlive. The determining influence on his career as a writer was a wise woman of extraordinary intuition, Lady Crewe[*], who recognized that his gift was biographical and that to realize it he required original material. Lord Crewe, as a result, gave him free access to the papers of his father, Lord Houghton[†], who, as Richard Monckton-Milnes, was a centre of cultural life in London in the middle of the nineteenth century and wrote the first biography of Keats. Originally intended as a short memoir, the book grew into a two-volume biography. This was not his most popular but is to my mind his most accomplished and durable book. The payoff was a volume on Lord Crewe. Hardly was this off the press when the telephone rang on my desk, and I heard James's voice

---

[*] Lady Margaret Primrose (1881–1967), daughter of 5th Earl of Rosebery, married 1st Marquess of Crewe, KG (1858–1945), Liberal statesman.

[†] Richard Monckton-Milnes, 1st Lord Houghton (1809–85), English poet and politician.

saying, rather contemptuously, that he had been asked to write the official
life of Queen Mary ...[3]

Pope-Hennessy had indeed established his reputation as a biographer with the
two volumes on Monckton-Milnes, which were published in 1949 and 1951. He
published his biography of Lord Crewe in 1955, a book which even he admitted
was less than inspired.

It was, however, the biography of Crewe that led to his appointment. Crewe's
daughter, Lady Cynthia Colville, had been a long-serving Lady-in-Waiting to
Queen Mary. She suggested him to Sir Owen Morshead, the Royal Librarian.
Morshead wrote to Pope-Hennessy on 13 June:

Dear Pope-Hennessy,

I wonder whether, after you have finished with Lord Crewe, you would
care to undertake the official life of Queen Mary? Your researches into the
period and circumstances of Lord Crewe's life would be useful: and no less
so would be your friendship with Lady Cynthia. John's experience at the V.
& A. would help you in that important aspect of Her Majesty's life. I would
give you every assistance in my power, and make free of all the papers.

The timing is not important; Wheeler-Bennett's life of King George VI
must appear first (because of the Abdication) and that will not be for 12 or
18 months yet. The financial arrangements and choice of a publisher would
rest with you.

I hope very much that you will feel able and free to undertake this task.
You are free to discuss it with Lady Cynthia: and for my part I would wel-
come the opportunity of a discussion with you either here or in London.
But I am in no hurry.

Sincerely yours
Owen Morshead.[4]

When offered the commission, Pope-Hennessy was determined to turn it down.
He even drafted a letter to Sir Owen telling him that 'with the deepest regret ... I
do not see how, at present, I can accept this flattering commission.'[5]

Two things changed his mind. His brother John was horrified that he intended
to turn the project down. He asked him to come and see him and gave him the
vital clue as to the tone he should adopt:

Royalty, I explained, were an endangered species, and this was an occasion to establish, through close inspection of a single life, the nature of the phenomenon.'[6]

The second was the promised discussion with Sir Owen which clearly put James's mind at rest and fired his imagination.

The commission was duly announced in the papers on 8 July 1955. *The Times* reported a statement from Buckingham Palace the previous evening to the effect that the Queen had been 'pleased to place the writing of a book about Queen Mary in the hands of Mr James Pope-Hennessy.'[7] This news was greeted with enthusiasm by two historians who had tackled royal biographies. Sir John Wheeler-Bennett, official biographer of George VI, wrote to Harold Nicolson, official biographer of George V:

He is an admirable choice, and indeed I cannot think of anyone who could do it better. I do not envy him the job, as I am afraid there is rather a paucity of material, and many of her associates are no more. However, there are bound to be a lot of letters about somewhere, if he can run them to earth.[8]

Nicolson then wrote to Pope-Hennessy:

I have a feeling that you will write a really first class book on this subject and that you will at least be able to indicate why this seemingly cold and unhappy woman managed to arouse much affection, and to remain a very interesting personality.[9]

Not everyone was so convinced. George VI's former Private Secretary, Sir Alan Lascelles, by then in retirement at Kensington Palace, had never met Pope-Hennessy. He telephoned Morshead to ask him 'why, and by whom, this unknown young man, who had probably never clapped eyes on Q.M. had been entrusted with writing her biography.'[10] Some time later he checked this with the Princess Royal, who confirmed the reason for the appointment: 'I rather think it was due to Cynthia Colville and Owen Morshead that he was chosen. You may remember he wrote a life of Lord Crewe.'[11]

As it happens, Pope-Hennessy had once met Queen Mary with Lady Crewe at her home, West Horsley Place in Surrey, during the summer of 1949. It was an event he had described to his brother John:

Bridget* [Lady Victor Paget] & I were at Horsley Saturday to Monday. Sunday was ruined by the arrival of Queen Mary to tea – in itself very interesting & enjoyable, but made hideous by Peggy's fussing all morning: she altered her mind about which room for tea 4 times, and had the butler put up 3 different kinds of table in the hall. It should have been a simple thing, as there was just us three, Queen Mary & Lady Cynthia. They arrived on the dot of 4, having hovered round Leatherhead because, as the roads are cleared by sirens, the journey had taken half an hour and she didn't want to be early. Lady C <u>read</u> to her in the car coming down, can you imagine a more awful task?

I was absolutely delighted by her, and immensely impressed. She is much larger than I expected, and looks miraculously new and clean – huge expanses of laundered chintz dress, a white lawn choker round the neck, with a colossal diamond suspended from it, a snow-white parasol and snow-white gloves, a little toque of pale magenta & pale blue violets – the whole incredibly appetising and agreeable.

I sat next to her at tea, and she was extremely agreeable, though not starting conversations ever, and Peggy kept thinking up something to say: 'Bridget never eats anything, Ma'am' – 'Yes I do' rather angrily. 'Perhaps you eat secretly?' asked the Queen. She has a very funny twinkle in her eye and is obviously capable of being great fun. She looked at everything, taking 3 hours, until our knees were cracking, & Lady Cynthia evidently counts it *lèse majesté* to sit down in a room in which the Queen isn't as long as she is somewhere in the house. Peggy moved Bridget & me about like pawns ('Now you had better go up to the Drawing room by the big staircase and I will bring her up by the little one'), and there was a great [deal] of hissing ('upstairs or downstairs, Cynthia?') about the washing

---

* Hon Bridget Colebrooke (1892–1975), younger daughter of 1st Lord Colebrooke, Permanent Lord-in-Waiting to King George V. Married 1922, as his second wife, Lord Victor Paget, divorced 1932. She had been a mistress of the Duke of Windsor, when he was Prince of Wales. She disapproved deeply of Mrs Simpson for addressing the Prince as 'David'. She said: 'In my day one either called him Sir or Darling.'

of the royal hands. She was genuinely interested in the Goethe autograph and the books I showed her.

Peggy telephoned thru' to London in the evening to find out (Bridget says) whether we'd passed muster and was told we were both thought 'enchanting', so we were given champagne for dinner and generally treated like good children.[12]

This story has a curious post-script. After his appointment as Queen Mary's biographer, Pope-Hennessy had access to her meticulously kept diary. Naturally he looked up the date to see what impression he had made on the dowager Queen. Turning to the page, he found Bridget Paget named, but he himself merely described as 'and ?'

* * *

Pope-Hennessy embarked on his three year quest for Queen Mary in 1955. It was to take him to many royal courts and to the lunch and tea tables of retired courtiers and ladies-in-waiting. He had access to a great number of private documents. He was shown royal residences both in England and in Europe. Part of the time he lived at the Gasthaus zu Scharfen Eck, Hagnau, Bodensee, in Germany, where the cost of living was cheaper and he was able to write quietly. As he went along, he kept notes of what he saw.

His approach to these interviews is well-captured in an exchange between the two brothers in 1958. John wrote to James of a lunch at Pratolino, the summer home of Prince and Princess Paul of Yugoslavia. Princess Marina, the sister of Princess Paul, was there, as was their cousin, Princess Irene, Duchess of Aosta (sister of Queen Helen of Romania). John wrote:

That barrage of royal questions is so difficult. 'How old is your brother?' Topic then changed. 'How much older are you than your brother?' Another change of subject. Then more questions. I do not understand why they cannot ask everything they want to know at once. James replied: 'I can easily give you a simile for royal questions. I see their minds like conveyor belts for luggage at London airport. First comes one's own suitcase, then someone else's typewriter, then *drei Stücke*, later another piece of one's own luggage. They usually forget what they have asked you when you are in the midst of a reply, and you find they have moved on to a discussion of flying-saucers or drinking habits in Zanzibar.[13]

And so James Pope-Hennessy set about researching one of the best royal biographies ever to have been published. The process took from the summer of 1955, when the book was commissioned, until the end of 1958. Extracts from *Queen Mary* were serialised in the summer of 1959, and the book was itself published that October.

It was to be a long journey for Pope-Hennessy, taking him to German castles, to Frogmore, Osborne, to meetings with the sources, and to others that Pope-Hennessy did not write up in that way. Between 1956 and 1958, he met the Landgrave of Hesse, Lord Stanmore, Prince Wolfgang of Hesse, Sir John Wheeler-Bennett, Monica Hesketh (who gave him letters from Queen Mary and oddments), Lady Phipps, Prince Ernst August of Hanover, Queen Helen of Romania, and Lord Hardinge of Penshurst amongst others. He was never short of encouragement, the Princess Royal writing at one point: 'It is so nice to hear from time to time how you are getting on.'[14]

On 10 February 1957 he met Sir Alan Lascelles, who was to play a signicant role in the production and eventual publication of the book. Tommy Lascelles took a liking to the young author and became a great supporter of his book, as did his wife, the former Joan Thesiger, daughter of Lord Chelmsford, one time Viceroy of India. Lascelles had lately lost his son John from cancer in 1951 and to a certain extent Pope-Hennessy filled this void.

Lascelles was a crucial witness to the key years covered in the book. He had served as Assistant Private Secretary to the Prince of Wales (later Duke of Windsor) from 1920 to 1929, at which point he had resigned in despair. He had returned to royal service as Assistant Private Secretary to George V in the late months of 1935. He never saw the King during this phase, because of his death the following January. Lascelles had then served Edward VIII under Sir Alec Hardinge in 1936, and been deeply shocked by the Abdication. He was Assistant Private Secretary to George VI from 1936 until 1943, when he effected the forced resignation of Hardinge, and took over as Private Secretary. He served George VI in that capacity until the King's death in 1952, and stayed with the present Queen until the end of 1953, thus overseeing the early days of her reign and the Coronation.

Following a dinner at the Beefsteak Club on 25 July 1957, Pope-Hennessy noted for the first time some of the things that Lascelles told him. Relevant to Queen Mary are the following:

Told me that King George V was far and away and without any question 'the most physically repulsive man' he had ever seen.

Reminded me of Queen Mary's reaction to the Prince of Wales's newly done up panelled room at St James's. He had had a copy made of her portrait, and framed in the panelling, and was in a great twitter about her opinion of the whole thing. When she came to see it with him, she merely looked round and said coldly: 'What a funny sort of room to find in a palace, David,' quite crushing and discountenancing him and his pride in the room.

That the story I had heard of King George V saying 'David' would never reign was nonsense; had he even suspected it he would have altered his will. In this he left Sandringham and Balmoral to his eldest son, so that the new King George VI had no property of his own and had to buy his brother out with a colossal sum. No-one at all, neither Baldwin, nor Queen Mary, nor Lascelles himself, ever *dreamed* up to the last moment that he *could* or *would* abdicate. When he heard it that evening, Sir A.L. was so stunned that he went out & walked 3 times round St James's Park in the darkness, thinking of James II.

That he agrees with my highish opinion of the Duke of Gloucester's I.Q.

That King George and Queen Mary were inexplicably disastrous parents.

That Queen Mary's low opinion of her father-in-law [Edward VII] is shown by the fact that she passed without comment the whole of the Henry Ponsonby book*, which was sent to her in typescript to censor.

That my view of Queen Mary's intense egotism was correct and well-founded. He thinks she can never have been in love in her life. On this point he again stressed King George's physical repulsiveness. He was much worse than most *strictly ugly* people can ever be. It sounded indefinable but very positive.

---

* *Henry Ponsonby, Queen Victoria's Private Secretary – His Life from His Letters* by his son, Arthur Ponsonby (Macmillan, 1942).

Major Wickham is roughly speaking mad, but I should see him …[15]

Lascelles put Pope-Hennessy right on many points concerning the Duke of Windsor and the Abdication, the reaction of Dominion Governments to this and so forth.

Later on, as he read the text, Lascelles advised him on how to deal with Sir Owen Morshead, and other problems:

What he wants is *cosseting* – stroke him continually like a cat, & he is yours for keeps. He has a suppressed inferiority complex, & he laps up friendly gestures like cream. You, with a very little effort on yr. part, can have him exactly where you want him.[16]

He agreed with Morshead about the portrayal of Princess Helena Victoria, daughter of Princess Christian, and therefore a granddaughter of Queen Victoria:

I told you long ago you weren't doing justice to poor Snipey – sending her down to posterity with nothing but a long nose. O.M. is quite right – she was an old pet, & I loved her. 'Much the best of those two Holstein girls,' the old D. of Connaught used to say.[17]

Pope-Hennessy began to write the book before he had finished his interviews. To do this, he kept copious notes on every possible aspect of Queen Mary's life. These are preserved in separate files, all beautifully typed, dated and organised. From these he wove his story. From notes in his day-to-day diary, it is not clear how much time he himself spent working in the Royal Archives at Windsor. He certainly went there from time to time, and the notes indicate considerable work carried out on Queen Mary's papers, either by him or by a research assistant.

Pope-Hennessy was approaching his work as a kind of ornithologist in quest of a rare species – observing with his sharp eye the figures who kindly helped him. But he never lost sight of the main quest: to present the life of Queen Mary to his readers.

In this, he was acutely aware of the various gates of censorship through which his book would have to pass. He kept his brother John informed of his progress. These letters give an insight into how he tackled his various problems. For example, while in in Hagnau, he reached 1892 and the illness and death of the Duke of Clarence. This preoccupied him for a month or so between April and May 1958:

I have begun today on the Duke of Clarence, irresistible; and highly tricky. I think I can get away with *murder* if everything is presented as making Grannie grander and stronger & *more utterly marvellous* – coming up *fighting* after *each* fresh trial, don't you see?[18]

He continued:

The drama of the Duke of Clarence passing of course can't be repeated twice in a lifetime, today I have killed off Princess Mary Adelaide, alas, also removed the Duke of Teck from the board – a tiny bit previous, but as he went mad so soon after her death we needn't think about him again – his daughter didn't. I have now got the Strelitz scandal which I daresay won't pass muster at the censorship but my idea is to write it *all* as it was, so as to deposit one copy at B.M. [British Museum] or somewhere, telling all the truth?[19]

He pursued the Strelitz scandal:

Am at work currently on Chapter 4 (= sixteenth chapter) in which Aunt Augusta's eldest Strelitz granddaughter, aet:19, is raped by one of the Palais footmen & gives birth to a bastard – the Duchess of York in her heroic way coping with all – *rather newsy*, in fact. Isn't Grannie turning out fine ? Surmounting all her difficulties & more admirable page by page – such is my aim & intention.[20]

To his brother he was also able to speculate in a way that he felt would be inappropriate in the final book. He posed John a question regarding the painter, Thaddeus Jones*:

Does it transpire to your accomplished eye that the Duke of Teck was in love with Thaddeus Jones, who was then removed (Chapter VII) by Prince William of Württ[emberg] (a notorious homosexual)?? 'Company of bright young officers' in earlier chapter also slanted that way, like a rocket-site.[21]

_____

* Henry Thaddeus Jones (1859–1929), Irish portrait painter.

By August he had reached the Coronation of King George V and Queen Mary in 1911:

> Motherdear [Queen Alexandra], in the fourth cycle of our drama, emerges as an ageing, saddened, heroic figure. Our heroine is wearing so many jewels upon what the present Queen would call her buzzum, that one is quite dazzled. Also 'the pink muslin with convolvulus' and 'the pinky *mousseline de soie* with hollyhocks'.[22]

In October he went to stay with Lady de Vesci, and wrote about the First World War. This completed some 500 pages of the book. The last 120 pages or so were finished in the remaining two months of 1958 (which included his memorable visit to Badminton, and his look into the Duke of Windsor's papers at the Mill).

By the end of the year, the book was effectively finished and had been read, chapter by chapter, by both Tommy Lascelles and his wife Joan. Lady Lascelles wrote to him: 'With a lump in my throat & tears in my eyes I have just put down your final chapters.' She commended what she called his 'keynote of simplicity and truth'.[23]

At about this time, Pope-Hennessy read Wheeler-Bennett's *George VI*, which had lately been published. He concluded that he did not like it, finding it 'poorly constructed, so *parti pris*, so undramatic yet at the same time unserene'.[24]

He departed for a much-needed break in Venice where he remained until 14 January. His long journey with Queen Mary was coming to an end. A week later he confessed to his brother: 'I feel like the Queen (ER II) who said : 'I cannot imagine a world without her'.[25]

* * *

To have finished the book was a significant milestone but by no means the end of the saga. The book had to be checked and approved. Throughout its construction, Pope-Hennessy had worried about this major hurdle. It was a process that lasted between January and May 1959.

Lascelles helped him a great deal behind the scenes. As early as September 1958, Lascelles prepared the way by writing to Sir Owen Morshead:

> I've never read a biography that delighted, moved and amused me more intensely. I've no hesitation in calling it a masterpiece ... Indeed, I can and

shall, most truthfully tell the Queen that there is not one word in the book that cld distress her, or any member of the Family; if occasionally a harsh word is in the text, that word is from royal lips (letters or diaries) & never from the pen of the author. I am left with the strong impression that *all* the royals mentioned – even obvious scallywags – were really much nicer individuals, and better citizens, than one ever thought.

Another feature of the book wh I find interesting is the clear picture it gives of the roles played by minor royalties in the European world of eighty years ago.

As for the two Queens concerned – Victoria & Mary – I like them both far better than I ever did before. [26]

Pope-Hennessy had to face Sir Owen Morshead, whose knowledge of Danish was clearly limited, asking him whether it was really necessary to describe Queen Louise of Denmark as 'Droning Louise' – he wondered if this was an adjective 'denoting a silly old droner'. Pope-Hennessy was obliged to explain to Morshead that that was the Danish for Queen.

Sir Michael Adeane, the Queen's Private Secretary, pointed out that Sir Edgar Boehm was Austrian not German, that Craig Owen should read Craig Gowan, that it was George Andrew McMahon not Macmanus, and that though there were Counsellors of State, there was not actually a Council of State. He questioned the 'alcoholic rumour' on page 313. They failed to notice a few errors, such as that Mar Lodge was north, rather than south, of the Dee.

In a rare move for those days, Pope-Hennessy was given special permission by the Lord Chamberlain, Lord Scarbrough, to reproduce the portrait of Queen Mary by Sir William Llewellyn on the front cover of the dust jacket.

Proofs, beautifully bound in red cloth, were then sent to the Queen, the Duke of Windsor, the Duke of Gloucester, and the Princess Royal on 4 April, with a request that they be returned by 1 May. The Duke of Windsor liked what he read:

Both the Duchess and I like and approve the manner in which you handled the delicate subject of ourselves and the Abdication, bearing in mind the fact that you have had to deal with this episode from my Mother's angle. [27]

The Duke of Gloucester confined himself to a few neat proof corrections. In August the Duchess of Kent read the proofs and wrote 'a really intelligent & appreciative letter of congratulation' on what she called his 'achievement'. She added that her only complaint was that the book had to come to an end as she could have gone on reading forever. This conjured an image in Pope-Hennessy's head: 'a pretty picture for a Beerbohm drawing – that puzzled German profile bent over a biography as long as a Dead Sea Scroll.'[28]

Then Tommy Lascelles weighed in to settle the question of the book once and for all. He wrote direct to Sir Michael Adeane, his successor as the Queen's Private Secretary:

Dear Michael,

James Pope-Hennessy tells me he will be sending you the final proofs of his book, for The Queen's consideration, in the next few days.

At that very agreeable dinner-party to which The Queen invited Joan & me the other day, I had some talk about the book with H.M.; but I should like to give you my final opinion on it, for what that opinion may be worth. – I have read, and re-read it, chapter by chapter, during the last 12 months, and as they say in the show-ring, I can't fault it.

As you know, I had to do the same by John Gore, Nicolson, and Wheeler-Bennett, and have now evolved a pretty thorough technique of sizing up royal biographies. In this case, I asked myself, all the time, three main questions: (1). Is the book a worthy and sympathetic portrait of Queen Mary? – During the last ten years of her life, I saw a good deal of the Queen, who was always frightfully kind to me. I was personally devoted to her, and admired her greatly. So here I set myself a high standard, and, looking back, I was at first a bit anxious as to whether the book would reach it; but, quite early on, my anxiety on that score quite disappeared, and the net result is an unqualified Yes to my 1st question.

I am sure that all those who knew the Queen will agree with this, while all those who did not know her will wish to God they had.

(2). Is there anything in the book that could offend, or distress, The Queen herself, or any members of her family? – Answer, No, nothing. It is throughout written in perfect taste – the book of a gentleman, rare in these days – and I found that at the end of it I had a deeper affection and regard for every member of the Royal Family referred to than I had before. Especially Queen Victoria, about whom certain little-known and wholly delightful characteristics come out; and as for The Queen's great-great-aunt, the Grand Duchess of Mecklenburg-Strelitz, she will be my favourite woman to the day of my death. A thing that specially appealed to me was the discovery, which I suppose I ought to have made for myself years ago, that all that generation of the R. Family were brilliant letter-writers.

(3). Will the 'common reader' appreciate the book? – Here I can only say that Joan & I, who are average common readers, used to sit each side of the fire with sheets of typescript in our hands, wholly absorbed, and alternately laughing aloud, or wiping away surreptitious tears. (There are some very moving passages in it) – so I prophesy that it will sell like hot cakes here, in Europe, and in U.S.A. and India; further that when we are all dead and buried, it may still be recognized as one of the outstanding biographies in the English language. It will have considerable historical value, too, for it gives a very interesting picture of the part played – in the background – by members of the various Royal Families, English & Foreign (other than the Sovereigns themselves) all through the Victorian and Edwardian periods; and I don't know of any other book that does that.

I did, as a matter of fact, ask myself a fourth question – Would the King have liked the book? – I'm as sure as I can be that he wld have enjoyed it immensely, and wld have given us all some extremely amusing footnotes to it.

– April 4th to 12th, I shall, D.V., be on the Brora. Pula, pula. That sainted woman, Jessie Tyeser, has this year told me to bring Nicky Renton with me. He is a crazy fisherman – a chip of this old block – and, as you know, getting a son or grandson his first fish is one of the few real pleasures left to us old gentlemen,

Yrs ever
Tommy.[29]

In May Pope-Hennessy heard that his book had passed the royal censors and been approved for publication. He telephoned Lascelles, who was livid that he did not make a special effort to come round and tell the good news in person. If Pope-Hennessy appeared ungrateful, he made up for it in his generous acknowledgment to Lascelles' help in *Queen Mary*:

For constructive but unsparing criticism, and for constant encouragement in my work on this book I am also vastly indebted to Sir Alan Lascelles, Private Secretary and Keeper of the Archives to King George VI and to Queen Elizabeth II.[30]

* * *

Queen Mary was published to considerable critical acclaim in 1959. Just before its publication Lascelles addressed the issue of royal biographies in an article in *The Sunday Times* entitled *A New School of Royal Biography*. In this he distanced himself from the kind of books written by Sir Theodore Martin (on the Prince Consort) and Sir Sidney Lee (on Edward VII). Perhaps surprisingly for a courtier, he welcomed the 'authoritative portrait' of Queen Victoria, given by Sir Henry Ponsonby, her Private Secretary, who might normally be perceived to have betrayed the Sovereign for whom he worked. As Lascelles pointed out: 'The book does not detract one whit from Queen Victoria's greatness: the reputations of people of her unquestioned calibre are only enhanced by the knowledge that they were not immune from ordinary human shortcomings.'[31] Lascelles continued:

> The gradual realisation of such considerations brought about the wholesome revulsion from the 'pedestal' school of biographers, who, by sedulously concealing the weaknesses of their subjects, made their very strength seem unreal: who set them on a pillar so high that, like Lord Nelson in Trafalgar Square, they remain utterly remote from their fellow-creatures. That revulsion had its dangers, too, as does any pursuit of the narrow path of Truth. Alongside it grew up an 'anti-pedestal' school of professional 'debunkers' – the sensation-mongering, black-washing biographers, determined at all costs, and regardless of the claims of truth and decency, to be resoundingly iconoclastic; and, lower down the scale, appeared the moron who is in a continual ecstasy from the discovery that, in ordinary circumstances, Royal personages behave like ordinary people. [32]

Adopting the line that he had not yet read the biography of Queen Mary, Lascelles wrote of Pope-Hennessy:

> His earlier works justify the anticipation that this one has been written with artistry and delicacy of taste that characterised them; one may also expect so original a writer to have approached his present task in an original manner. If his immediate predecessors in the art of Royal biography, gave us, as it were, full-length portraits by Allan Ramsay or Raeburn, Mr Pope-Hennessy has, I expect, painted a conversation piece by Zoffany: a conversation-piece in which, perhaps, his subject will stand out – not too sharply – from a group of her kith and kin,

against a background of the social and political landscape of the age in which Queen Mary lived her long life. [33]

Pope-Hennessy's anonymous obituarist in *The Times* believed that he had been 'to some extent handicapped by the fact that earlier writers, Mr John Gore, Sir Harold Nicolson and Sir John Wheeler-Bennett in their lives of George V and George VI had covered a great deal of the period in which Queen Mary was active.'[34] On the other hand, no one had known much of the early life of Queen Mary, which he investigated 'most thoroughly.'[35]

Harold Nicolson also read a large part of the typescript in 1958, noting in his diary: 'It is a really remarkable work, dexterously combining factual narrative with imagination, humour and sympathy.'[36] To Pope-Hennessy he was enthusiastic in his praise:

It has all the virtues of a serious biography, of a studious social history and of a romantic novel. It is informative, amusing, vivid and admirably composed and written. It is perfectly respectful; yet one can see the angels smile, and the chuckle of the devils is so subdued that only an ear as acute as Princess May's own could detect their laughter ... It is a pointilliste portrait built up of a thousand significant details. In fact what surprises one most is the skill with which, without disturbing the smooth flow of the narrative, you catch the sparkle of every ripple ... It is a real creative feat to have brought Princess May from a shadowed background, hesitant and stiff, into a sudden blare of publicity ... I see in this a dramatic gift that I had not suspected ... [37]

Writing in the *Dictionary of National Biography* many years later, James Lees-Milne, gave his views on the book. He declared that, with the possible exception of Nicolson's *George V*, 'no other royal biography of the century has so successfully combined sympathetic character-study with social history in such brilliant narrative form.'[38]

* * *

When the book was serialised in *The Sunday Times*, survivors popped out of the woodwork to add their own comments and occasional niggles, the fate of all authors who venture into publication. After a spirited exchange, it was settled that

Queen Victoria had indeed died in the arms of both the Kaiser, and her physician, Sir James Reid, at Osborne House.

Sir Shane Leslie took exception to Pope-Hennessy's description of H.P. Hansell, tutor to Queen Mary's elder sons and to Sir Shane. He stated: 'The trend in Royal Biography is set against him.' Leslie gave several examples of his wit and humour: 'As the Norfolk goalkeeper he could convulse a crowd with his goose-step out of goal.'[39] The niece of Miss Mary Blomfield complained of Pope-Hennessy's description of her aunt's disruption of a royal court, suggesting that she did not cry out, 'Stop torturing women',[40] but said to the King in a low voice: 'For God's Sake, Your Majesty, stop forcible feeding.' She and her sister were led from the Throne Room, and the King deputed an Equerry to serve them champagne and sandwiches before they left for home.[41]

For his work on *Queen Mary*, he was appointed CVO in 1960. Kenneth Rose commented that Sir Harold Nicolson was given a KCVO in 1953 for *King George V*, and Sir John Wheeler-Bennett a KCVO in 1959 for *King George VI: His Life and Reign*. He added: 'As Mr Pope-Hennessy's book can hardly be rated inferior to these works either in style or content it would seem that the standards on which awards have been made are hierarchical rather than literary – a KCVO for the life of a Sovereign, a CVO for the life of a consort.'[42]

In the years following *Queen Mary* he became quite involved with the Duke and Duchess of Windsor, who even visited him on one occasion at his home in Ladbroke Grove. The Duchess rang him up once in the middle of the night to suggest that she had a project for him which he might find 'quite dignified', presently adding, 'It's also financially rewarding.' This proved to be articles by the Duke, ghosted by James, reflecting changes in men's fashions. Pope-Hennessy backed down when he detected a political slant to it. Nor was he inclined to work with Jack Le Vien on a film version of *A King's Story*.

Tommy Lascelles was infuriated with Pope-Hennessy when, in 1964, he wrote an adulatory article in *The Sunday Times* in favour of the Duke of Windsor for his 70th birthday, in which he suggested that the Queen and Royal Family should relax their distant attitude to the couple. However, Lascelles was prepared to help him with a considered appraisal of the Duke's qualities and otherwise for a stock obituary being prepared. This was published in *The Sunday Times* after the Duke's death in 1972.

It had been hoped by the Windsors that Pope-Hennessy might be the Duke's official biographer. It is greatly to our loss that such a book did not materialise, since he looked at the Duke with interest, a certain affection, but also through unblinkered eyes. And he would possibly have taken a welcome non-establishment approach to the Duchess. It was certainly the hope of John Utter, the Duke's last Private Secretary, that Pope-Hennessy would be assigned that task.

However, Pope-Hennessy was becoming increasingly difficult as the years went by, due to his heavy drinking. As his older, unfailingly incisive brother, Sir John Pope-Hennessy, wrote in his autobiography:

> James was incurably extravagant (this he inherited from his father), and from 1964 on his life was clouded by insolvency ... I have a portrait of him, painted in the last years of his life, in a style derived from Tchelitchew, by Cecil Beaton, who had photographed him from the 1930s, on. In it, his haunted face registers despair.

And yet, fraught though the last years of his life were, James continued to work and write regularly. In 1959 he edited the letters between Queen Victoria and Princess Victoria of Prussia*. He published a study of his grandfather, *Verandah: Some Episodes in the Crown Colonies 1867–1889* (1964), which some consider his most original book, *Sins of the Fathers* (1967), *Half-Crown Colony* (1969), and *Anthony Trollope* (1972). Finally, in 1973, it was announced that he had been appointed official biographer of Sir Noël Coward, who had died earlier in the year.

The book was never written. In January 1974 Pope-Hennessy had spoken too openly of the advance he had received. This was overheard and it was thought that he was keeping this in cash at his home.

He was reading in his flat at 9 Ladbroke Grove, when three men entered the premises, bound and gagged him, and beat him savagely, evidently searching for the money. Pope-Hennessy's valet-housekeeper, Leslie Smith, arrived home and tried to rescue him. He was taken to St George's Hospital, where he died aged sixty. Though the assailants were jailed for manslaughter, and given stiff sentences by Mr Justice Melford Stevenson, on 11 July 1974, the sentences were reduced by the Court of Appeal. In May 1975 Lord Justice Scarman accepted that Pope-Hennessy suffered only superficial injuries, and died after choking on his own blood from a lip wound.

----

* HRH Princess Victoria of Prussia (1866–1929). She had hoped to marry Prince Alexander of Battenberg, but after his death, married Prince Adolf of Schaumburg-Lippe, and later Alexander Zoubkoff.

When *Queen Mary* was published, it was widely praised and widely read. And it has survived the passage of time. A.N. Wilson wrote of it: 'But there is one book toweringly greater than anything else he wrote, and that is his life of Queen Mary. It is not so much that he had at last chosen a great subject, but that he had found a subject to which his pen was perfectly suited.'[43]

That was not the end of it. In 1980 Peter Quennell published *A Lonely Business*, a mixture of letters, diaries, and some of the interviews that James Pope-Hennessy undertook for his Queen Mary biography. The aim was to give a portrait of him as a writer.

Pope-Hennessy had not intended the royal interviews to be published for fifty years (i.e. until 2009). He described them as follows:

> To supplement the manuscript and printed sources I kept a private and confidential file recording in considerable detail the conversations I had both with Queen Mary's immediate descendants, related German, Danish and Norwegian royalty and with surviving members of the Court of King George V and Queen Mary. None of these interviews have been published, nor could they be until a lapse of fifty years. They are strictly confidential and form, I believe, a not uninteresting study of royal psycholology as it was and as it largely remains today.[44]

Quennell was an elegant writer himself but, being then nearly seventy-five, he did not exert himself as an editor. His footnotes left much to be desired. While he told the reader that *Orlando*, a book Pope-Hennessy was reading, was 'by Virginia Woolf, 1928', he did not bother with matters outside his immediate knowledge. When Pope-Hennessy visited Nigeria in 1965, his driver spoke of the hated Premier, Chief Akintola: 'Of course, Sir, we will kill him, but if not today, soon, soon.' It would surely have been interesting to have been informed that a month later, on 15 January 1966, the Chief was indeed murdered. Nor did he identify Phyllis Shand Allfrey in Dominica. She was a well-known politician and author of *The Orchid House* (1954).

The lasting value of *A Lonely Business* was to be found in its third part: *Royal Portraits – Notes for the biography of Queen Mary*. These added considerably to readers' knowledge and appreciation of Queen Mary, without in any way detracting from the official life.

In 1980, for a variety of reasons, only about 31,000 words were published.

This compilation contains the full 73,000 words, expanding with notes to over 100,000 words.

In editing it, I have placed the interviews in chronological order, so that Pope-Hennessy's research unfolds like a journey. The book has several points of interest. It is a portrait of a by-gone age of royal life. Furthermore, when read chronologically, the interviews provide rare insight into the practice and method of biographical research, thus allowing them to be read on several levels. These portraits were of course written quickly, almost immediately following the interviews in question. Sometimes they were merely brief notes – a kind of aide-memoire, as with Lady Cynthia Colville or Miss Wyndham; at other times, full portraits, such as with the Windsors and the Gloucesters. While making every effort to preserve original spontaneity, the occasional solecism has been corrected silently and irregularities have been conformed.

I have introduced the figures that Pope-Hennessy interviewed, and added some footnotes to put certain people and events in context. I have tried to keep my interpolations to a minimum, since Pope-Hennessy himself needs no embellishment.

* * *

I nurture a fantasy that though I never saw Queen Mary, she may well have seen me. I was a Hyde Park baby, taken there regularly in my pram by either my mother or my nanny. My mother told me that on these excursions she would sometimes see Queen Mary being driven round the park in her Daimler. Since I was born in November 1951, and Queen Mary last drove out in February 1953, it may well be that she glimpsed my pram. I hope so.

I first became properly conscious of Queen Mary a few years later, when I was given a Coronation scrapbook. I must have been eleven or twelve. I still have it. Flicking through the pages, there are images of the Queen's grandmother taken at the end of January 1953, captioned 'one of the last pictures of Queen Mary'. The photograph was taken on her return from Sandringham, a holiday, most of which she had spent in her room. She was wearing one of her toques, and what I now know to be her wig was in place, as were heavy drop earrings, and a necklace. Her dignity was complete. Next to it is pasted the dramatic photograph taken at the Lying-in-State, in which Queen Mary wore full Tudor mourning for her son, King George VI. There were earlier photographs from her life, and a memorable photograph of the young Queen Elizabeth II, in black with a very full veil, and a minute waist. Next to her stands the young Duke of Edinburgh in naval uniform, both arriving at Westminster Hall for the Lying-in-State. These images impressed themselves on my young mind.

Soon after this, at the age of thirteen, I first read Pope-Hennessy's *Queen Mary*. It took me several weeks, but I read it from cover to cover during the Lent term of 1965 at Eton. As I have all too often related, I purchased my copy in a second-hand bookshop (which closed all too soon afterwards) in Thames Street, Windsor, opposite the Hundred Steps up to Windsor Castle. I paid fifteen shillings for it on the afternoon of Sir Winston Churchill's State Funeral, 30 January 1965.

I cannot claim to have mastered every word or nuance, but it was the grounding for an interest in royal biography, and I will forever be grateful that Pope-Hennessy's masterly work was the one that I fell upon. As was written in *The Shadow of the Wind*, 'few things leave a deeper mark on a reader than the first book that finds its way into his heart ...'[45]

I re-read *Queen Mary* with equal pleasure on a morale-restoring visit to Scotland in September 1989, which doubled as an exploration of royal and stately homes. I was conscious that I could hardly set myself up as a royal expert without knowing where Balmoral was in relation to Birkhall, Abergeldie Castle or Loch Muich, or without having visited Glamis.

For this project, after I had annotated the records that Pope-Hennessy left of his visits to the various sources, I sat down to read the book for the third time. In so doing I was interested to see how the author used his source material: what he put in, what he left out, how he told the story.

There is a curious postscript to my interest in the Queen Mary biography. From time to time I would pick up copies in secondhand bookshops in order to give them to friends. One day, in November 2010, I was browsing in a bookshop on the Gloucester Road and spotted a copy. Did I really need another one? I thought I would check the price. There, on the endpapers, was an inscription: 'To Darling Richard from Aunt Mary, Christmas 1959.' It had been reduced from £10 to £7. Recognising the handwriting immediately, I snapped it up. It proved that the Princess Royal had liked the book enough to give it to members of her family as Christmas presents that year.

I have always believed the book to be a masterpiece, but equally I felt I had learned much that was interesting about Queen Mary from his notes – much that he had not felt able to publish in 1958. Principally this included the significant information that Princess May had been in love with another man before she was engaged to either the Duke of Clarence or the Duke of York, and much about her feelings about other members of the Royal Family, those she liked and those she did not.

Modern biographers, royal or otherwise, authorised or unauthorised, tend to add weight to some of their statements by attributing opinions and anecdotes to the sources who revealed them. Pope-Hennessy did not normally do this. In fact he told one of his sources, Lady Willans, that he 'did not intend to put *people* in [his] book at all'. Thus we have Queen Mary explaining 'to someone who asked her'[46] how her parents met, but not saying who that person was. Nor did he reveal his source in an excellent account she gave as to how children were meant to remain mute in the company of their elders and betters, but then 'scintillate in sparkling conversation' when in company.[47]

It has frequently amazed me how much, as it were, Pope-Hennessy got away with in the writing of this book, which was certainly read and scrutinised by the Royal Household on behalf of the Queen. It would be a shame to stress every nuance or irony as this would deflect from a reader's pleasure in the biography, but the tone was well set in the second paragraph, when Pope-Hennessy wrote: 'Sure enough, with a precision that marked her actions throughout the course of her long life, the child did in fact appear in that lovely month [May] and upon the very day the doctors named.'[48] And the author had fun in describing her mother, Princess Mary Adelaide, as 'a personage of unusual girth,'[49] with many similar references to her enormous fatness in subsequent pages.

It might have raised the eyebrow of a censorious courtier to read his first reference to Prince Albert Victor, Duke of Clarence as one 'who flashed into Princess May's later life as her fiancé, only to leave it six weeks after for the tomb.'[50] But it is good. So too was his description of Queen Mary's aunt, Grand Duchess Augusta of Mecklenberg-Strelitz, as having 'something of the look of a complacent partridge.'[51] and Princess Catherine of Württemberg as 'their purple-faced hostess of the Villa Seefeld'.[52] He had fun describing the decline of Duke Alexander of Württemberg: 'The heart-shaped face was embedded in rolls of fat; two double chins brimmed over the collars of the uniforms he would still sometimes wear ...'[53] There are many further such examples scattered throughout the book.

A biography inevitably tells you a certain amount about the biographer while relating the life of the subject. There is a telling line in *Queen Mary* concerning her governess, Hélène Bricka: 'When the Frenchwoman came to White Lodge in 1886 she had had no previous experience of living with royal persons, and this gave her a salutary detachment and independence of mind.'[54] Pope-Hennessy brought just such detachment to his work.

But it was still an authorised royal biography. It does not seem that much pressure was put on him to remove passages, though undoubtedly he operated a discipline of self-censorship. When we reach the pages about Hopetoun and the Tecks' stays there in the early 1880s, Pope-Hennessy knew but did not say that Princess May loved the heir, Lord Hopetoun, who later became 1st Marquess of Linlithgow. Her Lady-in-Waiting, Maggie Wyndham, told him that she loved him in such a way that she had no love left after that. Thus when she was engaged to the Duke of Clarence in 1891, she accepted her fate, more with excitement at the distant prospect of becoming Queen Consort, than in entering a marriage of love.

These days a biographer would not be able to resist making such a significant point, which could have led to an interesting examination of the success or otherwise of arranged marriages. Pope-Hennessy makes no hint at any affection for Lord Hopetoun, though he does make one glancing reference to him when considering the kind of husband that Princess May might have expected to marry. 'Only a very rich member of the peerage, like Lord Hopetoun, or the Marquess of Bath's heir, Lord Weymouth, would be in a position to marry Princess May and provide her with an appropriate social position.'[55] It would require a reader with a deeply conspiratorial mind to conclude that Princess May had been desperately in love with the former peer. That is the only reference to him that I found, and I have read the book with razor-sharp eyes in quest of another.[*] (Now, of course, I wonder if Pope-Hennessy stumbled on some affectionate leanings on Princess May's behalf in favour of 5th Marquess of Bath[†])?

Nor is there so much as a hint of another romantic intrigue – the love that Princess May felt at some point for Prince Henry of Battenberg, husband of Queen Victoria's youngest daughter, Princess Beatrice. Princess May was not at

---

[*] There is a formula sometimes adopted by biographers, in which something is written in code, so that if further information comes to light later, then critics will realise that he knew but he did not say. I have used this code myself more than once, most particularly in my life of Queen Elizabeth The Queen Mother. Years ago, I showed Frances Donaldson a review in *books & bookmen* by Christopher Sykes of her admirable biography of Edward VIII, in which he criticised her for not mentioning the drug addiction of Prince George, Duke of Kent. She read it and commented: 'Of course I knew that. It's all very well for people like him to say those things. I am a biographer, not a gossip columnist.'

[†] 5th Marquess of Bath (1860–1946), married 1890, Violet (d. 1928), daughter of Sir Charles Mordaunt, 10th Bt.

their wedding in 1884 as the Tecks were in mourning for the Duke of Teck's father, Duke Alexander of Württemberg. The romance, if such it was, must have occurred between 1884 and 1895 (when Prince Henry sailed away on the Ashanti Expedition from which he never returned alive). It is likely that it was after her marriage to the Duke of York in 1893, but we shall never know. At any rate both parties evidently saw the dangers and it never became a threat.

Likewise, as we have seen, many of the sources gave accounts of the illness of Queen Mary's father, the Duke of Teck. The conclusion seems to be that soon after the death of the Duchess of Teck, he was confined to their home, White Lodge, Richmond Park. The implication is that he suffered from dementia. It was no secret that he had been ill. C. Kinloch Cooke wrote in his authorised biography of the Duchess of Teck, as long ago as 1900: 'When the book was first contemplated, I had every reason to hope for the co-operation of the Duke of Teck, but the serious illness which succeeded his wife's death, I regret to say, made it impossible for him to take any part in the work he was so anxious to see accomplished.'[56] Kinloch Cooke described the funeral of Princess Mary Adelaide in 1897, adding: 'In the few days that had intervened since Princess Mary passed away, the Duke of Teck had aged greatly, the once erect form was bowed with grief, and the handsome face bore visible traces of mental anguish. The shock of his wife's death completely overwhelmed him, and from that sorrow he has never recovered.'[57]

It was more serious than that. Pope-Hennessy referred to manifestations of the Duke's peculiarities as early as 1882 (fifteen years before his bereavement): 'How he would chain-smoke one pipe after another, shout at his boys and, on occasion, in a fit of temper, even yell in public at the Duchess, who managed to maintain a serene dignity in the face of his guttural outbursts.'[58] And again, in 1884, he referred to a scene made by the Duke about a hotel room, concluding: 'The point needs lightly stressing, since [Queen Mary's] father's tendency to public tantrums were as embarrassing to a growing girl as her mother's volubility and anxiety to make Princess May talk.'[59] He tells us that the Duchess of Cambridge wrote of his 'attacks' describing them as times 'when his brain feels as though loose and moving in his head.'[60] The engagement of Princess May to the Duke of Clarence inspired her aunt Augusta to enquire: 'What does poor Franz say? does he *cry* or *swear*?!! perhaps both! I hope it won't be too much for his head ...'.[61] After the death of Princess Mary Adelaide, the Duke was 'now mentally in a very bad way indeed,' and after his death in 1900, the Prince of Wales (later Edward VII) wrote that he had 'virtually been dead to us for nearly two years!'[62]

Yet the various sources, some of whom remembered the Duke of Teck, told Pope-Hennessy that he was completely mad. And in the Getty Museum in Los Angeles, there is a whole file on the madness of the Duke of Teck.

A particular feature of the book is the way he described the various royal residences and places where Queen Mary spent her childhood. It was the Duke of Teck who had interested himself in decorating White Lodge. Indeed he had little else to do except that and gardening. 'Into this small and narrow room [the Boudoir] a good quantity of furniture had now, under the Duke's directions, been compressed,'[63] wrote Pope-Hennessy. Having lived in Germany for the best part of the writing of the biography, the author was able to visit a number of the places where Princess May lived or visited as a child. He did not hesitate to describe them both as he found them, and as they would have been in her day. He was particularly good on Schloss Rumpenheim, Neu Strelitz and Reinthal.

A visit to Balmoral in the summer of 1957 inspired him to describe the decor as 'dark marmalade'[64], while he made no attempt to disguise his dislike of Sandringham. 'The grounds about the house, full of dells and pretty eminences, and the lake beneath the stone terrace, are the only fine features of Sandringham, for the house itself, built and designed in one of the worst periods of English taste, resembles a golf-hotel at St Andrews or a station-hotel at Strathpeffer.'[65]

Pope-Hennessy dealt skilfully with the many German personages that appear in the early chapters of the book. I have already been taken to task for my extensive knowledge of such princely figures, when sourcing the Pope-Hennessy notes. He mentioned that Queen Mary 'alone of all her family could remember the connections of the English Royal House with such persons, and could in a trice explain who was who and which was which in the most complex of continental genealogical trees.' I was fortunate in having worked on one of the many excellent reference books inspired and edited by the late Hugh Montgomery-Massingberd, in this case, *Burke's Royal Families of the World, Volume I – Europe and Latin America* (Burkes' Peerage, 1977). Pope-Hennessy threw off genealogical complications more lightly than I did, as witness his masterly race through the Württemberg succession.[66]

As Princess May grew up, the challenges facing the official biographer became more delicate, in particular when confronted with the character of the Duke of Clarence. The Duke of Gloucester had asked Pope-Hennessy if the Duke of Clarence was a homosexual and/or suffering from syphilis, and many theories had been advanced to him during his research.

The plan that Princess May should marry this prince arrived, as he put it, with 'the brutal force of a douche of cold water received full in the face.'[67] Pope-Hennessy chose with care the words he used to describe Prince Eddy – 'wayward and self-indulgent'[68] – his 'mind was volatile and his emotions were variable' – 'his life was shapeless'[69] – 'backward and utterly listless'[70], and so on. He quoted Queen Victoria on his 'dissipated life', adding, 'These dissipations were, incidentally, sapping his already feeble physical strength.'[71] Subtly, only some time after the descriptions of the Duke of Clarence's death, does Pope-Hennessy state that Princess May never loved him.[72]

Whenever he had a difficult point to make, Pope-Hennessy told the reader he was making it in order to explain an important aspect of Princess May's psychological development. In this way he justified telling a story that might otherwise be deemed prurient. The most striking example concerned the impregnation of her cousin, Duchess Marie of Mecklenburg-Strelitz.

Duchess Marie was the daughter of Duke Adolf Friedrich V of Mecklenburg-Strelitz (1857–1914) (son of HRH Princess Augusta, and thus a first cousin of Queen Mary), and his wife, Princess Elisabeth (1857–1933), daughter of HH Friedrich I, Duke of Anhalt. The drama with Marie was caused by a palace rule that a male servant carried the gas lamps into the palace rooms, including the girls' bedrooms. This gave him an opportunity of which the footman called Hecht took full advantage. Marie fell pregnant to Hecht. He was dismissed for 'stealing' and later made his story public.

The courts of Europe buzzed with the tale, Queen Victoria declaring that the girl must have been drugged, others that she had been hypnotised. Queen Mary was supportive to Marie, and to her aunt Augusta, who adopted the daughter. But Marie was disowned by her parents. In 1899 she married Count Georges Jametel (1859–1944), son of a rich merchant, with considerable support from her English relations, but he proved unfaithful, most notably with Infanta Eulalia of Spain, who had been his mistress since 1896. Marie applied for a divorce in 1908, at which point, apparently, her brother, Duke Karl Borwin (1888–1908), challenged Jametel to a duel in which the former was killed. Then in 1914 Marie married Prince Julius Ernst of Lippe (1873–1952). She died at Obercassel, near Bonn, on 14 October 1948.

To be fair, Pope-Hennessy did tell this story as fully as he felt necessary, while explaining: 'The scandal at Strelitz, which made such radical newspaper headlines in its day, is only of interest to us since it shows us Princess May's wisdom and open-mindedness, as well as her loyalty and affection, at their best ...'[73]

The incident of the intruder at Marlborough House in 1950 was not mentioned at all in the biography, though it had been well reported in the press at the time. I knew nothing of this until I read the Pope-Hennessy notes, but soon tracked down a detailed account in *The Times*. Had I been writing Queen Mary's life today, I would have described this if only as an example of Queen Mary's *sang froid* and her attitude to the stabbing of her housekeeper.

Of course, the incident is more interesting to the present-day reader following the serious breach of security at Buckingham Palace in 1982 when an intruder managed to get into the bedroom of the present Queen, an incident widely reported in the media, which nearly led to the resignation of the Home Secretary, William Whitelaw.

This is what happened to Queen Mary:

On the evening of 23 June 1950 Queen Mary took her seven-year-old grandson, Prince Michael of Kent, to Beating the Retreat on Horse Guards Parade. Late that night the housekeeper, Mrs Alice Knight (then aged sixty-five) was in bed and her window was open. A man later identified as Gerard O'Brien (aged twenty-six), at one time a gardener from Royal Parks, and originally from the Republic of Ireland, vaulted in through the window. When she challenged him, he beat her about the head and tried to strangle her. She cried out and the assistant housekeeper, Winifred Ralph, rushed in, only to be punched. She ended up with bruises about the face and superficial injuries, whereas Mrs Knight was in fact stabbed nine times with a penknife, one cut behind the ear requiring four stitches. O'Brien leapt out onto the flat roof, his pockets filled with jewellery and lipstick. He fell down onto the fanlight, got into the house again, and fell into the boiler room, where he was sick. When apprehended, he repeatedly said: 'Please, Sir, will they hang me for this?'

The two housekeepers were taken to St George's Hospital on Hyde Park Corner, while Queen Mary remained undisturbed in her bed, unaware of the drama of the night. Lord Claud Hamilton led a thorough search of the house, including the bedrooms, and also of the grounds, which strikes me as a somewhat comical performance. O'Brien was taken to Cannon Row Police Station where he later made a signed confession. On 13 July he was imprisoned for eight years. It emerged that he had twice before been convicted of violence, one time for robbery with violence. It was said in his defence that he was 'normally a mild little man, whose prime interest in life was ballroom dancing,' but that he suffered from a stomach complaint which meant that he should never drink.

Questions about royal safety were asked in Parliament, and *The Times* produced a leader which said: 'A bedroom in the heart of London, in a royal mansion, patrolled by sentries of the Brigade of Guards and watched over by the police might be thought to be safe from the hazards to which other homes are freely exposed.'[74] A few weeks later a parrot was captured in the gardens of Marlborough House after a long pursuit. This bedraggled bird, which had bitten the hand of a gardener, was returned to its owner in Enfield.

Pope-Hennessy did not eschew modern or unusual expressions in his text – he wrote of the Duke of Clarence that he was to be sent 'circling the globe like a *sputnik*'; of Queen Victoria's 'excellent family intelligence service, and her instinct like a Geiger-counter', and the invitation for Princess May to stay at Sandringham in 1891, giving 'a signal as clear, as swift, as dazzling as a Bengal rocket'.[75] He described marrying for love as a 'motive', and was not afraid to be brutal in his descriptions. When Princess Alix of Hesse turned down a proposal of marriage from the Duke of Clarence, Pope-Hennessy wrote: 'Thus firmly did the future Empress Alexandra Feodorovna of All the Russias take the first step down the fatal path which led her to the blood-stained cellar at Ekaterinburg.'[76] There were many other references to impending death, it being a feature of royal life that many engagements and festivities had to be cancelled when a distant relative died, perhaps unregretted but dutifully mourned.

He had a neat way of saying a lot with few words: 'The King of the Hellenes had withdrawn to his villa on Corfu to avoid the rigours of Passion Week in Athens.'[77] And a favourite passage of mine about Queen Mary in old age, back at Marlborough House, after the war:

> In the midst of this shimmering Georgian enclave in bedraggled postwar London, visitors found Queen Mary herself, upright, distinguished, dressed perhaps in blue velvet or in pale grey, around her neck her ropes of matchless pearls. Awed strangers spoke of Queen Mary at Marlborough House as representative of another epoch, but this was a misjudgement, for the Queen Dowager was in no way isolated, a magnificent relic, in these eighteenth-century surroundings. She would sally forth from Marlborough House to listen to the proceedings at a court for juvenile delinquents – 'It was most interesting but I have never heard so many lies told in my life' – or to enjoy *Oklahoma* or *Annie Get Your Gun*.[78]

There were some splendid figures in the book employed as witnesses, most notably the ever-disagreeable Lady Geraldine Somerset, whose jealousy of the Duchess of

Teck and her daughter found many outlets in her private diaries. And there was the magnificent Aunt Augusta, Grand Duchess of Mecklenburg-Strelitz, Queen Mary's favourite confidante. The letters between them enrich the book, and sometimes they startle. In August 1900 she addressed the question of anarchists:

> *My* plan would be, to forbid and close all meetings, Associations, and to muzzle the Press entirely, then, take up every man or woman, expressing anarchist views, have them flogged daily, and if decided murderers, have them tortured then blown off from a Gun! *that* is what *I* would decree!'[79]

There were hilarious characters too, such as the enormously fat Duchess Eugene of Württemberg: 'Aunt Vera suffered from an unusually virulent form of St Vitus's Dance. She was always attended by a sergeant of the Olga Dragooner, whose duty it was to pursue her down the palace corridors and catch her before she bruised herself against the furniture.'[80] Pope-Hennessy relished these eccentric figures. Of Queen Mary's aunt, Princess Claudine (sister of the Duke of Teck), he wrote: 'Princess Claudine had in her later years become increasingly eccentric; she would rise at four-thirty in the morning to ride about the countryside on a white horse, followed by her dogs but unattended by a groom. She wore her white hair cut short like a man, and was entirely absorbed in her little farm. When she went down to church on Sundays at St Peter in Graz her coachman would remain at the church door holding her dogs on a leash.'[81]

In the book Pope-Hennessy did not overplay the lack of sympathy between Queen Alexandra and Queen Mary, about which he had been told a lot. As the story approached the present day, he did not spell out all the difficulties and rows between Queen Mary and the Duke of Windsor after the Abdication, or hint other than that the marriages of King George and Queen Mary's children were happy ones. For each he found a positive quote welcoming the new bride into the family.

We now know much more about the way George V treated his children. Reading between the lines, Pope-Hennessy has said it all without quite saying it – how gruff he could be with them, how they were afraid of him, how Queen Mary passively deferred to her husband. When dealing with these sensitive issues, he employed the literary device of litotes: 'She [Queen Mary] had no automatic or spontaneous understanding of a child's mind or ways' – 'Yet it cannot be denied that, between them, King George and Queen Mary managed to be rather unsuccessful and unsympathetic parents.'[82] – or 'This habit of reserve [on the part of Queen Mary] might be thought to have nicely counter-balanced the outspoken and indeed intemperate criticism which King George would without warning launch, like some ballistic missile, at now one, now another, of his sons. In fact it did not have this effect, nor did it make it easy for Queen Mary's children to confide in her, to tell her what they were really thinking, nor to fathom what she really thought.'[83]

Pope-Hennessy let us know of the 'granite conservatism' of the King, of his 'philistine tendencies' as well as the dimness of his sisters, especially Princess Louise, 'whose hold on reality, like her health, was imperfect.'[84]

When it came to the Abdication, the author rightly concentrated on Queen Mary's reaction to it. All that has emerged since on that subject does not alter fundamentally the essence of what he told us.

And yet, as we shall see, Pope-Hennessy knew so much more about Queen Mary than he revealed in his biography.

A CHRONOLOGY OF
QUEEN MARY'S LIFE

1867

Queen Mary was born at Kensington Palace on 26 May as Her Serene Highness Princess Victoria Mary (May) of Teck, the only daughter of HH The Duke of Teck and his wife, Princess Mary Adelaide of Cambridge. She had three younger brothers:

HSH Prince Adolphus of Teck – Marquess of Cambridge (1868–1927)
HSH Prince Francis (Frank) of Teck (1870–1910)
HSH Prince Alexander of Teck – Earl of Athlone (1874–1957)

Her father, The Duke of Teck, came from a morganatic branch of the Württemberg family, while her mother, HRH Princess Mary Adelaide of Cambridge, was a granddaughter of King George III.

1883–85

The family lived partly at Kensington Palace, partly at White Lodge, Richmond, but, on account of debts, from 1883 to 1885 they lived in Florence.

1891

Princess May was engaged to the Duke of Clarence, elder son of The Prince of Wales (later Edward VII). He would have succeeded his father as King, but for his early death in 1892.

1893

After a suitable period of mourning, Princess May married the Duke of Clarence's younger brother, the Duke of York. The Duke and Duchess of York, as they were then styled, had six children:

HRH Prince Edward – Prince of Wales, Edward VIII and Duke of Windsor (1894–1972)
HRH Prince Albert – Duke of York and George VI (1895–1952)
HRH Princess Mary – Countess of Harewood and Princess Royal (1897–1965)
HRH Prince Henry – Duke of Gloucester (1900–74)
HRH Prince George – Duke of Kent (1902–42)
HRH Prince John (1905–19)

They set up home in St James's Palace, in the apartment of Queen Mary's late grandmother, the Duchess of Cambridge, and this was then called York House. They also lived at York Cottage on the Sandringham estate in Norfolk.

1901

Queen Victoria died. The Duke and Duchess of Cornwall and York, as they were then known, made a seven and a half month sea voyage to and from Australia, where the Duke delivered the royal message at the opening of the Federal Parliament.

On their return, the Duke was created Prince of Wales, and they were known as the Prince and Princess of Wales until 1910, living at that time in Marlborough House.

1905

The Prince and Princess undertook a tour of India.

1910

King Edward VII died and they became King George V and Queen Mary. They were crowned at Westminster Abbey in 1911, and at the end of that year, again visited India for the Delhi Durbar.

1914–18

These were the years of the First World War. The King and Queen celebrated their Silver Wedding in 1918.

1922 and 1923

Princess Mary married Viscount Lascelles (later Earl of Harewood) in 1922, and the following year, the Duke of York married Lady Elizabeth Bowes-Lyon. The future Queen Elizabeth II was born in 1926.

1925

Queen Alexandra died at Sandringham.

1934 and 1935

The Duke of Kent married Princess Marina of Greece, and the following year the Duke of Gloucester married Lady Alice Montagu-Douglas-Scott. 1935 was also the year of the King's Silver Jubilee.

1936

In January 1936 King George V died. Queen Mary moved into Marlborough House. In December King Edward VIII abdicated and King George VI ascended the throne.

1937

Queen Mary was the first Dowager Queen to attend a Coronation – that of George VI and Queen Elizabeth.

1939–45

Queen Mary spent the duration of the Second World War at Badminton House in Gloucestershire, the home of her niece, the Duchess of Beaufort.

1947

Queen Mary's granddaughter, Princess Elizabeth, married Lieutenant Philip Mountbatten, who became the Duke of Edinburgh. Their first two children, Prince Charles and Princess Anne, were born in Queen Mary's lifetime.

1952

King George VI died at Sandringham on 6 February and was succeeded by his elder daughter as Queen Elizabeth II.

1953

Queen Mary died at Marlborough House on 24 March at the age of eighty-five.

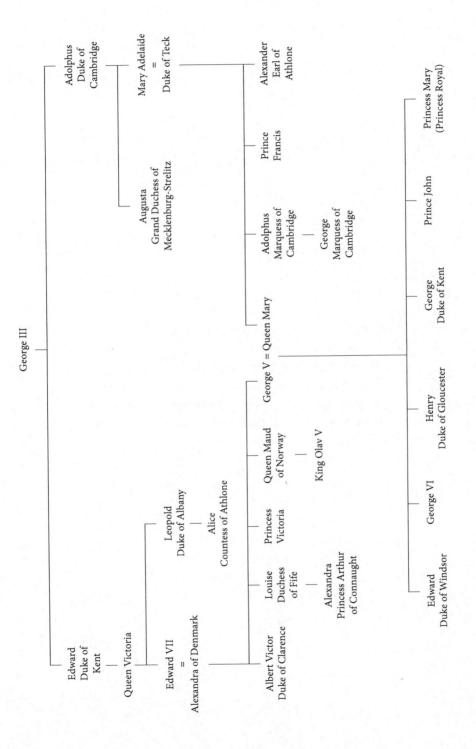

EDITORIAL NOTE

The idiosyncratic style used by Pope-Hennessy in these interviews has largely been maintained, and only occasional lapses in punctuation and spelling have been corrected to make it easier for the reader.

PART TWO: THE INTERVIEWS

By James Pope-Hennessy

James Pope-Hennessy spent from 1955 until 1959 researching and writing his book. He began, as Sir Owen Morshead had suggested, by asking Lady Cynthia Colville to help him.

In August 1955, Princess Alice, Countess of Athlone wrote to Lady Cynthia: 'Of course we will both gladly give him [P.-H.] any information he may be seeking ... Alge [the Earl of Athlone] could tell him quite a lot about that year spent in Florence.'[85]

On 12 September he saw the Princess Royal, and on 16 November he had a talk with The Duke of Gloucester. On 8 December Harold Nicolson invited the Marquess of Carisbrooke (son of Princess Beatrice and grandson of Queen Victoria) to meet him.

On 17 December he received his first letter from Sir Alan Lascelles, former Private Secretary to King George VI and to the present Queen, who was to play such an influential role in the development of the book.

1955

ONE

LADY CYNTHIA COLVILLE

16 August, Horsley

Lady Cynthia Crewe-Milnes, later Colville (1884–1968), was the twin daugh-ter of 1ˢᵗ Marquess of Crewe, by his first wife, Sybil, daughter of Sir Frederick Graham. When she was young she studied the piano at the Royal College of Music. In 1908 she married Hon George Colville (1867–1943). In 1923 she was appointed a Woman of the Bedchamber to Queen Mary, serving until Queen Mary died in 1953, following which she gave a memorable broadcast tribute on the BBC Home Service (the precursor to Radio 4).

It fell to Lady Cynthia to break the news of the deaths of the Duke of Kent and of King George VI to Queen Mary, as she happened to be in waiting at the time. When the King died, Sir Edward Ford, the Assistant Private Secretary, came in person to Marlborough House with the news. Lady Cynthia was flus-tered: 'Oh dear! It's very difficult. Queen Mary's never forgiven me for telling her without any adornments that the Duke of Kent had been killed.'[86] She tried to get Ford to tell her that the King was very ill, but in the end she went in and told her.

Lady Cynthia was also a keen social worker. In 1963 she published her memoirs, Crowded Life. *In later life she lived at 4 Mulberry Walk, in Chelsea. Princess Alice, Countess of Athlone attended her memorial service at St Peter's, Eaton Square.*

These few notes set the scene for some extraordinary revelations, few of which found a place in the final book.

1. Francis, Duke of Teck* died insane.

---

* HH Prince Francis, Duke of Teck (1837–1900), from a morganatic branch of the Württemberg family, married 1866, HRH Princess Mary Adelaide of Cambridge (1833–97), granddaughter of George III.

LADY CYNTHIA COLVILLE

2. Shyness originally casued by overwhelming effect of Duchess of Teck* and her exuberant charm; overshadowed as a girl.
3. Queen Mary once told C.C. she saw her father hurl a plate at her mother's head across the dinner-table.
4. C.C. thinks she was not in love with either Prince Eddie[†] or King George[‡]: 'It seemed ambitious ; and in a way it was' – the new engagement. She *was* in love with Prince Henry of Battenberg[§], who reciprocated: they agreed to behave well and stop seing each other. She was much attached to 'her cousin the Cardinal Otto something, and always enjoyed seeing him.' (Who was this ?)[¶]
5. Not long before she died Queen Mary told Cynthia that in the early days of their marriage she & the Duke of York had terrible rows, but things settled down later.

---

* See above.

† HRH Prince Albert Victor, Duke of Clarence (1864–92), elder son of HRH The Prince of Wales, and grandson of Queen Victoria.

‡ HM King George V (1865–1936), King from 1910.

§ HRH Prince Henry of Battenberg (1858–96), known as 'Liko' in the family, one of the sons of Prince Alexander of Hesse, who married morganatically. In 1885 he had married HRH The Princess Beatrice (1857–1944), Queen Victoria's youngest daughter, to which union the Queen had only agreed on condition that the couple remained at court. Prince Henry never felt fully accepted in England, and attempted to prove himself by taking part in the Ashanti Expedition, but he died from fever before seeing a shot fired. Princess May of Teck must have fallen for him after his marriage to Princess Beatrice. When he died, she wrote: 'Isn't it too sad about poor Liko? Poor At.[Aunt] Beatrice it is awful for her, her whole life ruined, one's heart bleeds for her in her fearful sorrow.' [*Queen Mary*, p. 317]

¶ HRH Prince Carl Alexander of Württemberg (1896–1964), third son of Albrecht, Duke of Württemberg; he became a Benedictine monk as Dom Odo in the Abbey of Beuron. He and Queen Mary were distant cousins. He was a spy for the FBI during World War II and sent in disagreeable accounts of the Duke of Windsor and his politics. Pope-Hennessy met him in 1958.

1956

TWO

MR HOUGH, Under-Footman to the Duke and Duchess of Teck

5 January

For his first fully transcribed interview, James Pope-Hennessy relied on his old friend, Ralph Dutton (1898–1985), the owner of Hinton Ampner, near Alresford in Hampshire. He was the author of a number of architectural and topographical works, including The English Country House *and* The English Garden. *In 1960 he suffered the shock of part of Hinton Ampner burning down, but at once set about restoring it. In old age Dutton succeeded a distant cousin as 8ᵗʰ Lord Sherborne, and commented that you could get anything you wanted so long as you no longer wanted it. He was blind in one eye.*

Mr Hough had been Ralph Dutton's butler at Chapel Street from 1939 to 1945. He was born in about 1867, and had served as under-footman to Queen Mary's parents, the Duke and Duchess of Teck. He now lived in Fulham with his wife.

At 11.30 on Wednesday 5 January 1956 Ralph Dutton took me to see his old retired butler Mr Hough, of 57 Stanbridge Road, off the Wandsworth Bridge Road in the Borough of Fulham.

Mr Hough, a smooth, well-kept looking old man in his eighties, with placid light blue eyes which seemed at times to be gazing into the past, went to White Lodge* in the late summer of 1893, as steward's-room boy and under-footman to the Duke and Duchess of Teck. It was just after the return of the Duchess and Princess May from abroad, whither they had gone when the Duke of Clarence died. Mr Hough, though mind you it was only gossip, had said he was always told

---

* The Tecks moved to White Lodge in Richmond Park in 1869, and were permanently settled there from August 1870 until 1883, when they moved abroad due to debts. They returned in 1885 and both died there. Originally it was a hunting lodge, built by George I, and enlarged by George II. It was the home of George III's daughter, Mary, Duchess of Gloucester until her death in 1857. The future Edward VIII was born there in 1894. Today it houses the Royal Ballet.

that she had never wanted to marry the Duke of Clarence at all – 'an arranged sort of an affair,' said Mr Hough.

Asked how old he was at that time, Mr Hough did not rightly know, about 17 he should fancy. The trouble in those days was that in private service you always had to alter your age – you were too young for some places, too old for others; hence you ended by really forgetting how old in fact you were.

The male staff consisted of a butler, two 'match footmen', one under butler, one Groom of the Chambers, one steward and one steward's room boy. The Duchess had two dressers, one of whom was called Miss Farrell; Princess May had two dressers, Miss Adams and another; they took it turn and turn about, alternate days on and off duty, doing mending etc. on their off-day. The cook was a female, assisted by a kitchen maid and a scullery maid. There were three or four housemaids, under old Liza, the head housemaid. There were three laundry-maids who worked in the laundry at 'the end of the passage'.

The Tecks kept one barouche, one landau, one brougham, one wagonette and one dog-cart, there were four carriage-horses, Jumbo the phaeton horse, and perhaps one other horse. There was Kitchener the head coachman, a 1st and 2nd coachman, with strappers and helpers. Hough was often on the box. Kitchener was admired by his employers for having such big hands and getting them up to London so quickly, though of course in fact it was the police clearing all traffic points for them which effected this. When the family went up for the evening from White Lodge, the carriage and horses put up at Collins', the job-master livery-stable in St James's Street opposite the Feathers. The footmen would put their livery coats in the boot and go off to a Music Hall.

Mr Hough had heard that the Tecks had been forced out of Kensington Palace[*] by Queen Victoria[†] because the Duchess of Teck never paid the tradespeople and they talked. The Duchess of Teck once said 'since it seems the tradespeople are so fond of talking about me I shall stop the beer, bread and cheese' (which they had in the kitchen): 'But of course nothing was ever done.' Queen Victoria put in a controller, the

---

[*] The Duchess of Teck had been granted an apartment at Kensington Palace on her marriage in 1866, where Queen Mary was born in 1867.

[†] HM Queen Victoria (1819–1901). She was also a granddaughter of George III, and thus a first cousin of Princess Mary Adelaide.

second of whom was the Honourable Alexander Nelson Hood[*], and it was in his reign that the arguments about the chemist at Sheen occurred. He said 'Why do you go to a chemist at Sheen when you can get it all at the Army and Navy Stores' whereupon the chemist at Sheen said if they withdrew custom he would not supply anything if any of them got ill in the night; so again 'nothing was done' – seemingly the tone of the household. The books were very orderly, rendered quarterly to the Comptroller; all the servants were permanently on board wages (he emphasised this). The Duchess, who was very kind, used often to give the servants rabbits etc. when game was sent.

The Guild Parcels bulked large in life at White Lodge, and were sorted in the Steward's Room.

The servants' Christmas Tree (perhaps in the drawing room he could not re-member) had stands round it for their presents – good quality presents of socks, jerseys etc. – there were long bamboo sticks with sponges on the end to put out the tree candles.[†]

When the Duchess and Princess May got back in 1893 from abroad they were *not* still in full mourning – 'on and off'.

Princess May and the Duke of York[‡] were engaged at a garden party at Bute Lodge[§], the Duke of Fife's. The Duke and Duchess[¶] wanted to be 'out of the way' so they each took a separate carriage up to London. Princess May and her fiancé announced it on their return from London; it was meant to be a secret, but Hough heard it that night 'down in the garden' from some other servant.

Hough remembers Queen Victoria at Prince Edward's[**] christening at White Lodge.

He remembers Princess May as 'a tall, slim young lady', 'very nice-looking, and very polite'. He had of course little to do with her directly.

---

[*]   Hon (Sir) Alexander Nelson-Hood (1854–1937), 4th son of 1st Viscount Bridport. Comptroller to the Duchess of Teck 1892–97, later Private Secretary to Queen Mary (when Princess of Wales) 1901–10, and Treasurer 1901–19.

[†]   Pope-Hennessy noted a reference to the typescript of Mabel Hunt's *Record of a Friendship*.

[‡]   HRH The Duke of York (1865–1936), later King George V, second son of Edward VII.

[§]   Actually it was called East Sheen Lodge (J.P.-H.).

[¶]   Alexander, 1st Duke of Fife (1849–1912), married 1889, HRH The Princess Louise (1867–1931), later the Princess Royal, elder daughter of Edward VII.

[**] HRH Prince Edward of York (1894–1972), later Edward VIII. Abdicated 1936, and thereafter HRH The Duke of Windsor.

The Duchess was always bowling up to London, often to stay in Stratton Street with 'the Baroness' (Burdett-Coutts).[*]

The hospitality in the servants' hall was always tremendous.

There were 'flusters' and 'hullaballoos' over such incidents as a parcel containing a present from the Duchess to her newly married daughter which a footman stuck under the seat of the carriage going up to York House; he had told Hough who, being busy helping the coachman with the horses, had not listened; the present had to be sent up next day at Hough's expense.

There was another fluster over the opening of the Richmond Theatre, when the Duchess insisted on 3 carriages – the Duke of Teck grumbled and said 'why change carriages to come back from Sheen in' – it was a characteristic extravagance of the Duchess.

When Prince Adolphus of Teck married Lady Mary Grosvenor,[†] Hough was on the box on the way back – WELCOME HOME was spelt in red lights on Richmond Hill and the horses reared at this so much Hough nearly fell off the box.

The Duke of Teck was 'a funny gentleman'; must elucidate this. Having left at some previous date, Hough was not there when the Duke went off his head.[‡]

General impression: generous, nice people, harum-scarum, constant rushing about and fluster.

End of first interview. We are taking Mr Hough to White Lodge in the warmer weather (D.V. and *unberufen!*).

Pope-Hennessy sent his notes on the meeting with Mr Hough to the Princess Royal, who was interested to read them. (For some reason, though there are several letters from the Princess Royal in Pope-Hennessy's papers, he did not keep a record of any of his interviews with her).

---

[*] Baroness Burdett-Coutts (1814–1906), granddaughter of Thomas Coutts, founder of the bank, Coutts & Co, thus thought to be the richest woman in England. A noted philanthropist. She frequently came to the financial rescue of the Duchess of Teck.

[†] HSH Prince Adolphus of Teck (1868–1927), later 1st Marquess of Cambridge, eldest son of the Duke of Teck, married 1894, Lady Margaret Grosvenor (1873–1929), fourth daughter of 1st Duke of Westminster. They were married at Eaton Hall, Chester.

[‡] By the time of the Duchess of Teck's death in 1897, the Duke was 'mentally in a very bad way indeed' [*Queen Mary*, p. 338]. Even before that, he made few excursions. As a widower he was not seen in public, but was cared for at White Lodge by a doctor and male nurses. When he died, the Prince of Wales noted he had 'virtually been dead to us for nearly two years'. [*Ibid*].

THREE

9 January

One of the people Pope-Hennessy was keen to see was King Haakon of Norway, but he was told that the King was in hospital. Instead he was given an appointment with the Crown Prince.

Thus, on 7 January 1956 he flew from Stavanger to Oslo in Norway to meet members of the Norwegian Royal Family, and members of the Norwegian Courts. He arrived four hours late after bad flight delays.

Crown Prince Olav of Norway (1903–91) was the son of King Haakon VII (1872–1957) and Queen Maud (1869–1938), Edward VII's youngest daughter. He was therefore a first cousin of George VI. Since his mother did not always enjoy life as Norway's Queen, she spent the winters at Appleton House, near Sandringham. Therefore he was brought up close to the British Royal Family and saw them often. He was educated at Balliol College, Oxford.

During the war, after the Germans invaded Norway, he set up a Norwegian government in exile in London. He continued to pay frequent visits to London for the rest of his life, and paid two State Visits to the present Queen. As late as the 1980s, he was invariably present on the balcony of the Home Office for the annual ceremony at the Cenotaph on Remembrance Sunday.

He was also a great sportsman, particularly in the field of yachting. He won a Gold Medal at the Amsterdam Olympic Games in 1928.

His mother, Queen Maud, took part in the Coronation of George VI in 1937, and died in London after an operation in a nursing home there in November 1938. At the time of Pope-Hennessy's visit, old King Haakon was still alive, but, immediately after the State Visit of the Queen and the Duke of Edinburgh in June 1955 (Britannia sailed on 26 June, and was still in the Oslo Fjord at the time), he had slipped and broken his thigh. As the King's biographer put it : 'He who had prided himself on being so straight, especially perhaps in his later years when age had bent so many of his contemporaries, felt that a king could not appear before his people in a bath-chair, and because he could not stand, straight and erect as he had stood throughout his

life, he preferred not to appear at all.'[87] Crown Prince Olav became Regent on
30 June 1955.

The Crown Prince had been married to Princess Märtha of Sweden, but
she had died on 5 April 1954.

THE CROWN PRINCE OF NORWAY

Arriving at Oslo, after a tedious flight due to bad weather conditions, I found a
message from the British Ambassador[*] to say that the Crown Prince Olav[†] would
receive me at 11.15 a.m. on Monday, 9 January. I accordingly took a cab up the
street to the palace, was received by an elderly servant who said 'good boy, you
are on time', and was shown into a first floor room of great height containing a
porcelain stove, some large 19th century pictures, and a somewhat tongue-tied
naval ADC at his desk. After a few minutes of laughter-from-the-next-room a
General came out of the Crown Prince's office, my letter from Arthur Salter[‡] was
taken in, and I was soon asked to follow it.

The Crown Prince is a capacious-looking personage full of good humour,
dressed in a grey double-breasted suit, his face full and good-natured, his head
slightly peaked like that of some members of our own royal family. He has the
Duke of Gloucester's[§] laugh. He asked me to sit down.

He said he had known Queen Mary well, and was perhaps less frightened of
her than her own children had ever been (this I prompted out of him by saying
many people were frightened of her). It was natural, he said in a royal way, for
children to be terrified of parents, and also natural that nephews and nieces
should be less so. He said her sense of humour 'off duty' was very pronounced
and very amusing indeed. Of Sandringham he recalled the immense squash

---

*   The Ambassador was Sir Peter Scarlett (1905–87), in Norway 1954–60.

†   HRH Crown Prince Olav (1903–91), son of King Haakon VII, and Princess Maud, succeeded his
father as King of Norway in September 1957.

‡   Arthur, 1st Lord Salter (1881–1975), government minister.

§   HRH The Prince Henry, Duke of Gloucester (1900–74), third son of King George V and Queen
Mary. Married 1935, Lady Alice Montagu-Douglas-Scott (1901–2004). Pope-Hennessy had met
the Duke once before at a luncheon at Buckingham Palace. He was to stay with the Gloucesters
at Barnwell in May 1957.

CROWN PRINCE OLAV AND
CROWN PRINCESS MARTHA OF NORWAY

at York Cottage* as the children 'got bigger' and so took up more room. King George's devotion to his mother† (he said) had prevented his asking her to leave Sandringham, but the whole arrangement 'had lasted far longer' than anyone would in the ordinary course of events have supposed it could. He said the building of Sandringham House itself had been haphazard, as the Wales family expanded. His mother's house at Appleton [on the Sandringham estate] was now empty and the Duke of Edinburgh‡ said he would like them to live in it as Sandringham was now too big, but the Crown Prince felt that Appleton would be on the other hand too small. What was the effect of pulling down English country houses now? Perhaps some were improved by the removal of billiard rooms. Had I seen the Duchess of Beaufort?§ How angry Q.M. had been to be forced to leave London for Badminton¶ in the war – 'not at all the thing'. King George and Queen Mary had only been to Norway once, and never to Oslo; that was for the coronation of King Haakon (June 1906) when they had stayed on the royal yacht *Victoria and Albert* at Trondheim, 'a good thing, too, there were no hotels' (Duke of Gloucester neigh of laughter). He recalled they had stayed three weeks and gone fishing.

One of the most remarkable things about Queen Mary was the way she 'kept up' with even minor and remote royal connections – all included in her sense of 'the family'. His mother, Queen Maud, used to talk to him of 'Aunt Maria', the Duchess of Teck. On the relationship between Queen Mary and Princess

---

* When at Sandringham, George V and Queen Mary lived at York Cottage from 1893 until Queen Alexandra's death in 1925, since she continued to occupy the 'Big House'. Not noticeably small, it is more the size of an English rectory, but would have been cramped when filled with a large family, courtiers and servants. It is now the Estate Office.

† HM Queen Alexandra (1844–1925), daughter of King Christian IX of Denmark.

‡ HRH The Prince Philip, Duke of Edinburgh (b. 1921), born a Prince of Greece and Denmark, son of Prince Andrew of Greece, and his wife, Princess Alice of Battenberg.

§ Lady Mary Cambridge (1897–1987), elder daughter of Queen Mary's eldest brother, 1st Marquess of Cambridge. Married 1923, Henry, 10th Duke of Beaufort (1900–84). They lived at Badminton in Gloucestershire. Pope-Hennessy went to stay with her in November 1958.

¶ Queen Mary spent the war years staying with the Beauforts at Badminton.

Victoria* he was discreet, saying that he had heard that long before his time there had been difficulties. How good Harold Nicolson's life of the King[†] had been, it gave one the impression that he had begun the book bored with the subject and with no respect for him and had ended up with an immense admiration. No, he had not read *Good Behaviour*[‡], he had tried to order it; certainly he would be most grateful if I send him one. He thought he must have met Harold Nicolson; had he not been in the diplomatic? I said Vita[§] had made him leave it – 'what a pity, what a pity – but then how lucky for him. It's no life at all, you know, acquaintances everywhere and no friends'.

Was not the Princess Royal[¶] of great assistance to me? So close to her mother, so close, and in manner very like. Not of course that the sons were not close too – no, he did not think the Duke of Kent** a particular favourite – there was no favouritism at all (here he became royal and anodyne). No, Queen Mary did not loathe shooting; she just did not like it, but went out with the guns every day at Sandringham, an example of her unfailing sense of duty to her husband.

So Queen Mary had kept a diary? How interesting. No opinions in it, he supposed, very characteristic of her that, very characteristic of that whole family. But by dint of being in a certain position for a certain length of time you couldn't fail, he found, to get to know about politics and foreign politics too; you ended by knowing more than the experts themselves sometimes, just by being there, don't you know. Funny, but true. I said Queen Victoria was a good example of this fact; he agreed. And of course the secret of politics was that nothing ever changed – the same elements constant but arranged in slightly different patterns – nothing

---

* HRH The Princess Victoria (1868–1935), second daughter of Edward VII and Queen Alexandra. She was George V's favourite sister. Queen Mary found Princess Victoria hostile and philistine. The Princess took delight in reporting the misdemeanours of her nephews, the Prince of Wales and his brothers.

† Hon Sir Harold Nicolson (1886–1968). His official life of George V was published in 1952.

‡ Nicolson's book, *Good Behaviour*, a study of certain types of civility, was published in 1955.

§ Hon Vita Sackville-West (1892–1962), married 1913, Harold Nicolson.

¶ HRH The Princess Mary (1897–1965), the Princess Royal, only daughter of George V and Queen Mary. Married 1922, 6th Earl of Harewood (1882–1947).

** HRH The Prince George, Duke of Kent (1902–42), fourth son of George V and Queen Mary. Married 1934, HRH Princess Marina of Greece and Denmark (1906–68).

changed fundamentally; I said how disappointing that sounds; he guffawed and said yes isn't it disappointing, very disappointing.

As he said that the Queen of Sweden[*] would be very helpful I ventured to hint about his own father[†] and said how sorry I was the leg hadn't mended. He said it *had* mended and that I could see him in a year's time; this accords with rumours that the King is really not well in any way. I told him I had nearly broken my back slipping in the icy street yesterday in a new pair of shoes – 'ah that is easily done, you cannot be too careful here'. We chatted a bit about Oslo and Lillehammer and Ferdinand's island, and then I took my leave. I went to see the ambassador, who has put in an official application to the archives department about my seeing papers.

On the vexed question of Q. Mary's shyness Prince Olav had always understood she had been very shy when young and had put herself into 'a steel case' from which afterwards she did not have the capacity in public to emerge.

The Crown Prince gave an impression of a capable as well as most amiable man, lonely perhaps, somewhat jovial but without the coarseness of the Duke of Gloucester. He is not entirely easy to talk to, but then are any of them? The Palace is immense, built at the time of the Union [of Norway and Sweden]; great pilastered front dominating the city, huge processional stairway with columns, made all the larger by a little housemaid peacefully using an old-fashioned carpet sweeper on the acreage of red turkey carpet. There were two somewhat doltish looking young sentries in odd uniform at the entrance. The Crown Prince's desk was a barricade of books lying on their sides, some of them seemingly art-books. He is not at all the boob Ava[‡] and others had said.

---

[*] Lady Louise Mountbatten (1889–1965), married 1923, HM King Gustaf VI Adolf of Sweden (1882–1973). Pope-Hennessy went to visit them after his Oslo visit.

[†] HM King Haakon VII of Norway (1872–1957). As noted, in the summer of 1955 the King fell and broke his thigh-bone, never fully recovering from this accident. From 30 June 1955 Crown Prince Olav acted as Regent.

[‡] Ava, Viscountess Waverley (1896–1974), married to Sir John Anderson, 1st Viscount Waverley (1882–1958), a former Home Secretary.

QUEEN MAUD OF NORWAY

10 January

MISS VON HANNO

Pope-Hennessy arrived to see Miss von Hanno at 3.30 pm.

On the afternoon of the day after that on which I had seen the Crown Prince I went again to the Palace, to the other side, to see Miss von Hanno*. A Lady-in-Waiting to Queen Maud, Miss von Hanno is now attached to the King and has apartments in the Palace. She sees him every day at luncheon. When originally asked by the Ambassador to see me she put up the sales resistance usual in courtiers and said she must be so careful. She admitted this to me, blaming it on Crawfie's† books; 'one feels so protective about the family' she explained. I knew this and so had asked the Crown Prince to put in a word for me at lunch, which he did with the result that she was most forthcoming.

I was shown into her apartments – a lofty darkish room in which we sat, perhaps a bedroom next door. She came hobbling out of her corner to greet me, leaning on a cane as she had injured her hip, or had an operation on it. She is an immensely subtle and jolly old character, half sea-captain, half-cocotte, but also well bred; laughed a great deal; drank a lot of sherry – 'or do you prefer whiskey? It's all here' (3.30 p.m.); white curly hair slightly dyed, and face made up. She had known Queen Mary well and always visited her when she came to England. Said emphatically how perfectly charming Princess Victoria was and how much loved in the family (not true). Much impressed always by Queen Mary's kindness.

'Shall I describe a Sunday at Sandringham to you?' With much giggling: 'Yes I will do that.'

They would walk to church. They would walk back from church. They (King Haakon and Queen Maud, or just Queen Maud and Miss Hanno) would lunch either at Appleton or at Sandringham. They would change from their church

---

* Miss von Hanno attended Queen Maud at the Coronation of George VI in Westminster Abbey in 1937. After Queen Maud died, she helped close Appleton House at Sandringham.

† Marion Crawford (1909–88), governess to Princesses Elizabeth and Margaret, who was tricked by her husband and some unscrupulous American editors into giving her name to articles, later encapsulated into books such as *The Little Princesses*. As a result she was ostracised by the Royal Family for the rest of her life.

clothes and go round the stables, looking at King George's yearlings, the gardens, the cow-sheds and the carving school; at the latter each guest could choose a piece of carving for himself or herself. When Miss von Hanno once remarked to King George that it was *most* unhygienic to have milk in buckets and that it would never be allowed to stand about in that way in Norway and should be pasteurised, he evinced great surprise: 'Really? really?' he said. Luncheon guests might be a bishop or a statesman such as Smuts* or once a Maharajah (Bikanir she thought) who would bow frequently with his hands pressed together. They would also go round the tenants' cottages of a Sunday.

I asked why royal families always *stood*. She said it was the most natural way of doing things, as it didn't embarrass people when the personage moved away. She agreed it was very exhausting for the entourage. Royalties have very good legs.

She thought I should see Lady Ponsonby†, Chaffinch's Farm, Birdham, nr Chichester, Sussex.

QUEEN MAUD'S DAMES D'HONNEUR AT TRONDHEIM (1906)

Pope-Hennessy then visited some of the late Queen Maud's Ladies-in-Waiting at Trondheim, where he also visited the cathedral.

On the subject of the Trondheim coronation, 1906, Ferdinand Finne's‡ old uncle, Iohn Egerborg, recalled that three of the four Maids-of-Honour of Queen Maud at that time were, rather remarkably, still alive:

1. Petra von Tongen, – who lives in Oslo but is at present staying with her daughter Mrs Roger Corbett-Millward, Bramcote Manorway, Lee-on-Solent, Hants. Generally agreed she would be the most useful. Miss von Hanno confirmed.
2. Mimi Krahg, widow of the Master of Horse. Tracked down by telephone Fru Krahg was very voluble. She was in bed and could not be seen because her

---

*   Field Marshal Jan Smuts (1870–1950), Prime Minister of South Africa.

†   Elisa Broch (1892–1977), married 1921, as his second wife, Sir George Ponsonby (1878–1969), Comptroller and Private Secretary to Queen Maud of Norway 1919–38. She was the daughter of Captain Hendrick Broch, and served as Lady-in-Waiting to Queen Maud of Norway.

‡   Ferdinand Finne (1910–99), painter and author.

'bones had fallen to pieces' but was none the less cheerful. Yes, she had seen Queen Mary and Princess Victoria on a number of occasions at that time. Princess Victoria stayed on after the Prince and Princess of Wales had left, and in fact came to Oslo and stayed in the Slott. Visually she remembered that both the Princess of Wales and Princess Victoria seemed essentially very *tall*; she was impressive, elegant and extremely 'imposant' (Norwegian meaning dignified). Frankly they had all thought her rather stiff. She attached herself to no-one and did not talk at parties in the Stiftsgaarden. She spoke English only, so far as Fru Krahg knew. Princess Victoria seemed especially tall because Fru Krahg's husband was so tall. The Princess of Wales was dressed in a pale embroidered gown with a tiara; the Kaiser Wilhelm* came *after* the Waleses had left. (Is this true?) Immediately after the coronation they all went fishing at Laerfossen near Trondheim. The King was very proud of landing difficult salmon. Princess Victoria and Queen Maud wanted to fish too but couldn't come out into the falls, so 'my husband took Princess Victoria on his shoulders, and Nansen took Queen Maud on his shoulders' and they fished like that. Several times I saw this happen. Later they each had their own small boats.

3. Alexandra Rader, née Hvitfeldt. Tracked down through her daughter, Fru Rader said she could remember nothing. I went to see her next morning at Hoffterrasse 4, when she repeated this statement. She had eyes only for Queen Maud, it had all looked splendid and beautiful, she was only twenty and of course at twenty you didn't notice anything, you felt so nervous over your own frock. A silly little woman, not unlike Cecil Beaton's mother,[†] with fluffy white hair, living in a flat crammed with creeping plants and small tables, thick yellow lace curtains draped over the windows; a modern flat in one of the new blocks which are very prettily arranged out of Oslo up the Drammensveien and towards Jar. She showed me a group of the King, Queen, etc. after the crowning which seemed, oddly, to include

---

[*]   HIM Kaiser Wilhelm II, Emperor of Germany (1859–1941), son of HRH The Princess Victoria, the Princess Royal, and thus grandson of Queen Victoria.

[†]   Esther (Etti) Beaton (1872–1962), mother of Sir Cecil Beaton (1904–80), photographer, designer, diarist, and writer. Mrs Beaton was the butt of many jokes amongst Cecil's friends.

Sir F. Knollys.* When I told Miss von Hanno about my disappointing talk with Fru Rader she said 'I will telephone to Alexandra myself. Such nonsense, although of course I imagine she didn't *remember* she didn't *know* who was who.'

FRU BRANDT

Journalist Walmot kindly took us to see one of the town's star turns, Fru Brandt who is ninety-two. She lives over a bookshop attached to a massage establishment run perhaps by a daughter. There was a small dark dining room with bookshelves up to the ceiling and all along one wall; some plants; tall chairs round the table; and a single scarlet ostrich feather in a special vase by itself. We waited here while the journalist explained who we were. There were sharp cries of excitement from Fru Brandt and her old sister, who was more dapper and active, and anxious that she should be seen at her best. Fru Brandt, a very large soft-looking puffy old lady with dead white face and hair and wire spectacles, and slightly coddy eyes, was half sitting half lying at a table covered with newly written letters. She was knitting in white silk, and on her shoulder sat one of the largest green parrots I have ever seen; it kept talking to her like a familiar. This room was as crowded as the other one, with a grand piano laden with family photographs extending to many generations, a large tank of gold-fish, several tables and two or three chairs. Christmas decorations were still up and on the table was a large tablecloth embroidered with bulky scarlet gnomes and Christmas trees.

Fru Brandt, while an interesting spectacle in herself, was not much help. She had, it finally transpired, sung in a subordinate capacity in the choir at the Coronation – mostly Grieg. There had been French waltzes at the party at the Stiftsgaarden. It (the cathedral) had glittered with candles and diamonds and pearls. Queen Maud was modest, retiring, won peoples' hearts by her manner, those who got to know her fell in love with her, she had great charm of manner at presentations, was tall, stately and regal. It suddenly transpired that Fru Brandt thought I was writing the life of Queen Maud.

(*En parenthèse*, Ferdinand's family and other Norwegians were convinced Queen Maud was a bad case of arrested development, around 14; she gave constant

---

* Sir Francis Knollys (1837–1924), later 1st Viscount Knollys, Private Secretary to Edward VII, 1870–1910, and to George V, 1910–13.

offence by dancing a whole evening through with one single English midshipman when she should have been doing her duty by the Norwegians. She was evidently considered too English and *not* a patriotic Norwegian queen.)

Fru Brandt thought 'an English military band' paraded through Trondheim's streets; perhaps the band from the yacht?

Before leaving Trondheim, Pope-Hennessy visited Fru Victoria Bocke, whom he described as 'the Lady Sybil Grant of Trondheim, but much more cultivated and with great drive'.*[88]

APPENDIX: TRONDHEIM NEWSPAPER FILES

The files of Addresseavisen for June 1906 show (as will Q.M.'s diary etc.) that the Waleses left England on the 16th in the Victoria and Albert, arrived on the 20th and anchored off Ravnkloa (between island and town). The King and Queen of Norway, with little Prince Olaf, went on board, the King in a British admiral's uniform, wearing the Order of the Bath. The crowd cheered constantly from the shore; the yacht hoisted the Norwegian flag; God Save the King was played; they remained on board 50 minutes, then all went on shore, talking happily, the two 'white-clad children' (Prince Olaf and Princess Mary aet: 9) as well. More shouting and bands.

Pope-Hennessy returned to Olso on 14 January.

---

*   Lady Sybil Grant (1879–1955), eccentric daughter of 5th Earl of Rosebery. She was a writer and designer of ceramics. In later life, she spent much time in a caravan or up a tree, communicating with her butler through a megaphone.

FOUR

KING GUSTAF VI ADOLF AND QUEEN LOUISE OF SWEDEN

16 January

Pope-Hennessy then made the short journey to Stockholm to see the King and Queen of Sweden. He stayed at the Grand Hotel.

King Gustaf (1882–1973) had reigned since 1950. He had first married Princess Margaret of Connaught, but she died of peritonitis in 1920. He had then married Lady Louise Mountbatten (1889–1965), daughter of the 1ˢᵗ Marquess of Milford Haven, the former Prince Louis of Battenberg. She was the sister of Princess Andrew of Greece (mother of the Duke of Edinburgh) and of Admiral of the Fleet Earl Mountbatten of Burma. She was a great-granddaughter of Queen Victoria and had thought herself destined for a life of spinsterhood.

The King enjoyed whatever he did, whether inspecting troops, giving a banquet or tending his garden. He relished life. He was also a connoisseur and collector. As a young man he had been given a Chinese pot, which inspired a love of Chinese artefacts. He studied these like a scholar, long before he visited China, returning with a boatload of treasures, some of which were shown at the British Museum in 1972. Bernard Berenson described him as 'a work of art in himself'.

Queen Louise had nursed in the First World War, where she learned to swear like a trooper. During the Second World War, Sweden being neutral, she had acted as an intermediary between her various royal relations in different countries. She was extremely modest, and when she visited London, stayed at the Hyde Park Hotel. She carried a note in her handbag, reading 'I am the Queen of Sweden' in case she was knocked over, which members of her family thought was the surest way to get herself locked up.

Arriving in Stockholm from Oslo on Sunday 15 January, I lunched with the King and Queen of Sweden the next day. They were at Drottningholm, the 17ᵗʰ century palace on a lake twenty minutes out of Stockholm, which they use for four or five weeks annually over Christmas-time.

I was fetched at the hotel and taken to the palace in the town, where, after waiting around with a naval ADC, I made my bow, entered the King's car and drove with him to Drottningholm. He said we would lunch alone and discuss Queen Mary after lunch.

(*Hand-written note in margin:* I described this in letter to John P.-H.)

Grand Hotel, Stockholm
Tuesday 16 January 1956

The King is *greatly* impressed by your V. & A. arrangements, and much admires it all; I said the rooms were recalcitrant being 1855, and he said the 1909 ones were worse – 'Why waste space on processional staircases, one does not process through museums.' He is really most awfully cultivated, simple and nice; very hewn-looking, with a high, thoughtful head like a Rodin, and spectacles; and hair like an old negro. She [the Queen] is small and stooped and somewhat wizened; they both look severe in repose but light up quickly and have a funny sense of humour.

After a lot of telephone calls from the Court Marshal's secretary it was arranged for a car to fetch me here and take me across the bridge to the palace. Here I was received by one of the usual tongue-tied ADCs royalty specialise in, a naval officer who stood with me in the Hall of Mirrors, a smallish 19th century room with others leading out of it. I now think that half the difficulty of royalty comes from the form of paralysis they cast over their employees or which these *generate*; they speak jerkily to one for twenty minutes, not listening, one ear cocked for the sound of a royal shoe on the parquet.

When the King appeared it was of course from the door out of which he was not expected. He is a tall, oldish man, swinging a brief-case which he flung at the ADC, saying abruptly 'Tak'. He then cross-examined me about *who* had asked me to write about Queen Mary, seemed satisfied and we were put into a huge motor-car and covered with a fur rug. My coat was held up by a diaphanous-looking military aide with pale brown hair, the lining of the left sleeve is torn and of course my arm got inextricably jammed between the lining and the coat.

We drove out past the modern town hall which the King explained to me, and we compared it to the Oslo town hall, and talked of modern Norwegian painters and of *Trondheim*. He has never been there so I bored him with this for some time, including the beauty of the theatre

THE KING AND QUEEN OF SWEEDEN

and the high standard of the *acting*. He then talked of B.B.[*] and said was I you and who was Mamma and then we got it all straight. Drottningholm is splendid when you approach it, standing upon a frozen lake; Queen Louise said she was married in the winter and always thought all the frozen expanses in Stockholm & at Drottningholm were meadows until the spring – this is pretty royal?

It is a very large palace built by a widowed queen[†] in 1670 or so, quite untouched inside except for some Gustaf III[‡] improvements and one or two *dreadful* rooms done by King Oscar[§] and the present King's grandfather[¶] – 'don't look at this room' he would say taking me through after lunch 'I'm afraid my grandfather was responsible'. The ADC had already told me we were to be alone, which I gathered was an honour; we drove right round the palace past sentries and stopped at a tiny door almost in the basement which *flew* open.

We took off our coats and the ADC gave me a powerful Swedish nudge to show I was to hang my coat on another coat stand than the King. We then went through several empty rooms to a large beautiful cube room with painted ceiling and tapestries lining the wall, a Spanish carpet on the floor, and here was the Queen, and a silent Lady-in-Waiting. Lunch took place two rooms away in a small square room; we helped ourselves to meatballs and sweetcorn and lemonade and claret and salad and cheese ('*salade à la Française*, I like that' remarked King Gustaf IV). It was awfully agreeable and intelligent, the conversation, and one's only difficulty was to remember to toss in 'sirs' and 'ma'ams' and 'as I was saying to the King'.

After lunch the suite withdrew and I sat between them in front of the fire and we had a long technical Queen Mary talk which I have put in my notebook. They then both showed me over the palace for 3/4s of an hour, she is very erudite too and has excellent taste: 'oh that's where they put that

---

[*] Bernard Berenson (1865–1959), art collector and historian, living at Villa I Tatti in the hills above Florence. The King of Sweden first met him in 1923. B.B. was struck by the then Crown Prince's knowledge of Far Eastern objects and respected him as a serious archeologist.

[†] Queen Hedwig Eleanore (1636–1715), married King Carl X Gustaf of Sweden (1622–60).

[‡] King Gustaf III of Sweden (1746–92), said to have reigned during Sweden's 'Golden Age'.

[§] King Oscar I of Sweden (1799–1859).

[¶] King Oscar II of Sweden (1829–1907)

desk, you see, we never know' she kept remarking. They think B.B. *so* lucky to have 'that young Mr Mostyn-Owen" with him, can he continue the work after B.B. dies? Nicky Mariano[†], poor soul, pour soul, breaking her ankle, and no thinner about the waist-line than the year before last. Was there some scandal about Leigh Ashton[‡]? 'it was the Queen saw his resignation in *The Times* and we have been wondering ever since.' What a pity your brother was not appointed,' said the King. 'But he could not go on writing, all that administrative work' said the Queen. It was all enjoyable, but I am waiting to leave Ava's note on the Crown Princess until the day I go (I consulted the ambassador about this) as I am *not* interested in royalty *per se*, and am quite surfeited for the time being.[89]

At the end of luncheon the Lady-in-Waiting and the ADC left us, and we sat in front of the fire in the saloon they use. I sat on a stool between them. We drank coffee and I was told I could smoke.

They had been wondering how they could help me, they said, and had evidently given the matter some thought. The Queen said her mother (Princess Louis of Battenberg)[§] had always been a close friend of Queen Mary, particularly in early days when she felt *sorry* for her; she being a young married woman when Queen Mary was still unmarried (this was not clear, it could have been the other way round).[¶] Her mother always said how shy she was. Both King and Queen re-emphasised her knowledge of The Family, her intense interest in remote relations, her demands for photos of every new infant; her photograph books, the Queen

---

* William Mostyn-Owen (1929–2011), English art connoisseur and writer.

† Nicky Mariano (1887–1968), Berenson's librarian, secretary, amanuensis, lover and biographer.

‡ Sir Leigh Ashton (1897–1983), Director of the Victoria & Albert Museum 1945–55. Of him Sir John Pope-Hennessy wrote: 'He made a late marriage [to the lesbian editress, Madge Garland in 1952]. 'Sir Leigh,' warned Queen Mary, with royal prescience when she came to the museum, 'don't let it spoil your work.' But it did precisely that, and he succumbed to drink.' [John Pope-Hennessy, *Learning to Look*, p. 162] Ashton was retired and spent his last years in the well-known psychiatric hospital, St Andrew's Hospital, Northampton.

§ HSH Princess Louis of Battenberg, née Princess Victoria of Hesse (1863–1950), later Marchioness of Milford Haven. She was a granddaughter of Queen Victoria, being the daughter of Princess Alice and Grand Duke Louis of Hesse.

¶ This was the correct way round. Princess Victoria married in 1884 and Princess May in 1894.

thinks, were arranged under branches of The Family. The Queen's mother had endless funny stories about the Duchess of Teck; they were so poor that as a girl she used to suspect that the sugar on the strawberries was mixed with powder, as it didn't sweeten anything. Once when the Duchess was opening a charity bazaar in Kensington, which had been greatly aided by Mr John Barker* the grocer, she had said 'And now I want especially to thank Mr Barker, to whom we owe so much' which caused great embarrassment as he was their chief creditor. Queen Mary's shyness could be attributed to her mother's ample nature, and her forthcoming manner, and way of flinging her arms about. Queen Louise does not herself recall 'Aunt Mary' Teck though she could in fact have seen her, she thinks.

The King used to see a lot of Queen Mary over her collections. 'We collectors' she used to say to him. He says her jades were late and not good, and his general attitude was somewhat affectionately patronising about her possessions. Queen Louise thought it a pity they weren't to be put in a museum – 'what can the poor little Queen† do with them all? She has too much already, at Windsor and Buckingham Palace'. The King said her catalogue system was first-rate and that I must emphasise this. Everything labelled and catalogued in her own handwriting. She was not easy at first with people, but once you had won through she was extremely friendly and kind; the getting going was difficult.

The King thinks I should see Frogmore House and her arrangements there.‡

While not producing anything startling, helpful or new, they were both clearly so fond of her that one got a distinct impression of someone admirable and loveable.

Pope-Hennessy left Stockholm on 22 January, returning to London.

---

*   John Barker (1840–1914), set up as a draper and ironmonger in Kensington, and in 1880 acquired 75 Kensington High Street as a grocery business, also taking on 12 and 14 Ball Street. The company developed into John Barker & Co Ltd and traded until taken over by House of Fraser in 1975.

†   HM Queen Elizabeth II (b. 1926), granddaughter of Queen Mary. She inherited all Queen Mary's possessions.

‡   Queen Mary turned part of Frogmore House into a family museum.

FIVE

24 January

Returning from Sweden, Pope-Hennessy dined with Harold Nicolson, and his elder brother, Lord Carnock (1884–1982), and they talked about Queen Mary's time in India. As Prince and Princess of Wales, they had visited India, sailing from Britain on 19 October 1905, and not returning until 6 May 1906. They sailed in the battleship, RMS Renown.

I met Lord Carnock*, Harold Nicolson's elder brother, on 24 January, when we all three dined at the Beefsteak.

It transpired that as a young man Lord Carnock was one of two sub-lieutenants on the RENOWN, which 'the Duke and Duchess'† boarded at Genoa in November 1905 for their Indian tour. There was a roster of officers to dine 'in the cuddy' with the Royalties, and so he frequently ate with them. They took it as a part of their duties and slightly disenjoyed it than otherwise. The Duchess had a conversational technique of her own, which was to probe searchingly into the home lives and families of the young men – a cover for her shyness. They thought her stiff. On the way out they all practised quadrilles, and he often had to dance with her. An innovation which he is certain was directly due to the Duchess was to include warrant officers at their table; the Duke as a professional sailor would never have dreamed of this himself. On one occasion when a warrant officer had to be sent home for stealing out of the safe there was some awkwardness as she had particularly liked him and kept asking about him: 'he was an odd character, and of course she saw that, and liked him'. The junior officers used to answer her questions with their minds on other things – whether they would be allowed to go pigsticking or not – and so on. She had a nasty temper; at Bombay the tide had

---

*   3ʳᵈ Lord Carnock (1884–1982). He became a Captain in the Royal Navy.

†   Before becoming Prince and Princess of Wales, George V and Queen Mary had been Duke and Duchess of Cornwall and York.

been misjudged and so she had to go down far too steep a gangplank and was furious. At Rangoon the officer of the watch had forgotten that at a certain point the time changed, and they were an hour late; she was very angry; Lord Carnock was standing at attention at the head of the gangplank, when the Duchess, fuming and gathering up her skirts, shoved her parasol into his hand remarking 'hold that, you idiot!' The quadrille practice was not just to pass the time but to get ready for entertainments in India.

SIX

23 March

Pope-Hennessy went to see the Dowager Duchess of Devonshire at 6pm.

Evelyn, Duchess of Devonshire (1870–1960) was the next consulted. She was the widow of 9th Duke of Devonshire, and was the grandmother of the then Duke. Born in 1870 as Lady Evelyn Fitzmaurice, she was the elder daughter of 5th Marquess of Lansdowne. In 1892 she married Victor Cavendish and he succeeded his uncle as 9th Duke of Devonshire in 1908. He was Governor-General of Canada from 1916 to 1921. From 1910 until 1953, the Duchess served as Mistress of the Robes to Queen Mary, and was thus in attendance on her at all state occasions. In 1937 she was appointed the first ever non-Royal female GCVO.

The Duchess had a difficult life. According to his grandson (the 11th Duke), the 9th Duke was 'an easy-going, ironic, laconic man', but in 1925 he suffered a severe stroke, after which he became 'bad-tempered and difficult to get along with'.[90] From that time onwards he could not bear his wife and hardly ever spoke to her. The Duchess's long-suffering secretary, Elsie Saunders, had to act as go-between.

The Duchess took over the running of Chatsworth. As John Pearson put it: 'Her chilly, strong-willed presence actually enhanced the authoritarian regime which still survived from the nineteenth century.'[91] The wife of one of the employees said of her: 'Duchess Evie – she was Queen Mary's type, very regal, wouldn't speak to you unless she wanted something, and I can't say she ever thanked you either.'[92]

The Duke died at Chatsworth in 1938, after which the Duchess lived at nearby Hardwick Hall, which before that had only been used for a few weeks each year. She occupied the Withdrawing Chamber, which she turned into a state bedchamber. A fine needlewoman, she restored the Verdure tapestry, and when parts proved impossible, she painted the missing pieces in onto beige repp of a rough texture. She often sat in a bay window of the Low Great Chamber (or Dining Room), working on her needlepoint with one of her daughters. She also introduced rush matting to the floors. As Mark Girouard wrote: 'For fifty years her strong character, lively curiosity and delicately incisive voice dominated the house.'[93]

Hardwick Hall was handed over to the National Trust in 1959, and the Duchess died in 1960.

On Friday 24 March 1956 I saw the old Duchess of Devonshire (who calls herself the Dowager, though she is no longer so)[*] at 22 York House, Kensington Church Street, a block of late Victorian flats. She is a tall, alert, *fine*-looking (in the French sense) old lady, with thinning white hair and great winningness of manner; a very acute face.

She began by saying she could not really help as, though one never believed it until one *was* old, being old *did* in fact make one forget things. Princess May was 3 or 4 years older than herself, and was 'the big girl' at the dancing class kept by Taglioni[†] in Connaught Square, to which the Duchess went as a girl (she is the daughter of Lord Landsdowne). Taglioni was then very old, very wizened and small; she had lost her money and had to open this school. There was drugget on the floor, and small gold chairs for parents when they came; the children used to giggle at the Duchess of Teck who was so large that she had to sit on two of these chairs at once. Princess May was always awkward and shy there, a big, pink and white, gawky girl; one of the lessons consisted in entering the front drawing room at Connaught Square draped in a chenille table cloth from the back drawing room as a train – teaching one deportment. Princess May was always horribly embarrassed by this effort, an intense one for her.

Princess May's hair was between gold and light brown; she had a very pretty complexion, but became much prettier later. Her hair, the Duchess thinks, was artificially curled. It was excessively thick; whereas most young ladies had it at night in four plaits 'with a piece of rag' at the end, she would have had perhaps six plaits. The Duchess remembers her envy as a little girl when Princess May appeared at the class with her hair half up and half down: up in front and hanging loose at the back.

---

[*] Lady Evelyn Fitzmaurice (1870–1960), married 1892, 9th Duke of Devonshire (1868–1938). Her son, 10th Duke had died in 1950, thus his widow, Mary, was officially the Dowager Duchess.

[†] Marie Taglioni (1804–84), famous Italian ballerina of the Romantic ballet era. Strauss composed the Marie Taglioni Polka in her honour. She retired from dancing in 1847 and taught social dance to children and society ladies.

THE DOWAGER DUCHESS OF DEVONSHIRE

She always understood that the Duke of Teck was an epileptic, his fits of rage when he threw plates and so on at his wife being 'epileptic tempers'.

The Duke of Clarence: He stayed with Lord Landsdowne* in Canada and (I gathered) in Calcutta. I said was he somewhat backward: 'That is putting it very mildly. He was a mental deficient. I remember him quite well.' He had inherited all Queen Alexandra's lateness – e.g. when half an hour late for a function in Calcutta, and keeping everyone waiting, he came downstairs, put his hand to his necktie, and then went up and changed it, taking another half hour. A mercy he died when he did. Very amiable, nothing against him, but just impossibly silly.

Queen Mary's dressers were always idle and disagreeable. Furious if you referred to them as 'maids' and very unpleasant to other people's servants – 'very airified'. At the end of her life they bullied her and were beastly to her.†

Q.M. a very bad sailor, getting a contraction of the muscles in the back of the neck in bad weather, very painful. Didn't like out of doors or Balmoral *at all*. Extraordinary discretion and tied-in quality; only *once* in many years of intimate collaboration was she ever relaxed with the D. of Devonshire; in a carriage in India, suddenly talked a bit about various personal things. 'Unlike other members of that family' she did read books or had them read to her.

Her shyness and restraint the result of her mother's ebullience and indiscretion and high spirits.

She could probably have been cleverer with her own children; less reserved, evincing more affection.

Very perceptive and quick. In Delhi the brick paths had been oiled to keep down the dust: trailing dresses would have got dirty. The Queen picked up her skirts which were not full enough to be picked up (fashion just on the change, 1912). The Duchess thought it absurd-looking but said nothing. The next day 2 little pages produced to hold the skirts, ended by frogwalking with them: Q.M. saying quickly 'Evie doesn't like me pulling up my skirt' – having twigged.

Queen Alexandra very stupid indeed. King George often short-tempered and snubbing with her.

---

* 5th Marquess of Lansdowne (1845–1927). He was Governor-General of Canada 1883–88, and Viceroy of India 1888–94. The Duke of Clarence visited India between November 1889 and March 1890.

† Most notably Miss Dunham. See later.

In March 1956 the art-dealer and bachelor socialite, Charles Harding, invited Pope-Hennessy to come to his rooms at 90 Piccadilly to meet Princess Marie Louise, daughter of Princess Christian, and a granddaughter of Queen Victoria. The appointment was set for 18 April. 'Would you please be here punctually at 5.45,' demanded Harding. It would appear that this meeting did not take place, possibly because the Princess was ill, or because Pope-Hennessy had to go to Sandringham. Princess Marie Louise died on 8 December that year, at the age of 84. On 22 April 1957, the Princess Royal wrote to Pope-Hennessy: 'I am too sorry you never saw Princess Marie Louise …'[94] She offered to help him meet the Duke of Windsor and Grand Duchess Xenia of Russia, and succeeded with both.

SEVEN

SANDRINGHAM

16–18 April

As the Spring came, Pope-Hennessy made a visit to Sandringham, the Royal Family's Norfolk home. Sandringham had been an 18th century manor house, and was bought by Edward VII as Prince of Wales in 1863 and rebuilt. It became, after 1910, the country retreat of his widow, Queen Alexandra, until her death in 1925. From the time of their marriage in 1893 until 1925 – effectively 1926 – the Duke and Duchess of York lived at York Cottage on the Sandringham estate. They then moved into the 'Big House', where George V died in January 1936.

In widowhood, Queen Mary never went to Balmoral or Scotland again, but she spent several summers at Sandringham, and, apart from the war years, invariably spent Christmas there with her family. This tradition continued right up to the end, though in December 1952, she scarcely left her room.

On Monday 16 April I went down to stay with Captain W.A. Fellowes*, the Agent for Sandringham, at his house in the hamlet of West Newton. We drove through Cambridge, Ely and King's Lynn, stopping at each, in fine Spring weather. There were daffodils and primroses everywhere.

I arrived at family tea-time, after which Fellowes, who is a charming, quick-witted Norfolk gentleman in a tweed cap and with an old-fashioned moustache (aet. circa 55) took me out for a preliminary look round. We walked up the road, through a gate into a yard where retrievers are trained, and on down a sloping path to York Cottage. This building has to be seen to be believed: it is grotesquely ugly, unarchitected, like something designed by a child – all gables, and beams and little balconies, and hexagonal turrets. It stands on the rim of a melancholy, reed-infested pond or 'lake', a leaden pelican looks into the water,

---

* Captain (Sir) William Fellowes (1899–1986), Agent to Edward VIII, George VI, and The Queen, Sandringham Estate 1936–64.

an iron bridge (replacing the old ornamental one) leads across to an untidy island, rife with primroses. (N.B. Mrs Bill* later showed me a letter written to her in Q.M.'s old age saying how odd it was that she had *never* seen the daffodils at Sandringham, not having been there at that time of the year). We went round to the front door, which is ornate, and into the house, after first looking at the dining room which is, like all the rooms, minute and has a bay, formed of the inside of a turret, which they used for breakfast. They would have tea under an awning stretched from the dining room French windows on warm days.

On the left of the door is King George's small study, still hung with scarlet serge† given him in France (v. the Ferays'‡ chateau to which I went last year), though it is now cleared of the shrubs which rendered it pitch dark in the old days. Downstairs are two or three more rooms and the drawing room, all of dwarf proportions. Upstairs Q.M.'s dressing-room, with Maple-like fitted furniture painted in white, for all the world like an hotel near the Gare de Lyon; her bedroom next door, where all but one child was born, is equally microscopic and claustrophobic, and looks out over the lake. The best room is the schoolroom, over the dining room and repeating the same bay. There is with it all a total lack of fantasy about the building; it was expanded from being the Bachelors Cottage (built by a Colonel Edis)§ by flinging on now one room now another, like a house made from several sets of toy bricks. It is middle-class, suburban, in some indefinable way pretentious and utterly uncosy. Of course it is now the estate office, and the paint is peeling off the outside woodwork; but even in its heyday it must have been peculiarly unattractive.

We then walked up to the Big House, which is as large as York Cottage is small. It is a preposterous, long, brick-and-stone building with a terrace behind it (no balustrading); once more hotel-like – Pitlochry or Stratpeffer perhaps – tremendously vulgar and emphatically, almost defiantly hideous and gloomy. The

---

*   Charlotte (Lala) Bill (1874–1964), nurse to Princess Mary and the younger children. She lived at Mary Cottages, West Newton.
†   Military broadcloth for soldiers' tunics. It remains there to this day.
‡   Jean and Thierry Feray, brothers, officials of *Monuments Historiques*; killed together in a car crash 1999.
§   Colonel Sir Robert Edis (1839–1927), architect. Pope-Hennessy would not have been surprised to learn that he also built 100 Piccadilly, the Constitutional Club, and the Grand Central Railway Hotel, Marylebone Station.

grounds round are very pretty, especially at this time of the year; good trees and shrubs, ground falling away into dells and rising to small eminencies, a larger lake, a vista of green lawns fading away towards the Church Walk and the church tower in the distance. A giant Chinese god, not exactly a Buddha, with a lascivious smirk on its face (rather the face of Kruschev)* sits under a pagoda-roof, flanked by Chinese lions: Admiral [name omitted] sent it from China for King Edward; the children, the late King told Fellowes, always called it 'Laughy' or 'Goddy'. The late King laid out a formal garden running from the house towards the Norwich Gates, and installed a stone figure of Father Time at the end of it; he also abolished some beds and ponds and extended the flat wide lawns. Queen Mary was always planting, as she hated to be pried upon by the public from the Norwich Gates, which are unexpectedly close to the house; it seems strange they could not have found a property more truly secluded. All the blinds of the sleeping formidable house were drawn, tall white blinds, and the windows glittered in the orange setting sun. It was all rather ominous and charged with implications of past unhappiness which, one could sense, but not grasp.

Capt. Fellowes, himself a source of fascinating stories and recollections of Q.M. in late years (he went there first in Edward VIII's brief reign) had arranged a series of interviews, over some of which he was charmingly and wittily apologetic. The first was with 'the great Lady Willens[†], who will tell you a lot of tosh'.

Lady Willens [*in fact Willans*] is the widow of Sir Frederic[k] Willens, one of the royal doctors, and of far more interest to me as the daughter of that Dr Manby[‡] who was the resident physician when the Duke of Clarence fell ill in January 1892,

---

* Nikita Khruschev (1894–1971), Russian President in the Communist era 1958–64.

† Wynefred Manby (1884–1964), daughter of Sir Alan Manby, married 1916, Sir Frederic Willans (1884–1949), Surgeon-Apothecary to HM Household at Sandringham 1924–45. As such he was in attendance at the death of Queen Alexandra in 1925, and signed the bulletins on the illness and death of George V in 1936. Lady Willans lived at West Newton House.

‡ Sir Alan Manby (1848–1925), Surgeon-Apothecary to the Prince and Princess of Wales and the Duke of York at Sandringham, 1885, attended the Prince and Princess of Wales on their Colonial Tour, 1901, continued with Edward VII, Queen Alexandra and George V.

and who sent for Broadbent* and Laking† (or did the *Queen* send for (?) Laking off her own bat??). Thus she was brought up on the place and lived there always; she now has a house at West Newton; a small, long-faced old woman, with a sharp hard air which is contrived to be quizzical, an affected down-to-earth clipped manner, a leg in an iron, a walking stick. She evidently has in her own eyes a reputation for speaking out, for she said, on reading me some peculiarly banal letter of Q.M.'s about Sir Frederick being ill ('I know what you are suffering, for I went through the same thing in 1928 with my husband' or some such) that she would not let me see the text, or have it for publication; also a parting shot 'now don't you go putting me in your book, I won't have it'. I replied I did not intend to put *people* in my book at all. She told me several totally pointless anecdotes, of how the King and Queen ('so different to nowadays') used to walk into her house and ask to scratch the pig in the pig-yard, for Lady Willans is one of that numerous and obeisant throng of royal snobs which flourish like fungi in the shadow of royalty. She did however say how remarkably interested Q.M. was in everything in the village: she would direct the women how to bring up or not bring up their children, visit the school, interfere in a high-handed but beneficent manner. They would seldom go out of the estate in early years; uncertain if Q.M. drove a trap herself; Queen Alexandra always did at a smacking pace. (Fellowes here said Q.M. had said to him driving one day along the twisting Princess's Walk (or Drive?) how terrified she had always been at the corners when driving with her mother-in-law, who apparently went like the wind round the bends). Lady Willans said Queen Alexandra's presence, continued sojourn rather, in the Big House was a source of acute grievance presumably (Fellowes said the late King used to talk of it, adding 'how that rankled') as she let the place go to pieces, moth everywhere. The general idea was of the King and Queen popping in and out of the village.

---

* Sir John Broadbent (1865–1946), Physician at London Fever Hospital, and expert on heart disease. He once declared that diseases such as influenza, pneumonia, measles and scarlet fever could be eliminated by the proper ventilation of offices and public buildings, the avoidance of overcrowding, the abolition of children's parties and if people ceased to indulge in indiscriminate kissing.

† Sir Francis Laking (1847–1914), Surgeon-Apothecary to Queen Victoria, and Physician-in-Ordinary to Edward VII and George V. His name was recently made controversial by the suggestion that he might have artificially inseminated Queen Maud of Norway with sperm from himself or his son. No credence was given to this theory.

The one capital thing she told me was that her father Dr Manby said it was quite obvious from the beginning that Princess May and Prince George were falling in love; when attending the Duke of Clarence in his bedroom that fatal time he could see, out of the window, P.M. and P.G. pacing the gardens hand in hand.

On leaving this crisp and unpleasing old lady we next called on Mrs Bill ('Lala') who was a mine of information, and a most delightful, simple woman, talking of them all with real affection and amusement and not in the least tainted by the royal atmosphere. She lives in a cottage, with a beautifully crammed and kept garden in front of it, and last year went round the world with Mrs Mabel Butcher*, the old retired housekeeper of the Big House. She has clear kindly blue eyes, peering out through gold-wire spectacles, pointed nose, pink cheeks, a felt hat pulled well down. She had got out her albums for me and begged me to snip out any I wanted but this I could not bear to do. Her information included:

1. She came to them in 1896, while Mrs Peters was still there (Lady Willans had told me that Peters was no good, nor was her *remplaçante,* so in the end they promoted the young Lala from under-nurse to full nurse, with 3 children under five on her hands; 'how I wish I could push out the walls of this nursery' she used to cry in despair at the cramped quarters at York Cottage).

2. *Duchess of Teck*: a smile lit up her face; 'a lovely lady', or some such phrase; always smiling, always late, always good-natured.

3. *Duke of Teck*: 'what was he like?' She looked straight at me through her spectacles and paused. 'A *trial,* oh what a trial! Such a tiresome gentleman.' The Duchess always so good with him; she imitated him wailing in a pathetic voice on a walk 'Mary, Mary, don't leave me behind' and the Duchess turning, smiling and encouraging him.

4. *Queen Alexandra*: always incredibly late, there would be the King 'stewing away inside himself in a carriage' and then she would appear beautifully dressed and smile and say 'How are you?' and he would almost explode. When the parents were away for the first time (1901–2?) the children went to the grandparents, who spoiled them. King Edward was *very* difficult and explosive, and would not let Mrs Bill keep the children to regular hours, while Queen Alexandra, combining grandmaternal care with silliness and

---

* Her correct name was Miss Sarah Butcher, and she was Housekeeper at Sandringham before Mrs Robertson. Housekeepers were known as 'Mrs' by tradition.

unpunctuality used to insist on bathing the baby, whatever the time or whether it was feeding hour or not.

5. *Prince John*[*]: I did not like to ask her, but from her photographs and tone he was obviously the favourite of them all (her own favourite, I mean). 'Johnny' she would say whenever we came to a snap of them. I said 'He died very suddenly?' 'Yes.'

6. *Household at York Cottage.* Terrible squash (some of her photos show herself and 2 nursery maids in starched white dresses and caps, looking enormous anyway). She has a photograph of the servants, including Mademoiselle Tatry[†], the French maid who was with P.M. before she married, a plump benign looking woman with puffed hair and glasses. There was 'the German girl' who was an under-nurse and talked German with them (I gather at meals) Mlle Dussau[‡], Princess Mary of York's governess. The dressers didn't answer to the name of maid, thought themselves a cut above that. Mrs Bill was at Balmoral at the time of the Czar's[§] visit, when the children had to be turned out into the agent's house.

7. *York House,* equally a dreadful squash, no proper space for the growing children (this the Duke of Gloucester had already told me).

8. I asked who could be an Anna Stephens who wrote to P.M. at the time of the Duchess of Teck's death, saying that little David understood it and was sad. She said there certainly was a nurse-maid, an Anna Stephens at the

---

[*] HRH The Prince John (1905–19), fifth son of George V and Queen Mary. His health was fragile, and he was sent to live at Wood Farm, Sandringham in the care of Mrs Bill. It was this prince that was the subject of the fictional film, *The Lost Prince*, made by Stephen Poliakoff in 2003.

[†] Marguerite Tatry (1852–1925), Queen Mary's maid when a girl, born in Aubusson, France. Later her dresser.

[‡] Mlle José Dussau (died in France, 1924). She came from a French wine family, her uncle, Louis Meyniac, being senior partner of Mestregat Meyniac of Bordeaux. She was found by Queen Mary on her 1901 visit to Australia, where she was governess to the children of 2nd Lord Tennyson (1852–1928), Governor of South Australia 1899–1902, and in attendance on Lady Tennyson. She became governess to Princess Mary and her brothers 1904–1910. The Tennysons were not pleased when Queen Mary hijacked her to teach her children French. Later she acted as a kind of Lady-in-Waiting to Princess Mary.

[§] HIM Tsar Nicholas II of Russia (1868–1918). He was Queen Alexandra's nephew. He came to Balmoral in 1896.

time, but that she had no business to go writing to the Duchess, it would not have been, I strongly gathered, her place. Later in the afternoon Mrs Bill walked down to the house bringing me Mlle Tatry's copy of Fortescue's Durbar book[*], given by Q.M.

9. *Madame Bricka*: Mme Bricka[†] was a very imposing woman. She showed me 3 snapshots of her, one standing in a large hat and boa, with a long walking-stick in her hand, by the gates at the bottom of church Walk. She taught the York children French from time to time.

We next proceeded, by the shooting-brake, twisting along the tarmac paths across the lawns, to the vicarage and church. The vicar, a new one, a genial handsome well set up young man in spectacles, and his wife, an English young woman with a long sharp bony nose and red cheeks, gave us some sherry in their drawing room, done up not unprettily in 'contemporary' paper, all very white and light. The church itself is a kind of minor mausoleum, profile plaques, life-size, of members of the Family on the walls, an encrusted altar as a memorial to Edward VII, and at the west end a memorial window of 3 saints, the central one, St Edward, having the head of the Duke of Clarence and Avondale with a halo behind it; there is another of these somewhere (St George's Chapel, or Down Street; check); very odd. Tablets commemorating Ed. VII's recovery from typhoid etcetera. Not, as the *books* say, like an ordinary country church in the least, but more like the private chapel of a family of ailing megalomaniacs: the shrine of a clique. The family sat sideways to the altar, in the choir-stalls, to right of altar as you face it; the household to left. Whenever one died a brass plate was affixed to the prayer-book stand running the length of the pew, saying that this had been the seat of e.g. Queen Alexandra, Prince Eddy, etc., for 28 or 40 or 32 years or whatever it may have been. The bas-reliefs are in white marble, on medallions carved upon oblong plaques. The place is kind of pretty full up.

I lunched alone with Capt. Fellowes who talked a great deal, and he told me many aspects of dealing with Queen Mary which I must log separately. After luncheon we attacked the big house, which was looking slightly more friendly in the spring sunshine, with its blinds pulled up for my benefit.

---

[*]   Hon John Fortescue, *The Royal Visit to India* (Macmillan, 1912).

[†]   Hélène Bricka (1844–1914), Queen Mary's governess when a girl. She died in Kensington.

We began with Mr Mannington, the tapissier, son of the previous tapissier, a baldish stoutish cockneyish man in horn-rimmed glasses, beneficently ready to show one everything. We started in the servants quarters and his store-room, where were stacked in cupboards the hundreds or thousands of small flower garden pictures, postcard size, with which Q.M. adorned her bed-room and dressing-room etc. I had a quantity of these out, and then attacked the photographs from her bedside and also from a panel she had made for them in her dressing-bath-room near the built-in cupboards. These were more or less what one would expect; although more of Prince Eddy than I would have imagined: a dreadful drawing in flat profile gazing out of the villa window at Heidelberg (or was it Dresden* he went to?) 1889; the hopeless heavy chin much in evidence; also photos of him, 3 in all I think. A very pretty water-colour of the Duke of Teck in youth in the uniform of some Imperial regiment. A large photo of the Duchess of Teck in the last year of her life, dressed as the Electress Sophia for a Jubilee ball†, powdered hair, looking very ill but still smiling poor old thing, the letter S embroidered on her gloves; no doubt the *last photo* taken but not a very personal one. A small tall Medici-shop-like Tuscan crucifixion, with 'In Piam Memoriam' and then the date of the Duchess's death in Oct. 1897 on the frame; somehow very touching as carrying one back to the happy Florence times. The flower-gardens (v. her Xmas cards) were innumerable, but there were also some pretty pictures by Rose Barton‡ of the York babies lying in gardens in the dappled shade. It is curious, for Fellowes says she did not like gardening especially was not interested in the growing of flowers; hated mauve flowers and had them all changed to pink in the beds; had more and more little beds made, but was *bored* by the processes.

We went through the china pantry etc. to the baize door into the house, where we met Mrs Robertson§, the housekeeper, an obsequious person with a large protuberant but not wide face (not a thin one, either), hair drawn back in a grey bun, dressed in black with a black cardigan and when you got close to her smelling faintly fusty or musty. We then went into the house proper, and the atmosphere closed in on one: the long narrow library, with coved ceiling, architected like

---

* The Duke of Clarence was sent to Heidelberg to improve his German in 1884.

† The Duchess of Teck wore this outfit at the Devonshire House Ball on 2 July 1897, as a tribute to her ancestress, Electress Sophia of Hanover.

‡ Rose Barton (1856–1929), watercolourist.

§ Jessie Robertson, Housekeeper at Sandringham for many years.

a passage in the London tube, is very authentic and untouched; originally the Bowling Alley, it was converted to a library (pretty, light-veneer bookcases) when York Cottage ceased to be Bachelor quarters, on the York wedding, and the bachelors had to be found rooms in the house, hence the alley went and the library came downstairs. At the so to speak *house* end of it is the smoking room, which forms part of it, and was there when the alley was (vide 'Duchess of Teck to her Chicks' about lionising Aunt Augusta all over the house). This is startling to say the least: oriental tiles, vivid artificial marbled walls and so on; very Leightonish and not unattractive because so emphatic. Next the billiard-room the only part of the house not affected by the fire (Edward VII had added it on to the earlier house); again very authentic, smelling of cigars, walls with Leech cartoons etc. Next the dining room, effectually disinfected by the Queen Mother* who has painted it lime green and hung the Goya tapestries in it; next the drawing room, which Mrs Robertson says is substantially the same, white and gold 1870 attempt at 1760, but less crowded now than of yore. In the panelling are set pictures (by Luke Fildes?)† of the Wales girls, and over the fireplace Queen Alexandra looking lovely, full-length. It is not at all an ugly room, and must have easily lent itself to the large house-parties, you could *see* them coming through the doors. Next a small sitting room, with the only 2 decent pictures in the house, Q. Victoria by Winterhalter and a self-portrait of Landseer, both installed by Q.M. Next the famous hall, where tea was always taken at a narrow oblong table, Queen Alexandra and subsequently Queen Mary, presiding at one end. Here again the ghastly good taste of the Queen Mother had been at work; Gobelins from White Lodge (beautiful, but unsuitable), the panelling pickled and the shine taken off it, the stuffed bear swept away; the piano original with very ornate carved brass hinges, at which Q. Alexandra would have played. There is a musicians gallery at one end of the hall. The hall is or was at the centre of the house, before the long tail was added: it opens on the carriage portico of the main entrance. (We had previously been into the downstairs bedroom – where I think George VI was found dead‡ – and into a little library or study used by the late King and his father for interviews or as a waiting room I didn't understand which). The tea-room and Chinese room,

---

* HM Queen Elizabeth The Queen Mother (1900–2002), formerly Lady Elizabeth Bowes-Lyon, married 1923, HRH The Duke of York (1895–1952), later HM King George VI.

† Sir Luke Fildes (1843–1918), portrait-painter.

‡ George VI died at Sandringham aged 56, on 6 February 1952.

Queen Mary's own arrangement, is one of the creepiest parts of this somehow frightening house: the tea-room was a small poky room with leather furniture in the middle of the house, with three windows (bowed inwards) looking out on to a conservatory; the glass was removed from these by Q.M. and the conservatory made Chinese with silk wall hangings, things like umbrella-stands, vases, jades, Chinese griffins and so on; while in it you feel you are being watched from the tea-room and a more worrying room I never saw, it was like something in a creeping nightmare. 'It's all so bewtyfool' Mrs Robertson kept chanting, snatching at the dust-covers to reveal some very garish and late silk hangings.

We went up a subsidiary staircase to the bedroom floor. The *main* staircase is almost incredibly gloomy, a great square windowless well of the same tangerine-coloured wood, with some family portraits by Angeli* hung at the bottom. At the head of the smaller stairs is a huge square picture of an 18th century king of Denmark, given to Q. Alexandra by some Danish city or organisation so far as I remember from Queen Mary's careful notes about the objects and pictures in the house, kept in a chiffonier in what was her boudoir. This boudoir is a large light airy sympathetic room, still with some of her French and English furniture, chairs covered by herself, glass topped table filled with Fabergé etc. It looks over the garden, or back of the house. A central heating system was installed but she would never have it connected, sharing Queen Victoria's liking for the chilly. Further down the corridor is her dressing-room, connecting by a narrow passage with her bedroom. These were Queen Alexandra's rooms: the bath-dressing room in white with fitted cupboards, all very maple-ish; painted white fetched in with a slightly greenish blue, a big carved blue-painted crowned monogram A over the cupboard; under which Queen Mary had put a smaller but similar monogram of her own. The bath, set in the wall in a niche of amber-coloured or marmalade-coloured marble is white tin, built in, with 2 sets of taps, one for a shower. The marble bath of Queen Alexandra was removed on Queen Mary's orders, the men having the greatest difficulty in heaving it out of the house. On either side of the bath alcove tall thin little hanging cases contain Fabergé and more of her miniature stuff. The passage to the bedroom is still closely hung with flower-gardens, like the ones in the cupboard in Mr Mannington's store. The bedroom itself

---

* Heinrich von Angeli (1840–1925), Austrian portrait painter, who painted Queen Victoria and many members of the British, German and Russian Royal Families. He was especially adept at uniforms and decorations.

is a large room, with sofa etc. of flowered needlework, firescreens painted with roses by disabled ex-servicemen etc. It is now painted an off-white or ivory colour and inhabited by our present Sovereign, who has moved Q.M.'s bed upstairs and installed one painted to look like bamboo. It is about the most de-personalised room I have ever seen outside a hotel: three pictures on the vast walls, hung not centrally nor symmetrically, Peter Scott[*], say, of duck flying and a vague picture apparently of Antibes. The dressing-table, blue and white, was a (?wedding) present to Princess May from her French maid Tatry, and was always used; Queen Mary herself having a triptych firescreen adapted and mirrored, then screwed on to the back of the dressing table. The present Queen objected to the cheap brass handles which have now been replaced by porcelain ones with pink rosebuds on them. It is now like the bedroom of an anonymous mouse. Q.M.'s own bed, stowed in a guest room upstairs, is evidently of mahogany painted over; a huge double bed, with padded top and end covered with a sort of cheese-muslin, the head embroidered with her monogram.

Through from the Queen's bedroom is the Duke of Edinburgh's boudoir, out of which leads his dressing room, loo and so on. Here there is evidence of a positive but somewhat vulgar personality, sofas and armchairs covered in virulent magenta chintz with huge medallions 'His Majesties' Shippes in 1672' in full sail on them; always the same shippes, whether on blue or magenta. Naval pictures and so on. In the passage caricatures, evidently by friends of the family. The bedroom in which King George V expired is next, small and uncomfortable (Fellowes says that Cynthia Colville once told him that to test how hard the bed was she slipped in one day when they were safely out and *jumped* up and down on it; it was like jumping on the floor). He died in his bed in a corner opposite the window. Just after he had died Queen Mary sent to 'enquire after Ruth Fermoy's baby'[†] I was told, a signal instance, they said, of her self-control and consideration for others.

Across the head of the main stairs is situated a truly sinister warren of small rooms, looking out on to the main front of the house, and turning the corner of it over the Equerries' Entrance. You go through, turn right and down two or three

---

[*] Sir Peter Scott (1909–89), ornithologist and painter, whose works are favoured by Prince Philip. Only son of the Arctic explorer, Robert Scott.

[†] Ruth, Lady Fermoy (1908–93), and her baby, Hon Frances Roche (1936–2004), later Viscountess Althorp and then Mrs Shand Kydd, respectively the grandmother and mother of Diana, Princess of Wales (1961–97).

steps in a very narrow carpeted passage; the first door on the left is where the Duke of Clarence died. This dim and cheerless hole is surprisingly small: opposite the door a window, to the right of the door a fire-place (*immediately*) on the r-hand wall then the brass bedstead, so that you could touch the mantelpiece with your hand if lying on the bed; along the other wall a cupboard and now a wash-basin, taps etc. How 14 people, including the Duchess of Teck crammed into this room on the morning of 14 January 1892 foxes me completely. Queen Alexandra kept this room as a shrine, visiting it almost daily if not indeed daily, strewing fresh flowers on the bed, looking at his uniforms and clothes ranged in a glass cabinet along the wall opposite the fireplace (Queen Mary swept this out and put it at the foot of yet another set of stairs with her miniature tea sets etc. in it). Even the soap and hairbrushes were left as on the day he died. On the exterior wall, under the window, is Prince Albert Victor's monogram in stone, with '14 January 1892' under it. It is clear from the constriction of this room and the narrowness of the corridor that Princess May, however much they tried to prevent her, *must* have heard his delirium and learned much.

Next to the death-chamber is the most sinister little room of them all, now used by Prince Charles* as his schoolroom. It must have been Prince Eddy and Prince George's sitting room, for it has a faded masculine air: books all round (with Q. Alexandra's double-A monogram on the cases, though), a fireplace and almost on top of it a dark red leather worn-out sofa. It is a dark room, very narrow, very poky, charged with some unpleasant happening or personality of the past. Here latterly Queen Alexandra would sit with Princess Victoria. I should not like to be alone in that room at night.

I then saw other rooms, of lesser interest save as giving or adding to the general impression – royal guest-rooms, other guest-rooms, the Lady-in-Waiting's bedroom, with a bell board like a butler's pantry – 'boudoir, bedroom, dressing-room' on china labels; the ladies' sitting room, the guests' sitting room, all seedy apartments like Victorian night nurseries long disused. In all these Queen Mary's hand has not been effaced, and her particular passion for hanging masses of small pictures one below the other on wires from the picture-rail much in evidence: she seems never to have knocked a nail or pin into a wall, the result being woefully untidy and stringy.

---

* HRH The Prince of Wales (b. 1948), eldest son of Elizabeth II.

To sum up: this is a hideous house with a horrible atmosphere in parts, and in others no atmosphere at all. It was like a visit to a morgue, and everywhere were their faces, painted, drawn or photographed: few pictures not directly relating to themselves: most curiously *borné* their horizon seems to have been, ringed in by their own family and their own likenesses, with an outer constellation of 'servants' of *every* class. Almost monastic in its seclusion, with the added safety that where a monastery would have religious paintings they lived with nothing higher than paintings of themselves.

From the house we went to the Woodcarving School in the stables, founded originally to train Boer War (?) disabled veterans in the locality, now teaching country youths to produce veneered furniture, boxes, ash-trays, etc. Several boys were at work, and the man in charge showed me the finished furniture, which is of a high quality. Queen Mary took a special interest in the School, and would send an Indian box, an English occasional table, some wooden beads from Antigua etc. as exemplars to be copied, and did all she could to encourage it. After that we saw Mrs Mabel Butcher, who lives in a converted stable-bungalow in the same yard: once a housemaid, then promoted housekeeper (and looked down on because she had started as the *housekeeper's housemaid*) she was a bird-witted little woman with stringy white hair. I felt too tired to ask her questions and in any case she was useless: yes, Queen Mary took a detailed interest in the running of the house, yes she arranged the Chinese room and so on. We then proceeded to the gardens, in which she took no special interest Fellowes told me – that is to say the big walled vegetable, cut-flower and fruit gardens in a separate walled enclosure along the main road outside the Norwich Gates. Arched apple-tree walk, very long, planted he says according to the different colours of the apples. Thence to the dairies and stables, and so to Queen Alexandra's Trianon, now never used, very pretty and odd and Scandinavian, at the same time very 1880-ish – a model dairy lined with Dutch tiles, a collection of Coronation mugs and jugs arranged by Queen Mary, flat white cream-pans; next to it in the same funny little Chalet the room where they would eat strawberries and cream, a small low room hung round with mock-Limoges plates (head of King Edward in a Tudor Ruff, head of Queen Alexandra ditto), exactly as it was with sofas and little tables and chairs, very creepy again like the Chinese room and tea-room; key unobtainable that day so we peered in through the window, a feeling of having people still about, nasty. Upstairs there is a loo with one narrow pipe carrying all drainage down into the earth.

Fellowes wants to pull down the rustic Hansel and Gretal lodge at this gate – gabled with fir tree beams; I urged not. Likewise a plaster maquette in the church for the Gilbert* memorial to Prince Eddy at Windsor which he says is *sans intérêt* and falling to pieces. I didn't see it, but I urged repair as I know it is the original of the never-finished monument and bought back by Probyn† when Gilbert was sold up as a drunken bankrupt (see relevant papers under *Death of Duke of Clarence*).

Home to sherry and a bath. Bill Fox‡, ex-10th Hussars, now a pupil of Fellowes, a big strapping blonde character with a cruel mouth, dined and after dinner we played a version of The Game called *What's My Line*. So ended my first visit to Sandringham. I will record Fellowes's remarks separately.

In May Pope-Hennessy went to Germany, where the Landgrave of Hesse showed him Rumpenheim. He also visited Hamburg, Marsberg, Salem (in Baden), Heiligenberg, Friedrichshofen, Rheinfall and Kronberg.

---

*   Sir Alfred Gilbert (1854–1934), who created the Duke of Clarence's magnificent tomb in the Albert Memorial Chapel, adjoining St George's Chapel.

†   Colonel Sir Dighton Probyn, VC (1833–1924), Comptroller to the Household of the Prince of Wales 1877–1901, Keeper of the Privy Purse 1901–10, Comptroller of the Household of Queen Alexandra 1910–24.

‡   William E.A. (Bill) Fox (b. 1932), farmed at Anmer Hall. His wife, formerly Carol Pease, was a godmother to Lady Diana Spencer. He later lived at Rudham Hall, King's Lynn.

EIGHT

LADY ESTELLA HOPE, South Park, Bodiam

15 July

*It was Lord Herbert (later 16th Earl of Pembroke and Montgomery) who
suggested to Pope-Hennessy that he should visit his aunt, Lady Estella Hope
(1866–1958). 'Her memory is excellent,' he wrote, '& I think you will be
amused by her.'[95] He suggested he should take tea with her. Lady Estella duly
invited him to South Park, apologising for 'the intense untidiness of this place.
I have only a small staff.'[96]*

*Lady Estella was the elder of two unmarried daughters of 6th Earl of
Hopetoun, an officer in the Life Guards, and Lord Lieutenant of Linlithgow
from 1863 to 1873. She had been one of Queen Mary's childhood friends and
playmates. Her mother, the Countess of Hopetoun, became a close and intimate friend of the Duchess of Teck, and she used to call Lord Hopetoun
'my Scottish son'. They lived at Hopetoun House, near Edinburgh, where the
Duke and Duchess of Teck and their family were frequent guests.*

*The Teck children loved coming to stay at what they called 'beloved
Hopetoun', their visits being 'red letter days in their calendar.'[97] Lady Estella's
brother became 1st Marquess of Linlithgow, having been Governor-General of
Australia 1900–2.*

At one point Lady Estella was a keen competitor in carriage-driving.

'I'm afraid I shan't be able to be of much use to you. I've only got a few photographs and these letters, the letters are nothing, just when my brother died and so
on. Oh except for this one, which Princess May sent to my mother* (*letter of 1883*)
thanking her for piercing her ears. Funny, wasn't it? But my mother had some little ear-rings that Princess May greatly admired, and one day my mother said she
would give them to her, but as her ears weren't pierced she couldn't wear them.
My mother had pierced our ears for us, so Princess May asked her to do hers,

---

*   Etheldred Birch–Reynardson (1835–84), married 1860, 6th Earl of Hopetoun (1831–73).

awfully dangerous wasn't it, because my mother was hardly an expert. Anyway she did pierce them and gave Princess May the ear-rings.

'Know them well? Of course we did, why they used to come and *settle* on us at Hopetoun *for months*. Let me see, the two boys* came with their tutor in 1880, then next year, when my brother† came of age, they all came for two months, and then again in 1882 for another two months. They loved being at Hopetoun and as we were all much of an age we used to play together all the time. I remember they loved to collect crystals and pebbles along the sea-shore (Hopetoun is on the sea) and even from the *gravel* in front of the house, we used to see them bending over collecting things, I supposed they liked them; once when we were doing our lessons Fraulein got very angry because we were watching the Tecks coming across the lawn with a basin, we couldn't make out what was in that basin, something red; do you know what it was? No? It was a giant sea-anemone that almost filled the bowl.

'Yes, Princess May was very, very shy. When my brother came of age we had to walk along a passage to the ballroom, and she hid behind my mother, and her teeth were chattering – partly I expect from the cold in the passage but mostly from fright. But she was not, as people seem to think, stiff in herself; she was very high-spirited and mischievous. Once, at the Henley Regatta, my sister Dorrie‡ had a new wide blue-silk sash on, and the Princess snatched it off and threw it in the Thames; I don't know why she did it and I don't think she was punished for it. We had tents and straw, and we used to play at settlers and all sorts of things. She was always dressed old for her age – just look at that frock in the photograph – awfully stuffy for a child, wasn't it: buttoned up round the neck and all that. Her hair? She was ash-blonde.

'The Duchess was enormously fat; she was even fatter than my mother, and *she* was stout (she had diabetes and died of it when I was quite young). She would have been beautiful if she hadn't been so gigantic; she corseted herself in as much as she could, though, and carried herself well; she walked and moved beautifully. She kept the Duke in order: 'Franz' she would say sternly, fixing him with her frog's eyes.

'The Duke? Well, but you mustn't put this in your book, mind you, he was *childish*. Oh yes *long* before he got softening of the brain. He was very spoiled and he had a terrible temper. He was a great trial to Princess Mary. He had a

---

*   Prince Adolphus and Prince Francis of Teck.
†   John Hope, later 1st Marquess of Linlithgow (1860–1908).
‡   Lady Dorothea Hope (1868–1943), younger daughter of 6th Earl of Hopetoun.

manservant called Jones and when he engaged him we were always told he said 'I will en-gage you, Joansss, if I can call you damn fool as often as I like'. When he went out shooting, on the way there in the brake, Jones would be sitting behind him with two pipes, and as soon as the Duke had finished one pipe, he would hand him a full one and then refill the other; he was eternally sucking on these pipes, very bad for him I should think, wouldn't you? He was very severe with the boys – 'Dolly, Frank I will trrrash you' he used to shout. Once he went into Edinburgh (he used to go there to do commissions for the Duchess) and he came back with those balloons that squeak as they go down; he had got one for every member of the household, including my great-aunt, Auntie York*: he handed them out solemnly 'One for Auntie York, one for Dorrie, one for Stella, one for Dolly' and so on; well naturally when we got hold of these balloons we ran about making a noise with them. He burst out of his room in a passion screaming 'Dolly, Frank I will trash you, unfortunate I can't trash Stella and Dorrie too'; wasn't it odd, when he'd given them to us himself? On another occasion he went in to Edinburgh to see a lawyer and at the end of the conversation said to him 'do you know you are wearing a most beautifull tiepin, Mr ----'. My brother used to collect these stories for us, we did like hearing them. Then when my brother came of age we found a terrible scene going on in the supper-room, with Princess May looking embarrassed and the Duke shouting at Prince Dolly – 'Dolly, I tell you again and again you do not sit down before your sister'; and then, later, on the dais he began shouting at the Duchess about their childrens' manners. The Duchess sat there, with her hands in her lap and her head up, gazing into space, and he yelled at her 'Mary, vill you not have that face; Mary, you are driving me mad vith that face; Mary, I VILL NOT HAVE that inferrrnal face' and he marched off the dais and down the ballroom and one of my aunts was sent to mediate and bring him back. She just sat there, with her frog's eyes staring at nothing.

'The Duchess's hair was very fair, and she wore a braid of it on the very top of her head, forward, so that it looked like a crown. Once when we were coming in from the harriers we found her in a beautiful dressing gown, but without the braid; she looked perfectly alright, but Princess *May* was horrified that people

---

* Etheldred Yorke (1812–99), younger daughter of Simon Yorke, of Erddig, co. Denbigh. Thus younger sister of Anne Yorke, Lady Estella's maternal grandmother, who married Charles Birch-Reynardson.

should know it was false hair and kept saying to her, 'Go back, Mamma, go back, Mamma.' I don't know why she should have minded so, do you?

'They adored food, they always said that when they got back to White Lodge they would only have eggs and bacon again. At Hopetoun they ate and ate and ate, and they made meals last two to three hours, so that we children were always trying to catch my mother's eyes to know if we could run back to our play. I have never forgotten the emphasis the Duchess put into the words 'rrrich crrream' – she hadn't a German accent at all, oh no, but she was always talking about rrrich crrream. Once she had been told to eat dry biscuits, and I can see her now, crumbling her horrible Abernethie biscuit and saying that the doctor had told her to eat it before rrrich crrream, not instead of it. People did eat much more then, of course, that's why they got so fat, and it wasn't considered ladylike to take exercise; though when the Duchess wanted to, she *could* walk.

'We always thought that if one of the royalties failed, Princessy* might marry my brother. My father died when I was six you see, and they let my mother stay on at Hopetoun to bring us up. What they loved at Hopetoun, too, was the swimming bath, very large with warmed water, and Princessy would never leave it; Mrs Ranger, their nurse (or the Hopetoun nurse??) used to stand at the edge and say in her whispering voice 'Princess, you must get out, come along Princess you must get out' but Princessy pretended not to hear and would just go on splashing about.

'The Duke had been a handsome man, I suppose in a way he still was.'

'Have you seen Lord Athlone?† Oh what a pity, baby is ga-ga now is he? We always called him baby. Frank was the one we liked best. When I saw Lord Athlone some years ago he said he had been back to Hopetoun to look at the straw we used to play in; he said it was still there.'

---

*   Princess May.

†   HSH Prince Alexander of Teck (1874–1957), later 1st Earl of Athlone, Queen Mary's youngest brother.

NINE

PAULINE, FRAU FURSTIN ZU WIED, PRINZESS VON WÜRTTEMBERG

21 July

In June the Princess of Wied confirmed her intention to receive Pope-Hennessy at the Gestüt Marienwahl, Ludwigsburg/Württemberg. She asked him to bring Herr von Radowitz with him as she had forgotten her English, and assured him that she could describe Villa Seefeld near Rorschach for him, and would be glad to help him 'as far as I can in getting informations about Queen Mary'.[98]

HRH Princess Pauline of Württemberg (1877–1965) was a rare survivor from an alien age. She was effectively the only daughter of King Wilhelm II of Württemberg and his wife, Marie, 3rd daughter of Prince Georg Viktor of Waldeck-Pyrmont. She was a cousin of Queen Mary. She was born in Stuttgart in 1877, and married in 1898, Friedrich, 6th Prince of Wied (whose brother Wilhelm was King of Albania between February and September 1914). They they had two sons, Hermann and Dietrich.

Princess Pauline was also a first cousin of Princess Alice, Countess of Athlone, through the Waldeck-Pyrmonts. In her memoirs, Princess Alice described an unfortunate occurrence when the Wieds attended the Prussian court in Berlin: 'My fat cousin, Pauline, daughter of my Uncle Willy, King of Württemberg, found herself parted from her husband, because she was a royal highness and he was only a serene highness. He had accordingly been directed by the Court Chamberlains into a lower room than his wife. She was so outraged she never went to court again.'[99] Princess Alice concluded: 'The protocol at the Prussian Court was quite overpowering.'

When Pope-Hennessy met the Princess, she was seventy-eight, and she lived until 1965, dying at Ludwigsburg. Her father had become King in 1891. He was a cultured man, with aesthetic appreciation – Pope-Hennessy described him privately as a 'notorious homosexual'[100] – and he ran one of the finest studs in Europe. He and his second wife, Queen Charlotte, were larger-than-life figures, as was the Princess of Wied herself.

The Duke of Windsor stayed with King Wilhelm and Queen Charlotte just before the Great War, when he was Prince of Wales. In later life he recalled :

THE PRINCESS OF WIED

'Their ample figures betrayed the justice they did to their four square meals a day'. When they went out riding in the afternoon, the King would doze off, and the Queen would jab him in the ribs when his hat slipped or he needed to return a salute.

The King had been appointed a Knight of the Garter by Edward VII in 1904, but his banner was taken down in 1915 as an alien to Britain. Then in 1918 he abdicated, and, as with all the minor German monarchies, the Kingdom of Württemberg ceased to exist. He retreated to the family hunting lodge, Schloss Bebenhausen, where he died in 1921.

Princess Pauline was the author of a most extraordinary book of royal memoirs – Vom Leben Gelernt (Ludwigsburg, 1953) by Fürstin zu Wied, Geb. Prinzessin von Württemberg. The book contains photographs of the Princess in full girth, and one family group in which her sister-in-law, Princess Elisabeth of Wied, is rigidly immobile, and on a kind of stretcher, concealed under her flowing dress. Later Pope-Hennessy loaned this book to Princess Alice, who returned it saying she was 'v. much interested knowing so much about her life & personality & the people she describes so well'.[101]

On Thursday, 19 July 1956, I flew from London to Stuttgart and took a taxi to Ludwigsburg, where I arrived at 11 p.m. at the Schiller Hospiz, Gartenstrasse, a very comfortable modern hotel next to the Y.M.C.A. and apparently connected with it. There was a copy of the bible in every room. Carol von Radowitz[*], who had kindly consented to interpret for me, arrived at ten the next morning from Frankfurt, and we later telephoned to Princess Wied, who sent a message to say she would expect us at five p.m. We feared this meant a heavy tea.

In the morning we walked in the garden of the Schloss[†], the interior of which I had visited (452 rooms) with Bridget Parsons[‡] this May. The gardens are

---

[*] Carol von Radowitz, presumably a descendant of the Prussian statesman and general, Joseph Maria von Radowitz (1797–1853). Something of a friend to the Duke and Duchess of Windsor, he would accompany the Duchess on her widowhood summer holidays to Biarritz in the 1970s. He lived in Frankfurt.

[†] Schloss Ludwigsburg was the Royal Palace of the Württemberg kings, built between 1704–35, and one of the most elaborate surviving examples of Baroque architecture. It is about twelve kilometres from Stuttgart.

[‡] Lady Bridget Parsons (1907–72), only daughter of 5th Earl of Rosse.

romantically arranged, with a pool, a sham castle ruin, masses of every sort of summer flower, great slopes of lawn and splendid trees. In the afternoon I went through Württemberg material and at 4.40 we set out for Marienwahl. Radowitz is of a landowning Württemberg family. His father (?Hof-Marschall to the old court, I think) is the figure riding at the head of the Olga Dragonen in the picture of which I have a postcard. He told me that Marienwahl had been built by King William for his first wife Marie, (mother of Pauline) whom he had unexpectedly adored; being entirely homosexual he had no further children by this* or his subsequent marriage. He had a small private house near the Schloss in Stuttgart to which he would repair on certain evenings to meet young Württembergers procured for him by his old valet. This continued until the end of his life. He was immensely popular and none of his subjects resented his well-known habits.

Marienwahl, a small 1840-ish stucco villa, not unlike a house in St John's Wood, is situated about a quarter of a mile from the Schloss at Ludwigsburg. It stands in small wooded grounds; you go through a stuccoed gateway and there it is, with some mossy grass in front of it, and heavy shady trees behind and around. There is an atmosphere of moss and ivy and tree-shade; the rooms (which we subsequently saw when going to call on the half-American Princess Dietrich ('Netty') Wied)† are dark and much as they always were; the drawing room divided into two by folding doors standing open, has many portraits in it, early and late 19th century, including Thaddeus Jones's‡ very pretty picture of Pauline as a five-year old child, painted to pair off with an Empire picture of Pauline of Württemberg as a child: the Jones one is full-face in a straw hat tilted back, fair hair, garland of flowers held (I think) in an apron by two pudgy hands. The inner drawing room is untouched and is lined with dark red cashmere, the low settees, armchairs etc. all covered with the same; through the window are the big trunks of trees. Many occasional tables, though Princess Netty said she had cleared a lot of these away. The dining room, which she is currently painting white and turquoise blue, is a long but not large room (about the size of our dining room in Avenue Road) with an ugly fitted shelf running all round at shoulder level and a central chandelier. It is on the right of the front door, which is itself at the side of the house.

---

* There was a stillborn daughter, 27 April 1882. Marie died three days later.

† Antoinette Julie, Countess Grote (1902–88), married 1928 HSH Prince Dietrich of Wied (1901–76).

‡ Henry Thaddeus Jones (1859–1929), Irish portrait-painter.

The old Princess Wied, who complained that her son gave her nothing of her jointure and so she has no money (her *eldest* son* who inherited the palace of Neu Wied, not Prince Dietrich who is an alcoholic and lives with his wife in the main house just described) has settled herself into a tiny cottage at right angles and across from the main house. We walked across gravel which a man and woman were raking in a fanatical German way, to the door of this minute abode, where we were met by a sort of housekeeper-companion with cropped grey hair, who ushered us through a cheerful little hall and dining room, where stood some jars for jam-making, and up the small staircase painted jasmine yellow to the upper floor. Then down a very short corridor to a door, which, on being opened, revealed Princess Pauline.

Princess Pauline was sitting in the smallest room I have ever seen inhabited. The walls were plastered with photographs of Carmen Sylva, the Kaiser† etc., and over her desk hung an enormous crayoned photo of herself as a girl. Between the two windows was a vast desk covered with efficient looking disordered papers. At right angles to this desk and jammed against it was a card table. Between the card table and a huge sofa on the other wall sat Princess Wied in a huge leather chair. On the desk were two bottles – Cointreau and some home-made plum liqueur. On the table was a huge box of mingled Turkish and Virginian cigarettes. She was facing the door, and sideways to her desk.

The Princess was one of the strangest figures I have ever contemplated. She is enormously fat, with a huge red face like an old baby, one tooth in her top jaw which she kept coyly covering with a *potelée* hand, clipped white hair like cotton wool (shaven at the neck like a general) and an expression of delighted benevolence; jammed against her table she looked like a greedy child on a high chair. Her wrists are colossal, the folds of her chin numerous, her eyes behind hornrimmed spectacles very bright and amused. She was not as I had been told to expect formidable but very welcoming and a shade nervous. She was wearing a tailleur of severe make, a starched collar with turned down points, a man's foularde bow tie. It was not till she got up, which she did with difficulty as there was no room to move, that I realised that she is almost as short as she is fat, a kind of genial old barrel of a personage,

---

* Hermann, Hereditary Prince of Wied (1899–1941), had in fact been killed in action in Poland during World War II. He had a son called Friedrich Wilhelm (1931–2000), who became head of the dynasty following the death of his grandfather in 1945.

† 'Carmen Sylva', Queen of Romania (1843–1916), born Princess Elisabeth, 4th daughter of Hermann, 4th Prince of Wied, and Kaiser Wilhelm II of Germany (1859–1941).

though at the same time consciously royal. When I asked some foolish question about the Tecks and the '*Hoheit*' she smiled royally and hissed the one word '*morganatische*', sounding the sssshhhhh part with tremendous relish and dismissing the subject with a little imperious wave of her hand.

As the conversation got easier, she rose, or more correctly stretched across the table (we were sitting at each of the free sides of it) and seized the bottles in her plump little hands, together with two thimble size glasses which we were constantly ordered to replenish. She also shoved the cigarettes about and when I began taking notes produced a block and pencils in the twinkling of an eye. One could see she had not run the German Red Cross in the last war for nothing. She was extremely competent. The room was most like an old schoolmaster's study.

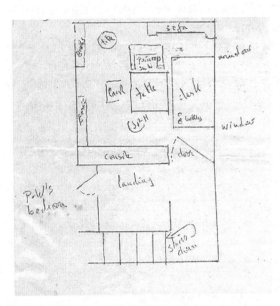

We were with her for about an hour and ten minutes. The room was hot and the evening sun streamed through the little windows. The beginning was distinctly sticky. I tried to kiss her hand but missed it. We then sat down and she gazed at us expectantly, like a baby waiting to be amused; I only realised later that what she likes is to *laugh*, which she does immoderately beating on the table with her fat fists and metaphorically throwing herself back in her chair – not *actually*, as there was no room and she is so large as to be thoroughly, occupationally static. She began with the customary nervousness at being asked anything indiscreet, a lot of generalities about how very very intimate she and Queen Mary had been as girls etc. etc. I then asked through Carol, at random for something to catch on to, who was Olga Uxkull.* This produced a cataract of information and laughter: she had been the Lady-in-Waiting of Marie, Pauline's mother, had retired but came back to Württemberg a lot was what it boiled down to. There was also some scandalous story relating to a brother Uxkull who had been the lover of Countess Hohenstall (afterwards Lady Paget)† at the Court of Berlin and had been caught making love to her by the Crown Princess Frederick‡ who had had to pretend to notice nothing; this accompanied by jellying laughter which made her shake all over. I then, unwisely, ventured on P.M.'s demeanour during the 1892 interregnum – was told she was in mourning and of course miserably sad over the Duke of Clarence, oh so terribly sad; and she put on a kind of funereal face.

Miscellaneous information followed. Tilly was Bathildis§ sister¶ of Q. Charlotte, which I knew. The Grand Duchess Vera of Württemberg** was Russian who married the cousin of the King, their daughter married a Schaumburg Lippe†† and lived in the Schloss at Ludwigsburg. The Grand Duchess had St Vitus's dance, in a particularly violent form, and at Friedrichshafen a sergeant of the Olga Dragoner was detailed to look after her as she was so very strong and when suffering from an attack would

---

* Countess Olga Üxküll–Gyllenband, Lady-in-Waiting to the Crown Princess of Württemberg, Princess Pauline's mother.

† Countess Walburga de Hohenthal (1839–1929), married 1869, Rt Hon Sir Augustus Paget (1823–96), Ambassador to Italy and Austria. She was a Lady-in-Waiting to the Crown Princess of Prussia (later Empress Frederick) (see below).

‡ HRH The Princess Victoria (1840–1901), married 1858, HIM Emperor Friedrich III of Germany. She was the eldest daughter of Queen Victoria.

§ HSH Princess Balthildis (1873–1962), second daughter of HSH Prince Albrecht of Schaumburg-Lippe. Married 1895, Friedrich, Prince of Waldeck and Pyrmont (1865–1946). In *Queen Mary*, Pope-Hennessy wrongly identifies her as an Anhalt-Dessau. She was a younger sister of Queen Charlotte of Württemberg (1864–1846), stepmother of Princess Pauline.

¶ Pope-Hennessy wrote: 'No, sister-in-law, I think.' He was wrong.

** HIH Grand Duchess Vera (1854–1912), married 1874, HRH Duke Wilhelm Eugen of Württemberg (1846–77); daughter of Grand Duke Constantine of Russia; sister of Queen Olga of Greece. She was immensely fat.

†† HRH Princess Elsa (1876–1936), married 1897, HSH Prince Albrecht of Schaumburg-Lippe (1869–1942).

suddenly dash off through the rooms and corridors, clad in a bath towel; Pauline as a child used to watch the sergeant chasing the Grand Duchess. More laughter.

The Villa Seefelt belonged to King William's mother Catherine,* Princess Wied's grandmother. They would play there with the Tecks, who were staying at an hotel at Bad Horn, and cross and recross the lake constantly.

The Duke of Teck was (a Colonel?) in the Olga Dragoner and would take part in the parades, and in the Dragoon parties at Mon Repos.

The Duke and Duchess of Teck always spoke to each other in English. The parents were both unpunctual, particularly the Duchess. This created in Queen Mary a need or urge towards punctuality herself.

The Duchess of Teck was bilingual. Her expansiveness accounted for P.M.'s shyness and reserve, though with the family or those she knew well she was not shy but fun. The Duchess's hair was darkish brown and little of it was her own (chuckles). The Duchess was 'funny-looking' but had such charm and conversational brilliance you forgot this when talking to her.

One day at Friedrichshafen little Affie† was coming up the winding staircase with her Uncle Waldeck‡, and asked him 'Are you taking the Fat One out today?' to which he replied 'I hope not as I don't want to break the springs of the carriage'. As they turned the corner they found the Duchess of Teck who was standing in an embrasure gazing(?) out of the window at the lake. There was a terrible to-do and the Duchess did not speak for 3 days. She then summoned Affie and scolded her roundly and ended saying charmingly – 'You see as it was about *me* it didn't matter, but it might have been about a Lady-in-Waiting and that would be unforgivable you must remember'.

The Duke of Teck's madness began when he was in Württemberg (I couldn't make out what date – '92?). A doctor there was a success with him for 6 weeks. They then sent him back to England where in the end he was shut up.

---

*   HRH Princess Catherine of Württemberg (1821–98), married 1845, Prince Friedrich of Württemberg (1808–70), parents of King Wilhelm II.

†   A family nickname for Princess Pauline.

‡   HSH Prince Friedrich of Waldeck-Pyrmont (1865–1946), brother of the Princess's mother, Marie, and of the Duchess of Albany.

The Wieds went to stay at Frogmore for Princess Alice's* wedding.

She had never met Aunt Augusta†, but it was she who had recommended and produced the hateful Miss Bradshaw. The Princess then settled down to describe with immense gusto the various methods she had invented as a child for persecuting Miss Bradshaw, and the rivalry between Miss B. and Mademoiselle Vanner, a very delicate refined person from Switzerland whom Affie liked. Miss Bradshaw was considered by Mlle Vanner to have loose morals, and she would entertain young men in her room; whenever Affie found this out she would sit in the next room and bang on the piano and when Miss Bradshaw ran out to scold her she would have run away by the other door. Miss Bradshaw finally was given notice, and when she bent down to kiss Affie goodbye the child struck her with her clenched fist (the Princess at this clenched her own fist and struck violently at the air). The governesses shared a footman and whenever Miss Bradshaw wished to go out, Mlle Vanner quickly arranged to do so first, and since they could not go out without the footman quarrels resulted. There was more in this vein, with much laughter.

She ended by again saying how very very intimate they had been as girls. Princess May's appearance never changed during her whole lifetime. No she was not pretty nor beautiful, her 'style' was always the same. What she looked like as an old woman she looked like as a young one.

At the end of the interview she waddled into her bedroom and gave me her book‡, writing in it thoughtfully but with violent upward strokes of the pen. On saying goodbye she suddenly turned to me and said in fluent English 'Please give my respects to Queen Elizabeth when you see her next, if she even knows who I

---

* HRH Princess Alice of Albany (1883–1981), daughter of Prince Leopold, Duke of Albany (1853–84), and Princess Helene of Waldeck-Pyrmont (1861–1922), aunt of Princess Pauline. She married Queen Mary's brother, Prince Alexander of Teck (later Earl of Athlone) at St George's Chapel, Windsor, in 1904.

† HRH Princess Augusta (1822–1916), elder daughter of HRH Prince Adolphus, 1st Duke of Cambridge, and sister of the Duchess of Teck. She married 1843, Friedrich Wilhelm, Grand Duke of Mecklenburg-Strelitz (1819–1904). She was the Aunt Augusta, of whose correspondence with her niece, Queen Mary, Pope-Hennessy made such good use.

‡ The inscription in this copy of *Vom Leben Gelernt* reads: 'Mr James Pope Hennessy dem Verfossen eines buches inher Queen Mary, mainer so sehr verehrten w. geliebben Cousine – Fürstin zu Wied. 21 Juli '56'.

am or that I exist, which she most probably doesn't. She had clearly understood every word I had said through the interpreter all the time.

We went over to see the daughter-in-law Netty Wied who was charming and showed me the Jones picture and a visiting book with the Teck signatures; it was bound in vellum with a little water-colour miniature of Marienwahl set into the cover, and violets. Also a silver étui inscribed with the Teck parents and Princess May's signatures, given to someone (? Queen of Württemberg) on one of those ever-recurrent birthdays. She indicated that her mother-in-law was very difficult. Her younger son*, she said, now works as a garage-hand in Oberammagau.

---

* There were three sons, the younger two being Prince Ulrich (1931–2010) and Prince Ludwig (1938–2000).

TEN

HON MARGARET WYNDHAM, West Horsley Place

12–14 August

Pope-Hennessy stayed frequently at West Horsley Place, the enormous house in Surrey belonging to his great friend Peggy, Marchioness of Crewe. She was the daughter of the Earl of Rosebery. Staying there for a few days in August 1956, he met the Hon Margaret Wyndham (1879–1965), youngest daughter of 2ⁿᵈ Lord Leconfield. She had served as Woman of the Bedchamber to Queen Mary from 1938 to 1951, and in retirement was an Extra Woman of the Bedchamber from 1951 until Queen Mary's death in 1953.

West Horsley was bequeathed by Lady Crewe to her daughter, Mary, Duchess of Roxburghe, who in turn left it to Bamber Gascoigne.

While staying at Horsley, Pope-Hennessy wrote to his brother, John:

> I am sitting in the Geraldine room at Horsley ... there is an atmosphere of unparalleled mortality, not modified by Miss Maggie Wyndham who is in the final stage of decrepitude and very frightened of P. [Peggy]. I pump her all the time about Q. Mary which is necessary but there is a distasteful feeling of working against time with her, and though her information is copious, psychological & invaluable (she evidently liked her no more than any of the others *or* Mrs Waterfield [P.-H's secretary], *or* I do) I am so dead sick of dealing with the dead and regret my novel more and more.[102]

This interview is particularly striking as Miss Wyndham appeared to have revealed to Pope-Hennessy the name of the man whom Queen Mary had loved when young, before it was mooted that she should marry the Duke of Clarence. Later, in a letter, she corrected herself, having remembered it wrongly.

Significantly, as was the way with official royal biographies, Pope-Hennessy did not even put a veiled hint about him in the biography. Nor has his name ever been mentioned by other biographers of George V and Queen Mary, in the years that followed.

Records of various conversations with Miss Wyndham, who was with Queen Mary during the whole of the war at Badminton and after, and had long talks with her about the past. They are set down at random, with no particular order.

~

Q.M. on end of Indian Empire: 'When I die India will be found written on my heart, as Calais was upon Queen Mary's'*

~

Her adoration for military marches: 'I should like to die to the sound of a military march' she remarked one day. She knew and recognised them all, and would almost march to them, beating time with her hands. At Badminton they got her a gramophone and discs of marches.

~

Conversation on the Duke of Clarence:

M.W. (One day in the motor-car; she added that only in cars would Q.M. speak frankly; she felt away from royalty, pages etc., and at Marlborough House would always answer 'I don't know' to any question. Miss W. is fortunately very inquisitive.)

'I sometimes think the Almighty has a special providence for the Royal Family, Ma'am.'

'Whatever *do* you mean, Maggie?'

'I was thinking of the death of the Duke of Clarence, Ma'am and the fact that Your Majesty married the better brother. Not but that Y.M. would have made a go of it but it would have been uphill work.'

Q.M. (placing her hand on Miss W's knee): 'My dear, how right you are. I even realised it at the time I got engaged. My father-in-law was always saying to me "See that Eddie does this, May" or "Make sure Eddie does that, May" so that I got

---

* Mary Tudor, Queen Mary I.

so worried I went to my mother and said "Do you really think I can take this on?" "Of course you can" she replied.'

~

Another day: 'My husband was not in love with me when we married. But he fell in love with me later.'

~

Before 1891 Princess May had been truly in love, the only time of her life, with Someone whose name Miss Wyndham cannot remember. She had used up her capacity for loving then; 'as much in love as she ever could be'. Someone she could not marry.

~

Both engagements seemed natural to her as she put The Throne above everything else and all personal feelings. Miss Wyndham would sometimes ponder on what it *could* feel like to have an abstract passion like this which you *never* swerved from.

~

Queen Mary was never a skilled needlewoman (Miss W. being one of the best in England). They put together some squares of woolwork and called it Queen Mary's carpet. The cupboards at Marlborough House were full of similar squares, probably are so still.

~

Not musical, though could face Italian opera. Passion for the theatre, 'I often thought the more gruesome the play the better she liked it'.

~

Terrible effect on the Duke of Gloucester and the Princess Royal. Both liberated and much improved since her demise.

~

At Sandringham if the King were present they put on Garter ribbons, tiaras and diamonds for every family dinner even without guests. At Xmas time they would, thus arrayed, pull crackers and put on funny paper hats over the diamonds. *Miss W.*: 'I sometimes thought' (and she is an arch encrusted Tory) 'that it *did* seem all very artificial – well somehow very *archaic*, our way of life with them all.'

~

No royalty is ever expected to do anything disagreeable, this was why Cynthia Colville gave Lady Airlie[*], Q.M.'s oldest attendant and friend, notice.

~

Towards the end of her life she suffered agonies of unhappiness from a sense of powerlessness. Nothing she asked for was done – e.g. cutting trees in the Mall – no-one asked her advice. She was deeply shocked at the Duke of Edinburgh's riding with the sovereign in the Coronation procession. She should have been alone. She felt ignored. She hated Princess Margaret.[†]

~

What she would have liked above all else was to have been Queen Regnant: 'But she wouldn't have been a very constitutional Queen, you know.'

~

---

[*] Lady Mabell Gore (1866–1956), daughter of 5th Earl of Arran. Married 1886, 6th Earl of Airlie (1856–1900). Extra Lady of the Bedchamber to Queen Mary 1910–17 , Lady of the Bedchamber 1917–53. There is no official indication that she was dismissed.

[†] HRH The Princess Margaret (1930–2002), younger daughter of George VI, thus granddaughter of Queen Mary. This feeling was reciprocated.

Sir Dighton Probyn and Miss Charlotte Knollys* were in love but decided they would see more of each other by sticking to Queen Alexandra and not marrying. In the Lady-in-Waiting's bathroom at Sandringham there is nothing but mirrors, and over the door: 'C. from D'. He had done it up for her.

∼

Miss Wyndham read both John Gore and Harold Nicolson in typescript to the Queen.[†] A passage in the former about her sufferings from Queen Alexandra and the sisters-in-law:

'Now do you think I should pass that, Maggie? Should that be published?'

'I think it only just, Ma'am.'

'Well you may be right. They are all dead. If Maud[‡] was alive of course I should refuse. It had better stand.'[§]

On the same subject Princess Victoria horrid to her and thought to be an epileptic.

∼

When they returned from India in 1906 the parents sat on a sofa with Prince John between them, and, looking at each other, said 'But *can* this be *our* Child?' Yet she often said he was the most *physically* beautiful of all her children.

∼

---

*   Hon Charlotte Knollys (1835–1930), Woman of the Bedchamber to Queen Alexandra. Part of the small circle that remained with Queen Alexandra in her widowhood at Sandringham.

†   John Gore (1885–1983) wrote *King George V: A Personal Memoir* (1941), and Harold Nicolson (1886–1968) wrote the official biography, *King George V – His Life and Reign* (1952).

‡   The Queen of Norway, her sister-in-law.

§   John Gore wrote : 'For the Duke [of York], at any rate, life was an idyll in the 'nineties. If it were not a biographer's first duty to seek the truth and fearlessly set it forth, one might leave it there, an idyll unalloyed for the royal couple. Perhaps with a little more sympathy from the Prince and Princess [of Wales] and Princess Victoria, it might have been no less for the Duchess'. See Gore, pp.128–9.

Explained her relationship with the Master[s] family: 'You see my mother was always short of money, and Mrs Master[s]* paid for things for her at bazaars.' Humiliated by parents' extravagance and exile.

~

Q.M. was *not* generous; she was parsimonious; and then suddenly she would commit an extravagance, like saving the Royal School of Needlework from bankruptcy, thousands of pounds. Also endless Xmas present lists.

~

Duke of Luxembourg† suggested as a suitor. Turned down on religious grounds (*when?*).

~

Miss W. watched from White's Club the wedding procession, 1893. The Duchess of Teck in the carriage with Q. Victoria, bowing extravagantly to right and left, the Queen quite eclipsed, tiny, and fluttering a small hand.

~

J.P.-H. (leading *and* disingenuous question): 'Of course Queen Mary must have had a very funny sense of humour?'
  M.W. 'It was indeed a *funny* sense of humour.'
  J.P.-H. 'I meant a really *good* sense of humour?'
  M.W. 'She had no sense of humour at all. What she had was a sense of the *ridiculous*, which I never think is at all the same thing. We often had good laughs

---

* John Henry Master, JP (1831–1919), formerly of the Indian Civil Service, and his wife, Gertrude Begbie (1842–1924). They lived at Montrose House, Petersham. Gertrude 'assisted the Duchess of Teck in the management of local charities' in the Kew area. Gertrude was in Cannes when the Duchess of Teck visited the South of France in 1888.
† HRH Grand Duke Wilhelm IV of Luxembourg (1852–1912), married 1893 HRH Princess Marie Anne (1861–1942), daughter of Infante Miguel of Portugal, sometime King of Portugal.

on our way back from some royal function, mind you, and sometimes I would catch her eye at one of them and we would wink at each other. But it was purely a sense of the ridiculous. Like all Royalty, as a matter of fact.'

~

*Lady Crewe** (at tea) 'Now, Maggie, how long at a time did you have to read to Queen Mary for?'

M.W. 'Oh the longest used to be seven hours.'

L.C. 'Seven hours?'

M.W. 'Oh yes, but that was not always usual.'

J.P.-H. 'It sounds rather inconsiderate?'

M.W. 'Well she *was* inconsiderate about that sort of thing. We would come back from some function dog-tired, and she would lie on the sofa and rest and we would have to read to her. Sometimes she would say "Maggie, you're getting hoarse. Hadn't you better stop for a few minutes?" and then I would take a lozenge and go on reading. It might interest you to know that she *worked when she was asleep.* She was the *only human being* I have seen doing that. I would be reading to her and she would be doing her woolwork, and I would see that she had dropped off; I would wait till she got into an uncomfortable position (which was fairly soon) and then I would begin again; but the most singular thing was that while she was asleep she was working away methodically with her needle; and when she awoke I had to take out all the stitches she had done in her sleep – oh they were all over the place, believe me.'

J.P.-H. 'And what did she like having read to her? Novels?'

M.W. 'No, history and biography; novels she would read to herself at night. I was often surprised by what she liked – for instance she discovered *The Magic Mountain* by Thomas Mann, and she loved that. And then she discovered Dostoievsky – *Crime and Punishment* she particularly liked. I wanted her to let me read *War and Peace* to her but she wouldn't. "I'll leave out all the battles, Ma'am" (which I have often done when reading that book myself), but no, she wouldn't have Tolstoy. She would read the evening paper to herself, but we would have to read *The Times* – though often she had read a good part of it before we had begun.'

---

*   Lady Margaret (Peggy) Primrose (1881–1967), younger daughter of 5th Earl of Rosebery, married 1899, 1st Marquess of Crewe (1858–1945).

~

There were only two women who were allowed to do or understood how to arrange Queen Mary's wig.* Once at Badminton they were both ill at once and nobody knew what to do. The Queen told Miss Wyndham that *she* proposed to do what she had done during the crisis of the King's illness (in 1931?), sleep with her head tied up in a scarf under her chin. She did this for seven days at Badminton – 'for seven days and nights she lived in that wig'. During the one air-raid scare at Badminton she made Miss W. wait *twenty minutes* before seeing her, whilst having her hair arranged.

~

She was smaller than she seemed. Her clothes fitted Miss Wyndham (who is 5ft 6 or 7) perfectly, 'except of course for taking them in at the chest and waist'.

~

Evie, Duchess of Devonshire once said to Miss W. '*You* should write down the things the Queen tells you, Maggie. She has never told anybody else'. Miss W. was surprised at the things she *did* sometimes tell her about the past, but in the later stages of her old age she stopped referring to the past at all.

~

She was sternly Anglican. 'If I wasn't, I wouldn't be here,' she once remarked.

~

On Monday 14th August Miss Wyndham remembered the name of the man whom Q.M. had confessed to having been (mutually) in love with, the only love of her life. 'It begins with an H. Have you got a Peerage to make sure if the dates fit?' J.P.-H. 'Not Lord Hood, by any chance?' 'Of course it was Lord Hood. We called him Gross-vee-Nor as a joke. It *was* Gross-vee-nor. I used to dance with him. He was

---

*   Queen Mary wore a silver wig by day and a gold wig at night.

neither handsome nor interesting, indeed awfully dull. I was *very* much surprised. Of course she could never have married him, nor would she have thought it *right*.'

Extract from Burke's Peerage:

GROSVENOR ARTHUR ALEXANDER, 5th VISCOUNT HOOD, succeeded his father 1907. Late Lieut-Colonel Commanding 7th Battn. The London Regt., formerly major Grenadier Guards, served in Ashanti 1895–6 and in South Africa 1900–2, O.B.E 1919.

B. 13 Nov 1868. M. (1) Primrose Stapleton-Cotton 1911 (who d. 1919) and (2) Marguerite, yr dr of late Hon Albert Hood, 2nd son of 3rd Viscount Hood. He died without issue 26 April 1933 and was succeeded by his nephew the present 6th Viscount (who is my acquaintance Sammy Hood, J.P.-H.).[*]

Note by J.P.-H.: He was evidently a connection, how close I must check, of the Hon Alexander Nelson Hood[†], son of Viscount Bridport, who succeeded Mr Sebright as Comptroller and Equerry to the Duchess of Teck (see Kinloch-Cooke, vol.ii, p. 191, footnote and index passim). Also see the old White Lodge footman's mention of him in Dutton interview (W.L. file). I think a first cousin once removed or so, and thus a natural escort on her early seasons when she was shy and knew few London young men. Also some old lady (which?) has mentioned Lord Hood's name to me as a suitor of the Duchess of Teck in the 50's – she said 'Princess Mary' I suppose and I misunderstood and misattributed the dating.

∼

Queen Mary was very fond of Jews and had several intimate Jewish friends – Mrs Mayer Sassoon[‡], Sir Lionel Faudel-Philipps[§] etc. This was partly on the collecting

---

[*]   As noted, there was not a single reference to 5th Viscount Hood in *Queen Mary*.

[†]   They were distant cousins.

[‡]   Mozelle Gubbay (1872–1964), married Meyer Sassooon (1855–1924). Philanthropist and art collector. In 1933 she presented Queen Mary with a dessert service of spoons and forks dating from 1777. These were sold in the Duke of Gloucester sale at Christie's, January 2006 (Lot 113).

[§]   Sir Lionel Faudel-Phillips, 3rd Bt (1877–1941), Trustee of the Wallace Collection.

side, but not wholly. One of the first questions she asked Miss Wyndham at their preliminary interview was 'so you like Jews?' 'I replied "I don't dislike them, Ma'am, and I have Jewish relations"' (Miss W. in a characteristically mischievous aside to J.P.-H. 'I always think of the Primroses as Jewish, you know.')

~

At King Edward's funeral[*], Queen Alexandra instructed all the female members of the royal family to wear heavy crepe veils. They obeyed, and she appeared unveiled and heavily made up, thus scoring off them but causing consternation amongst the crowds as well as those inside the Abbey.

~

Miss Wyndham is small, somewhat bent now, frail, over-refined looking, with snowy grey hair, horn rimmed glasses and occasionally a hearing aid. She was always ridiculed as a child and bears the marks of this in a nervous manner, but when alone or feeling a success or of interest is very astute and intelligent. She looks incredibly inquisitive, somewhat like an enquiring but timid mole or shrew-mouse. 'I didn't like to probe too much' she said, 'because that would have shut the Queen up. I just listened to what she told me, and then out of discretion forgot about it or put it at the back of my mind'. She is also liable to say 'the trouble with my doctor is he lives in the suburbs – Holland Park Avenue' or to talk of 'people of breeding'.

P.S. Miss Wyndham also confirmed, with vehemence, that Queen Mary had a 'terrible temper'.

Q.M.: On the Abdication: 'This might really be <u>ROUMANIA</u>!!'

------

[*] In May 1910.

A LETTER FROM MAGGIE WYNDHAM

14 October 1956

25 Hereford House,
North Row, W.1

Dear Mr Pope-Hennessy,

Alas! We did not meet in Florence after all & I have a confession to make & that is that my memory has come back to me & it was *not* Lord Hood but Lord Hopetoun: so the romance we made with the Peerage is I fear fictitious – Lord Hopetoun was older than Queen Mary & am I not right in thinking she was often at Hopetoun? Anyway I feel sure you will not mention this 'tendresse' in the memoirs. It was only to give an idea of her character & charm. I am sorry to have misled you & this sudden memory came to me just before I left for abroad a month ago.

I went to Brolio with the hope that Baronessa Ricasoli* (aged 97) would have some recollection of Princess May in Florence, especially as I was told the Baroness had a phenomenal memory – but alas! She remembered nothing that could be of use to you, only how pleasant was the Duchess, how good looking was the Duke & how charming the Princess.

I hope you had as pleasant a time & as much sun as I had in Italy.

Yrs. sincerely

Margaret Wyndham

LORD HOPETOUN

The man for whom Queen Mary had a 'tendresse' was the 7ᵗʰ Earl of Hopetoun, later 1ˢᵗ Marquess of Linlithgow (1860–1908), brother of Lady Estella and Lady Dorothea Hope. His father, 6ᵗʰ Earl (1831–73), was principally remembered as a great figure in the hunting world, having been a successful master of the Pytchley Hunt in the 1850s, when Charles Payn was the huntsman. His

---

* Baroness Giuliana Ricasoli Firidolfi (1859–1959), installed the Red Cross in the Ricasoli Palace in the First World War.

father-in-law, Charles Birch-Reynardson, was described as 'one of the keenest fox-hunting squires the sporting county of Lincolnshire ever produced'.[103]

Such is hunting lore that it was recorded that on 21 November 1854 the hounds ran for two hours and twenty-five minutes, made a point of eight-een miles and covered altogether twenty-six before they marked their fox to ground at Boughton Camp. Two hundred horsemen rode out at the start of the day, but only six saw the end of it. Lord Hopetoun was one of them. He had run his second horse to a complete standstill, but happened to come across his hack on the road, by chance. This does not sound the kind of activity that would much have interested Queen Mary.

The son, the 7th Earl, succeeded in 1873 when he was twelve. He travelled in the East and America, and at one point seemed set on a political career, as a rival to the Earl of Rosebery. He was appointed a Conservative Whip in the House of Lords, and Lord-in-Waiting in Lord Salisbury's first administration. From 1887 to 1889 he served as Lord High Commissioner to the General Assembly of the Church of Scotland.

In 1889 he was sent off to be Governor of Victoria, Australia. He was very popular, it being said of him: 'Dignity, impartiality, courtesy, tact, and sympathy characterised the acts of his administration. His manners were at once simple and charming. He was open-hearted and hospitable.'[104] He returned home in 1895 and was appointed Paymaster-General and Lord Chamberlain.

In 1901 he was appointed the first Governor-General of Australia, in the first Parliament of the Commonwealth. He was there to greet the Duke and Duchess of York when they arrived in Melbourne, and they invited him to dine on their yacht. As Governor-General, he was again generous, but he found he was spending £16,000 a year when his salary was only £10,000 a year. On this he was expected to run two Government Houses. Therefore he resigned in 1902. In 1905 he was appointed President of the Court of Sessions. Honours were bestowed on him in great profusion. He was a Privy Councillor, a GCVO, a GCMG, a Knight of the Thistle, and created 1st Marquess of Linlithgow.

More relevantly, he married on 18 October 1886, Hon Hersey De Moleyns, daughter of 4th Lord Ventry. They had two sons, the elder of whom became 2nd Marquess of Linlithgow, and then Viceroy of India; and two daughters, the younger of whom was Mary, Countess of Pembroke, a Lady-in-Waiting to Princess Marina, Duchess of Kent.

Lord Linlithgow's health was not good, though he kept a pack of beagles and harriers. He suffered ill health for a year before dying at the Villa Cecil in Pau *on 29 February 1908 from pernicious anaemia at the early age of forty-seven. His funeral was held at Hopetoun. As Princess of Wales, Queen Mary was one of those represented at his Memorial Service at the Chapel Royal in London.*

According to his grandson, Lord Glendevon: 'A man of integrity and charm, he had also been an extravagant spender and left his son, who adored him, a good many financial problems.'[105] In the weeks after his death his hunters and wines were sold.

It would appear that whoever wrote Queen Mary's obituary in the London Times might have known about the role of Lord Hopetoun in Queen Mary's life, for there is a veiled reference to this:

The Ophir arrived in Melbourne in May [1901], and the Duchess [of York] was given a warm welcome by the Governor-General (Lord Hopetoun) – one of her mother's closest friends.[106]

EXTRACT FROM THE DIARY OF MAGGIE WYNDHAM – 1940

At Badminton the Queen continued her interest in clearing up the grounds & park, the latter was with the object of increasing either pastures or arable as a lot of ground was to be given over to the plough – But as the days lengthened the Queen went further afield & we paid visits to Bath, to local houses & to factories. The Queen also interested herself in the Forces quartered in the stables at Badminton, arranging ENSA entertainments & films for them & also picked up hitchhiking servicemen & women on the road when possible. Once H.M. said to me that she felt like the soldiers, taken away from all her surroundings, interests & hobbies & from everything she held dear & found herself put down in a new part of the country without any of her known surroundings & for that reason felt she had so much in common with the soldiers in the same position.

I said she had made a place of refreshment in these new surroundings & quoted the Archbishop of Canterbury* as saying what renewed energy he had got from her

---

* Most Rev Cosmo Gordon Lang (1864–1945), Archbishop of Canterbury 1928–42. He used to stay with George V each summer at Balmoral, and visited Queen Mary at Badminton. She corresponded with him during the war.

vitality & vigour & that I knew Evie Devonshire had derived much pleasure from her visit. The Queen replied 'Thank you, my dear, it is nice to think one can do that'.

On 28 September Pope-Hennessy visited Frogmore.

ELEVEN

THE COUNTESS OF SHAFTESBURY

5 October

James Pope-Hennessy was a staunch Roman Catholic, which served him well for his next interview. The Countess of Shaftesbury (1875–1957) had been a Lady of the Bedchamber to Queen Mary from 1906 to 1913, and an Extra Lady of the Bedchamber from 1913 till 1953. Queen Mary used to refer to her as 'My Woman, Shaftesbury'. She was in attendance on the trip to India for the Delhi Durbar 1911/12.

Lady Shaftesbury was born in 1875 as Lady Constance Grosvenor, elder daughter of Earl Grosvenor, son of 1ˢᵗ Duke of Westminster. She married 9ᵗʰ Earl of Shaftesbury (1869–1961) in 1899. He was Chamberlain to the Princess of Wales's Household from 1901 to 1910, Lord Chamberlain to Queen Mary from 1910 to 1922, and Lord Steward from 1922 to 1936. They lived near Wimborne, in Dorset.

She was always known as 'Cuckoo Shaftesbury', and when Cuckoo was expecting a child, Queen Mary insisted she be told the name as soon as it was known. Lady Shaftesbury sent a telegram, which read: 'Dottie, Ma'am, Cuckoo.'

She died on 8 July 1957, a few months after this interview. The next generations of the Shaftesbury family suffered a succession of tragedies, as was widely reported in the press. The 10ᵗʰ Earl, her grandson, was murdered by his wife, a former nightclub hostess, in 2005, and his son, the 11ᵗʰ Earl, died of a heart attack aged twenty-seven soon afterwards.

Pope-Hennessy went to see Lady Shaftesbury at the Connaught Hotel at 5.45 pm.

On Monday 1 October 1956* I had tea with Lady Shaftesbury at the Connaught Hotel, having previously sat next to her by accident at Farm Street, to which she and Lord Shaftesbury, although not *exactly* Catholics, regularly go. I had previously

---

* His diary gives it as 5 October.

seen him some months ago at his daughter Lettice Ashley-Cooper's[*], when he was kindly but not in his best memory that day, but told me of the tiger-shoot, the story of which he had written down and sent for me to the Princess Royal. Lady Shaftesbury, while notorious always for her vagueness, was very much on the spot, in spite of trembly head and hands; she is infinitely benign, twinkling, perfectly delightful and quick, with the most charming old-fashioned manners imaginable; her hair in little corkscrew curls on her cheeks and forehead, clear blue eyes, quite amused by her own infirmities and age.

She began, as so often those I have been to see on this subject do, by a deprecatory series of remarks as to how little she feared she would be of use. She then became of great use, and first and foremost because both she and Lord S. who came in after tea and sat while we all drank sherry, spoke of The Queen as they call her with such genuine, amused, devoted and yet critical affection.

She began by an anecdote, to warm up so to speak. An old man of 103 at Osborne asked to see The Queen and Lady Shaftesbury went with her. They found two old men in a garden. The Queen approaching the elder said 'I am Queen Mary'. Old man: 'Why so you are, my dear, but you *have* grown!' 'Well, yes, perhaps I have,' replied the Queen.

She next said that the Queen had one strange attribute she had never observed in anyone else – 'almost frightenin', you know' – that of being able to hear what everyone was saying to each other at a dinner-table of 30; 'She never misused it, or repeated things wrong, but she always knew exactly what was goin' on, so I used to be pretty careful; other people who didn't know, weren't.'

She had known the Queen since childhood, Princess Dolly being 'my little aunt Meg'[†] to whom Q.M. was such a good sister as she was to her brothers too. 'Poor Prince Frank[‡], great charm but not satisfactory, we knew him so well I can't think why'. She remembers the Duchess of Teck 'comin' and beamin' at us' when they were young. 'She really was enormous.' In those early days Princess May was high-spirited, 'not above sliding down the staircase on a tea-tray and all that sort of thing'.

---

[*] Lady Lettice Ashley-Cooper (1911–90), known as 'Duchess'.

[†] Lady Margaret Grosvenor (1873–1929), fourth daughter of 1st Duke of Westminster, married 1894 Queen Mary's oldest brother, HSH Prince Adolphus of Teck (1868–1927), later 1st Marquess of Cambridge.

[‡] Queen Mary's second brother.

She said I was quite right about her shyness, but that she gradually got over this altogether; the world tours helped, and then 'we were always goin' on at her about it, tellin' her that anyone would be pleased by *anything* she said to them, no matter what it was'.

During the (? 1905) Indian journey they were somewhere or other where they were housed in bungalows with verandahs. Their boxes were outside. In the middle of the night the Princess of Wales woke up to hear torrential rain and, slipping a jacket over her nightdress rushed out alone to drag in her boxes so her things shouldn't get wet. This she thought typical.*

She was – 'luckily' – not of a passionate nature, nor emotional. Lady S. thinks she really did like Prince Eddy insofar as it was possible for her to like anyone, and was upset when he died and sad; but then Prince George was much more *fun* than Prince Eddy, who wasn't much of a creature. The King and Queen were devoted to one another, this especially showing during his bad illness some years before his death. Lady S., with a *particular emphasis*, repeated how happy and lucky it was that the Queen was not of a passionate nature.

Brought up a strong Protestant, she ended by being more and more High Church, and Lady S. had heard that she had been seen sitting (or praying) in a London Catholic Church later in her life. One of the last times Lady Shaftesbury saw her, Queen Mary suddenly said 'I suppose one must force oneself to go on until the end' to wh. Lady S. replied 'I am sure Your Majesty will'. This she thought remarkable because *so* unlike her usual reserve, an admission that her death was approaching.

Though fond of her children she was not maternal, but she was passionately devoted to Prince David[†], and the way he behaved hurt her more than anything else in her life. Princess Mary was terrified of her mother. King George too strict a father.

Terrible seasickness all through the voyages, they tried everything, swinging cradles and cots and so on, all to no avail. The Medina nearly sunk in a storm in the Bay of Biscay – the staff were some of them sleeping in the dining room – 'we were thrown about like billiard balls each time the ship rolled'.

She adored India and was *quite different* there.

---

[*] Probably Malabar Point – see Q.M. to Aunt Augusta of 7 Nov 1905. (J.P.-H. note).

[†] The Duke of Windsor, with his Abdication.

Lord Shaftesbury sat next to Aunt Augusta[*] at a Strelitz banquet when the Waleses had gone 'to the Berlin wedding'[†]; she was as deaf as a post, and kept asking him questions he couldn't understand, and there was suddenly a lull in the room and he was left shouting at her at the top of his voice.

Lady Shaftesbury subsequently told me on the telephone, with discreet precautions of no names mentioned, that magnanimity and breadth of mind were two major attributes of the Queen. These were evident, for example, in her treatment of Madame d'Hautpoul and her brother Harry Stonor[‡], for at one time there had been thoughts of an engagement between Prince George and Julie Stonor[§], impossible on religious grounds. She was always charming to her and tried to help her and was fond of them both.

Lady Shaftesbury telephoned again and asked me to go once more to the Connaught that Friday, 6 October. She was alone at first, and then Lord Shaftesbury came in.

She said it was impossible to describe how cosy and cheery evenings at York Cottage were, especially the children's' hour, when after King George had come in from shooting they would all sit in front of the fire playing a kind of Happy Families card game of the Counties of England. She always wanted to combine education with games for the children.

Bricka and Tatry treated Princess May as though she were still a little girl and she, amused, put up with it. Bricka dominated everyone and there were never any rows where she was concerned, as 'she was too frightenin''. Tatry on the other hand made endless trouble always.

She knew nothing of the relations between Queen Alexandra and the Wales sisters on one side, and P.M. on the other.

---

[*] Queen Mary's aunt, HRH The Grand Duchess of Mecklenburg-Strelitz.

[†] The wedding of the Kaiser's daughter, HRH Princess Victoria Louise (1892–1980) to HRH the Duke of Brunswick (1887–1953) in 1913.

[‡] Hon Julia Stonor (1861–1950), married 1891, Marquis d'Hautpoul de Seyre (1859–1934); and Hon Sir Harry Stonor (1859–1939), Gentleman Usher to Queen Victoria, Edward VII and George V. Deputy Master of the Household 1918–21. They were the children of Hon Francis Stonor, and were Roman Catholics.

[§] i.e. Prince George – later George V – and Julia Stonor, later Marquise d'Hautpoul.

She and Lord Shaftesbury went to the 1906 Spanish coronation*. Very grand as a sight, though the church was quite small. The Waleses behaved too beautifully after the bomb incident. Lord S. didn't believe the anarchist would have bombed the church, he would just have stabbed the King (and Queen) as they came by.

I asked her to define the difference between Bedchamber Women and Ladies-in-Waiting. 'The Women of the Bedchamber did all the work, poor dears, and the Ladies were, well more there for ornamental purposes.'

---

* This was actually the wedding of King Alfonso XIII of Spain (1886–1941) and Princess Victoria Eugenie of Battenberg (1887–1969), daughter of Princess Beatrice. A would-be assassin threw a bomb at their coach as they returned from the service, splattering blood all over the bride's wedding dress.

TWELVE

LADY JULIET DUFF

6 – 9 October

Pope-Hennessy was a friend of Lady Juliet Duff (1881–1965), who entertained frequently at Bulbridge, her house at Wilton. Her guests invariably included stage and ballet figures, writers and others connected with the arts.

Lady Juliet was born in 1881 as Lady Juliet Lowther, only daughter of 4ᵗʰ Earl of Lonsdale and his wife, Lady Gwladys Herbert, a sister of the 13ᵗʰ and 14ᵗʰ Earls of Pembroke. Her father died when she was one, and her mother then married Lord de Grey, later 2ⁿᵈ Marquess of Ripon. She married in 1903, Sir Robin Duff, 2ⁿᵈ Bt, and after he was killed in 1914, a man called Major Keith Trevor, from whom she was later divorced.

In her early days she had been a keen promoter of Diaghilev. Her wide circle of friends included Somerset Maugham, Maurice Baring, Hilaire Belloc, Cecil Beaton, Laurence Olivier and Vivien Leigh. Also frequently at Bulbridge was Lady Juliet's 'jagger' or 'walker', Simon Fleet.

While staying with Juliet Duff at Bulbridge (whence we went over to Osborne House[*]) from 6 to 9 October 1956 I had many talks with her about Q.M.; I had forgotten how well she had always known them all, through her mother's[†] intimate friendship with Queen Alexandra. Her recollections were random and, spaced over several days, hard to recall in detail.

She said, amongst other things: –

It was Prince Francis[‡], whom she knew *well*, who started Princess May on collecting. He had wonderful taste.

---

[*] Queen Victoria's home on the Isle of Wight. They visited it on 9 October.

[†] Gwladys, Marchioness of Ripon (1859–1917).

[‡] Queen Mary's second brother.

131

Princess May was never maternal. Showing Juliet one of the babies in its cot she once remarked: 'I wonder what it's thinking? Nothing at all, of course, stupid little thing.'

Juliet had the impression always that Princess May was frightened of and subdued by Edward VII, whenever she saw them together.

She was very conscious of being insufficiently royal by birth, and once said to Lady de Grey: 'Isn't it kind of them?' when telling her that the Emperor and Empress William were coming to lunch. Lady de Grey ticked her off over this.

Queen Alexandra was not always nice to her, and also was conscious that her daughter-in-law was not completely royal. Princess Victoria ditto.

Princess May once said: 'I always have to be so careful never to laugh, because you see I have such a *vulgar laugh*.'

P.M.'s descriptions of what she had been doing or seeing were often vivid and good, particularly her tales after the world voyages.

Her skin and complexion were lovely, also her hair. 'I suppose she really was very pretty, but one somehow never thought of her as pretty.'

Her Xmas presents used to be wonderful and carefully chosen, but tailed off into plastic handbags and rubbish.

Q: 'Didn't Queen Alexandra and her daughters make fun of P.M.'s clothes, thinking her less elegant than themselves?'

A: 'Well *they* weren't elegant at all, just one mass of sequins, they looked like Liberace.'*

Queen Mary disliked her daughter-in-law Elizabeth, now the Queen Mother. When they were engaged King George said 'She's a dear little girl, but I don't like her fringe'. Later he told her he didn't like her fringe and much to everyone's surprise all she said was 'Oh I *am* so sorry', and didn't take the hint.

Juliet, who shares the sane view that the royal family are not like human beings at all, says that contrary to popular belief they are faithful and monogamous: George V, the late Duke of Kent, even the Duke of Windsor are examples of this, Edward VII an exception.

They all *eat* enormously.

Sandringham was gloomy, dark and hideous, atmosphere of *pitch-pine*.

---

* Liberace (1919–87), flamboyant television pianist, noted for his over-the-top style of dressing and his white piano.

Miss Charlotte Knollys – '*she* was a funny old thing. She used to travel with more trunks than Queen Alexandra.'

The Wales sisters were totally uneducated. When they went abroad in the yacht and stopped e.g. at Naples, they looked at no sights, and only bought tourist knick-knacks.

Queen Mary loved the theatre, but King George would never go, so she didn't either.

Princess Louise, Duchess of Fife was noticeably idiotic. Princess Victoria very frustrated, and consequently mischievous and bitchy.

York Cottage was unbelievably dark, laurels pressing against the windows of King George's study, e.g.

Q.M. never forgave any of her ladies who had left her, even if this was at her own suggestion. They became 'Poor Mabell' or 'Poor Evie'* at once.

Juliet remarked, at the time of the Kent wedding†, how big the crowds had been and how demonstrative – 'almost more even than at the Duke of York's marriage'. 'Oh, yes,' Q.M. replied, 'but then you see Marina *is* a royalty.'

Q.M. extremely careful with money, even close. She could never be persuaded to give the Athlones a car towards the end of her life, when they were always on the bus. 'A car' she remarked 'would entail a chauffeur as well.' On the other hand she would give £1,000 for some object, admitting with a twinkle that it had cost far more than she should have spent on it.

Ld Claud Hamilton‡ says she *did* offer them a motor-car, he had the negotiations to do; the Athlones refused saying they could not afford to keep it up – 'which I think was all nonsense, between ourselves.'

---

* Mabell, Countess of Airlie, and Evelyn, Duchess of Devonshire.

† Prince George, Duke of Kent married Princess Marina of Greece and Denmark in 1934.

‡ Lord Claud Hamilton (1889–1975), seventh son of 2nd Duke of Abercorn; in George V's Household; Comptroller, Treasurer and Extra Equerry to Queen Mary 1936–53. Pope-Hennessy interviewed him in February 1957.

1957

THIRTEEN

PRINCESS ARTHUR OF CONNAUGHT

15 January

In November 1956 Margaret Wyndham suggested to Pope-Hennessy that he might like to see Princess Arthur of Connaught. She had talked to her '& she wonders if she could be of any use to you with her recollections of Queen Mary.' She continued: 'The Princess is bedridden with rheumatoid arthritis but very much on the spot & would be delighted to receive you if you think she can help you.'[107] Pope-Hennessy duly wrote, and Bettyne Blunden (1920–94), one of the Princess's nurses, confirmed the appointment in a letter dated 24 December 1956.

HRH Princess Alexandra of Fife (1891–1959), daughter of HRH The Princess Louise, Duchess of Fife and Princess Royal, and of 1st Duke of Fife. She was therefore a granddaughter of Edward VII. She was Duchess of Fife in her own right, but was more generally known as Princess Arthur of Connaught.

She had been a good sportswoman in her day, disposing of 75 stags in five weeks in Scotland, and then in December 1911 she nearly drowned with her family on their way to their annual winter holiday in Egypt. Soon afterwards, the Duke of Fife caught a chill and died, and she succeeded to his dukedom.

In 1913 she married her cousin, HRH Prince Arthur of Connaught (1883–1938), and they had one son, Alastair, Earl of Macduff, born in 1914. She could have been one of the most prominent members of the Royal Family, and had her husband not died before his father, she would have become Duchess of Connaught. But she was shy and nervous. She turned to a career in nursing rather than a life of royal duties.

Her career as a nurse was interrupted when her husband was appointed as Governor-General of South Africa between 1920 and 1923. On her return she worked as Nurse Marjorie at University College Hospital and Charing Cross Hospital, once amputating a patient's thumb. She opened the Fife Nursing Home which she ran as Matron for ten years.

Many tragedies struck in later life. Her husband died in 1938; her son, the 2nd Duke of Connaught, in 1943; and her younger sister in 1945. After

PRINCESS ARTHUR OF CONNAUGHT

that she took to her bed, suffering from chronic rheumatoid arthritis, which crippled her and prevented her from walking. After March 1946 she took no part in public life, living at 64 Avenue Road, just north of Regent's Park, and occasionally being taken out for a drive in a special ambulance car.

Her cousin, the Duke of Windsor, occasionally visited her, helping by providing her with drugs such as Hydrocortone and Meticorten from America. While confined to her house, she wrote two books, A Nurse's Story in 1955, and Egypt and Khartoum in 1956. She was working on a book about the history of big game hunting, but died at her home in February 1959, aged sixty-seven.

Pope-Hennessy visited her at her London home at 5pm, and she was quite forthcoming.

I went to see her at 5.00 pm on 15 February [January] 1957. A large roly-poly person, with bobbed hair and spectacles which she took on and off and brandished, lying on a small satin-upholstered truckle bed behind a large screen in an amber-coloured bedroom at 64 Avenue Road, her biggish modern house. She chuckles a great deal, especially about her illness; confined to her bed for eleven years, with two incurable kinds of arthritis *and* asthma, but very gay and brave about it all. Mercifully unroyal and making a lot of sense I thought (although others such as Lord C. Hamilton & Sir Alan Lascelles speak of her as mad). Writes, and gave me her two booklets, printed by Bumpus. Reads a great deal, mostly biographies, can't read novels. Has only a few of the usual royal preoccupations – e.g. lies there wondering why Princess Anne is not Pss. Royal and the present Pss. Royal the Dowagr. Pss. Royal. But far and away the easiest English royalty or collateral I've yet hit, human and educated.

When Princess Louise* was annoyed with her sister-in-law she would always say: 'Poor May, poor May, with her Württemberg hands'.

On the Sheen† engagement of P.M. and Prince George. 'I don't know whether he was shy in himself or shy of her or somethin' but I remember my mother saying he was just about to leave the house without havin' proposed so she said to him "Georgie, don't you think you ought to take May out into

---

* HRH The Princess Louise, Duchess of Fife, Princess Arthur's mother.
† Sheen Lodge, the Richmond home of the Duke of Fife, and his wife, Princess Louise.

the garden and show her the frogs in the pond?" and when they came back he told them he was engaged.'

Queen Mary's chief characteristic in *this* niece's eyes was her quality of 'never interfering'. She would *never* advise or suggest unless asked to do so. When coming to see Princess Arthur immobile in bed she never once suggested a new doctor or a new treatment, which most people were doing. Princess Arthur even thinks she didn't interfere over the Abdication until her appeal at the *very* end.

She had *no eye* for colour; always liked pale colours as she hated anything gloomy; always dressed in pinks and blues, but at the slightest opportunity would wear white. 'On one of those few hot summer's days we ever have, ye know, there she'd be, ever so happy, and dressed in white from head to foot.'

After the motor-car-lorry accident in the war* she stepped down the ladder from the overturned car completely tidy and as usual except for the handle of her parasol which was slightly bent to one side.

Princess Maud (Queen of Norway) was, P.A. thinks, her favourite sister-in-law; when she came over for a final fatal operation Q.M. spent all day at Claridge's with her to comfort her – 'that's the sort of thing she'd do, very thorough.'

I enquired about Princess Victoria: 'Oh full of tricks, full of tricks. We all suffered from her, trying to make mischief between my parents and then between my parents and us children. Not bad mischief, ye know, but just old maid's tricks.'

She believes, on what evidence I didn't gather, that P.M. was really devoted to Prince Eddy, though later she became fond of Prince George. I said I didn't think Prince Eddy would have made such a frightfully good king and she said 'Heavens no, a weak character; and then she would have found him difficult as he got older; people's characters don't always strengthen as they get older, ye know.'

She kept on repeating that she supposed Q.M. must have been devoted to King George as they told each other everything, and as she was good at *trying* about shooting and country life neither of which she cared for. But she sounded dubious and in need of reassurance.

Q.M. sometimes said unintentionally as well as intentionally funny things. On unpunctuality: 'I simply cannot understand unpunctuality. Why should anybody be late? *I* know exactly how long it takes me to dress.'

---

* In May 1939. See below in the Lord Claud Hamilton interview.

Queen Alexandra wildly unpunctual and always changing her plans. Once by changing her mind at the last moment she upset the whole timetable of all the continental expresses for 24 hours (refused to go somewhere as arranged).

The break between the Edwardian court and the George V court far less marked than between George V's and George VI's courts. 'It remained very Edwardian. They both used to say you had to move with the times, but in certain ways *they* could not do so.'

Q.M. and India: 'You know sometimes [it is] not the things people say but *the way they say them* that strikes one. I remember very clearly that I once mentioned India and Queen Mary said '*Beautiful* India, *lovely India*' in such a way that one realised how she felt about it.'

(I imagine a dreamy tone?)

Her being read to was, she thinks, a habit of the period. Once, on Maggie Wyndham, she said 'Maggie is so *stupid*. She gets hoarse and then her voice gives out' – rather, Pss. Arthur commented, as though Miss Wyndham were a gramophone needing a new needle.

When young P.M. was very attractive rather than pretty; before her marriage full of jokes and high spirits; afterwards markedly less so. When first married she must have had a very difficult time with Q. Alexandra, Pss. Victoria and the family. (This before marriage bit is hearsay, since Princess Arthur was not born till '91.)

'There's been too much written about the Abdication. Why don't you just leave it out? Old Windsor's book* was a lot of rubbish, wasn't it, and always repeating herself.'

'The Battenbergs are a sketchy lot, a sketchy lot' (immense chuckles) 'I believe the first one was a hairdresser or something.† But what does that matter so long as they do their job?'

Queen Mary was slightly dubious about the present Duke of Edinburgh. At the time of the engagement, Pss. A. asked her what she thought of him and she replied 'He ought to read more'. Later she was much excited and impressed by his scientific speeches.

Again and again stressed the non-interference theme.

---

* The Duchess of Windsor, *The Heart Has Its Reasons* (Michael Joseph, 1956).

† The Battenbergs were a morganatic branch of the Hesse-Darmstadt family. They were the progenitors of the Mountbatten family.

FOURTEEN

LORD CLAUD HAMILTON

13 February

Lord Claud Hamilton (1889–1975), was a son of 2nd Duke of Abercorn. He served as Equerry to HRH The Prince of Wales 1919–22; Deputy-Master of H.M.'s Household, Extra Equerry to George V, 1922–4; Equerry 1924–36; and Comptroller and Treasurer in Queen Mary's Household, and Extra Equerry, 1936–53. He lived at 8 Russell Court, St James's.
In 1933 he had married Mrs Violet Newall.
Pope-Hennessy called on him at 6pm.

Absurd-looking P.G. Wodehouse man, with a thin, tilted, highly-coloured some-what varnished-looking face, moustache, a nervous sniffle, very good old-fash-ioned manners. He popped in to St James's on getting my note, and explained that he now lived in Princess Marie Louise's garage, converted into a mews house, in Russell Court, Cleveland Row, opposite the main gate of the Palace. I went to see him there next day at 6.00 p.m., Wednesday 13 February 1957. Nervous and awkward to begin with, not helped by half a thimbleful of south african sherry which had to last me 1 hour and a ½. He began by explaining again that this was Pss. Marie Louise's garage etc., trying to put himself and me at ease.

Very diffident about mentioning himself, and felt he had nothing interesting to tell me. Points which emerged from a great deal of nervous fidgeting and snif-fling were:

1. *Punctuality:* Q.M. herself told him she was so punctual because of her mother's laxity in this respect. She was very often too early, and had to sit in her hall waiting to start.

2. *Generosity:* He said Ld. Spencer* had got the Royal School of Needlework story wrong, but didn't indicate how. Once when his own daughter[†] had TB before the war and they had to send her abroad, Q.M. cross-examined him about this, and suddenly and *most* surprisingly produced 'substantial financial help'.

3. Re. *presents* he said he had long been convinced that she selected these for the recipients by *colour* alone. Thus an unimportant clerk might get something valuable because of its colour, and someone close to her get a five-shilling tin tray because it was pink or mauve, I gathered.

4. *Shrewdness:* Unlike Queen Alexandra, who could never resist slipping a fiver into the answer to any rogue's begging letter, she was most judicious about helping people. 'No, I don't like this man's letter' she would say and she was almost invariably right. An excellent instinct for what was phoney.

5. *Trustfulness:* He had been astonished to find that once she took him on, she trusted him absolutely and entirely with all her money affairs. If she liked a page, she would equally trust him utterly.

6. *Emotional:* She was 'emotional' – 'I mean every now and then she might let a tear or two trickle out'. But she was fundamentally cold, had no use for people when they became infirm, and thought all mentally deficient children should be killed off. She was a good friend until someone became incapacitated by ill-health. Quite unlike King George who stood by his friends to the end.

7. *Selfishness:* 'In fact' (continuing above train of thought) 'the truth is she was *damned* selfish. One of the most selfish human beings I have ever known.'

8. *Dullness:*The lives led by King George and Queen Mary were inconceivably *dull.* There was a function every three months or so, otherwise they just lived in Buckingham Palace; every Sunday they would go out together without a lady or gentleman and motor to Coppins[‡] to call on Princess Victoria. The sixteen years of her widowhood she saw hardly anybody, no-one but perhaps the Athlones would come to Marlborough House.

---

* Jack, 7th Earl Spencer (1892–1975), grandfather of Diana, Princess of Wales.

† Lady Claud Hamilton had a daughter by her previous marriage, Pamela, now Baroness Sharples (b. 1923).

‡ Princess Victoria lived at Coppins, Iver, Buckinghamshire and bequeathed this to her nephew, Prince George, Duke of Kent.

9. *Democratisation:* She discovered democracy in the last war, and loved it. A very marked change in her manner, picking up American airmen in her car etc.; The first American airman they picked up, a blonde Scandinavian type, was very chatty and told her all about Al Johnson* who had visited his camp. He was sitting beside her on one of the bucket seats, Ld C., and two others in the back seat; 'Do you know who I am?' she enquired. 'You've certainly got me guessing there' he replied 'I am Queen Mary' 'Say, isn't that swell of you' he answered. (<u>Note in margin</u>: See also Miss Wyndham's diary for Q.M.'s own explanation of this.)

10. *Shyness:* She was incapable of making conversation. Lord Claud often watched her at, e.g. a military dinner when she was the only woman, amongst distinguished generals etc.; after dinner she would just stand there 'cleaning her teeth with her tongue' and saying nothing. Until the last war she never bothered about the Services.

Note on slip of paper attached to this sheet:

> 'And what do her ladies tell you?' he asked with a nasty toothy smile. 'That she was perfect, I suppose. Oh, you did see Margaret Ampthill†. No doubt she told you she was a Saint.'

11. *Balmoral:* She positively hated it. Ld C. saw more of her up there, for ordinarily he might go a month without seeing her to speak to, when in attendance on the King. He would go up after dinner there if sent for, and find King George sitting by the fire, Queen Mary on a sofa along a distant wall. I said 'I suppose they were talking?' 'Rather a long way off for conversation, ye know,' he replied. 'And the page outside the door, listening.'

12. *And her husband:* Lord Claud could never make up his mind if they liked each other or *not*. It was *quite* wrong to say she was frightened of him. She venerated the throne, and him as being on it. For *this* reason she would defer to his wishes.

---

* Al Jolson (1886–1950), American singer and comedian, starred in *The Jazz Singer* (1927).

† Lady Margaret Lygon (1874–1957), third daughter of 6th Earl Beauchamp, married 1894, 2nd Lord Ampthill, Viceroy of India ; Lady of the Bedchamber to Queen Mary 1911–53.

13. *Her collecting:* Her collections, when valued for probate, were not worth much. Her prized Clodion was pronounced by the experts 'so much cotton wool'. She never bought a good picture nor was she interested in them. Her water-colours of flower-gardens were valued at 'a quid a piece for the frames'. She bought family things chiefly, and up to the end would insist on e.g. saddling the Duke of Gloucester with a vast and impossible silver tea-urn because it had belonged to the Duke of Cumberland.* She could recognise ancestors wrongly labelled in antique-shops.

14. *And Frank Partridge[†]:* She was much attached to Mr Partridge, until he stored her possessions in the war. His cellars were damaged by water when incendiaries were put out, and she never forgave him (possibly never spoke to him again). She was constantly pointing to some damaged piece of lacquer on a cabinet – 'Just look what Partridge did to that, too stupid of him' – not realising or recognising that the whole lot might have gone up in flames.

15. *Food and drink:* The King and Queen liked food, but always the same thing repeated. At Buckingham Palace she seldom if indeed ever saw the chef; she would cross off or add items in the daily menu book. When going to Sandringham the menu had to go down days in advance. In 16 years at M.H. she *never* saw the chef once.

He drank whiskey and port, 'so he got a red nose, like meself' – she Sparkling Moselle – 'not what everybody would care for, you know'.

At Marlborough House she had breakfast and luncheon alone, dinner with a Lady-in-Waiting. Frightened of becoming fat, she ate almost nothing at all. Her lunch took ten minutes; the housekeeper might have been talking to her, would go downstairs at 1.14 and be summoned back at 1.25 when the Queen's lunch was over and the housekeeper hadn't had hers.

---

* The Duke of Gloucester possessed various silver tea-urns and soup tureens with royal provenance, which were sold at the Duke of Gloucester sale at Christie's in January 2006. A royal soup tureen from the service of William IV and Queen Adelaide fetched a hammer price of £55,000 (lot 65).

† Frank Partridge (1875–1953), founder of Frank Partridge & Sons (fine art dealers), then based at 26 King Street, St James's. His King Street premises received a direct hit during the war, and he opened next day with his surviving stock in Bruton Street. His philosophy was to sell quickly with a moderate profit. He used to tell his clients, 'I'm offering you a lick o'treacle.' [*The Times*, 11 and 13 August 1953]

There was no waste. *Exactly* the right quantity was sent up, nothing more. Say two tiny slivers of roast chicken, *no* potatoes, a little vegetable; and then a wafer. The Ladies-in-Waiting were often hungry – dinner consisting of a little fish, *one* potato for the Lady-in-W., a tiny sweet and a minute savoury.

16. *Marlborough House:* Hardly any heating.

After Buck. Pal. she couldn't cut down, and there were *sixty* servants at M.H. ('don't put this in, mind you, because of the Socialists'). For instance 'the page outside her door', and many other footmen etc. had to be doubled for relief. I asked *why* the page outside her door, and he said they always had them and did so because of the size of palaces and how long it takes for people from the nether regions to answer the bell. In the earlier M.H. days (1936 on) there was not even a front door bell and a man had to sit in the hall all day in case anyone called – 'nobody did of course, except occasionally Princess Alice, but still he had to be there in case'. The dusting alone at M.H. was a major operation, I gathered from Lord C. 'On the Queen's desk alone there were ninety-three different objects to be dusted each day – or was it seventy-three? I forget.'

17. *And her children:* Preferred the Duke of Kent because she thought him like her in his tastes. The King and she were 'simply dreadful parents, the most *awful* parents'. She didn't really care for the children at all.

18. *And the past:* Except for the punctuality and Dss. of Teck bit, she never talked to him about it, probably did more to the ladies. She talked on all sorts of subjects, and was very well-informed – they never found out *where* her information came from – she hated Sir Alan Lascelles* because she felt he kept information from her in G. VI's reign.

---

* Rt Hon Sir Alan Lascelles (1887–1981), Private Secretary to the Prince of Wales 1920–29, Assistant Private Secretary to George V 1935-6, to Edward VIII 1936, and to George VI 1936 –43; succeeded Sir Alexander Hardinge as the King's Private Secretary in 1943. Also Private Secretary to the Queen 1952-3.

LORD CLAUD HAMILTON

19. *Her calm and courage:* Extremely composed after the motor accident [in May 1939]*, the car keeled right over and she fell on top of Lord Claud. They got a ladder and got her out, toque etc. in place only the china parasol handle broken. They went to a house and were given cups of tea, but when Ld Claud said to the policeman 'will you please let Marlborough House know' he asked 'Where's that? A public house near here?' She was equally calm when the intruder came into M.H. and stabbed Mrs Knight the housekeeper in five places,† only indignant at anyone daring to get into a Palace and being able to do so.

20. *Driving habits:* She and the King sat on the 'bucket seats' not, as *I* have always thought, in order to be seen properly but so as not to be over the wheels. 'Horrible seats' you were nearly thrown out each time the motor rounded a corner.

21. *Well-read:* Queen Mary was exceedingly well-read. She 'sacked' her nicest lady, Cicely Vesey‡ (now resident at Windsor) for not knowing enough about books. She sacked Miss Wyndham for getting tired when she read. She liked being read to in the motor-car, which made Lady Constance Milnes-Gaskell§ feel sick and which Miss Wyndham flatly refused to do.

22. *Food (contd.):* Even the tea was on the morning menu. Very scanty, something like 'Biscuits Saxe-Weimar' – 'which were just a handful of coagulated sand'. She would sometimes buy small bars of chocolate at the shop in Curzon Street (?Bendix) and eat these at odd hours of the day. Never had soup.

---

* In May 1939 Queen Mary's Daimler was hit by a lorry carrying a load of heavy tubing. The car overturned, Queen Mary was much bruised and shocked. She emerged from the wreck with the help of two ladders. An eye-witness wrote : 'She climbed up and down these ladders as if she might have been walking down the steps at the Coronation. She had not her hat or one curl out of place ... The only outward sign of disorder was a broken hat pin and her umbrella broken in half.' See *Queen Mary*, pp. 594–5.

† After the intruder had been arrested, Lord Claud Hamilton led a thorough search of Marlborough House, including the bedrooms and the grounds.

‡ Lady Cicely Browne (1888–1976), daughter of 5th Earl of Kenmare. Married 1911, Col Hon Thomas Vesey. Woman of the Bedchamber to Queen Mary 1951–53. She lived at the Red House, Sunningdale.

§ Lady Constance ('Pussy') (1885–1964), elder surviving daughter of 5th Earl of Ranfurly. Married 1905, Evelyn Milnes-Gaskell (1877–1931). Woman of the Bedchamber to Queen Mary 1937–53.

23. *Lady Shaftesbury at the Durbar:* Lady S. was proverbially unpunctual. When all the carriages were lined up and ready to move off for the Durbar she was nowhere to be found. 'Where's Cuckoo.' And the whole procession which had begun to move, had to circle round and round until Lady Shaftesbury arrived.

As I left Lord Claud showed me his dining room, which has no outside windows but a glass partition between it and the pantry (which was filled with Lady Claud's underclothes being ironed by a daily woman); The glass has been painted with ferns and bees. As he took me through this to the front door, he said 'Of course, you know I had the *greatest* admiration for her, she was a wonderful old lady. What she minded most about, as we said, was the Monarchy,' he continued standing on the rainswept doorstep, 'the Monarchy – and of course the upper class and all that'. I said goodnight.

FIFTEEN

LADY REID

14 February

The Hon Lady Reid (1870–1961) was the widow of Queen Victoria's doctor, Sir James Reid, Bt, GCVO, KCB, who was in her medical Household from 1881. She was born Hon Susan Baring, third daughter of 1st Lord Revelstoke and of Louisa Bulteel, sister of Mary Ponsonby (wife of Queen Victoria's Private Secretary, Sir Henry Ponsonby). Susan was the granddaughter of the Lord Grey who introduced the Reform Bill. She was the younger sister of Margaret, Viscountess Althorp (mother of 7th Earl Spencer). She was a Maid of Honour to Queen Victoria from 1898–9. As such she was expected to be able to speak, read and write French and German, to sing and play the piano for the Queen's entertainment, to sketch, undertake needlework, and play household games such as backgammon and bridge. If no royal visitors were present, the Maid of Honour sat at the Queen's table and was thus expected to be well informed and to converse with confidence.

Her first period of waiting was at Osborne in August 1898, and by Christmas she was on terms of some familiarity with Reid. They became engaged surreptitiously, Reid informing his mother: 'She is not very pretty, nor has she much money; but she is clever, accomplished and sensible to a degree, and she likes me which is the chief point!'[108] Eventually Queen Victoria had to be told. She was dumbfounded, astonished and not especially pleased, since she did not like any of the gentlemen of her Household to marry, least of all with her ladies. The Queen forbade the engagement to be announced for an agonising period of time. She dictated her terms, which largely concerned Sir James remaining with her and closely on call. After a month, she allowed the engagement to be made public. The couple were married on 28 November.

Sir James Reid continued to serve the Royal Family after the death of Queen Victoria in 1901. Queen Mary used to take him with her to visit tenants and found that he, being Scottish, was of great assistance to her. He lived long enough to attend the wedding of the Duke of York and Lady Elizabeth Bowes-Lyon in April 1923, and died the following June.

Their descendants led interesting lives. Susan was the mother of Admiral Sir Lorne Reid, GCB, CVO (1903–73), and the grandmother of Richard Ingrams, Editor of Private Eye *and* The Oldie. *Michaela Reid, the wife of her grandson, Sir Alexander Reid, 3ʳᵈ Bt, edited* Ask Sir James *(Hodder & Stoughton, 1987), a fascinating account of the later years of Queen Victoria, as seen through the eyes of her doctor.*

I went to 24 Thurloe Square at 3.30 p.m. on this Thursday, to see Lady Reid. She is 86 and was Miss Susan Baring, one of Queen Victoria's Maids of Honour, and married the Queen's doctor (see *Osborne* file). The door was opened by a parlourmaid, and through this and the door to the inner hall one could see along to the back room of the house (door also open) where sat Lady Reid, somewhat hunched, in profile against the window. She got up as I came in; a very short, somewhat bent old lady, with a highly intelligent, plain long face, largeish nose; seated in a low armchair, dressed in a wool dress and cardigan of two dark shades of violet with a shawl of dark and lighter violet, crocheted in circular lumps the size of a shilling; she was evidently at work on a similar shawl in brown, red and white which lay in embryo on the worktable beside her. She is extremely gay and witty, with a photographic memory for the extreme past.

She began by thanking me for coming and telling me about the Kensington Palace dancing classes. I then told her about the bicycling story in P. May's letter of August '99 and she explained this amidst much laughter (see *Osborne* file). She then told me in graphic detail the story of her engagement, Miss Phipps,[*] the Queen etc., all of which Jack Wheeler-Bennett[†] has recorded. Talked much more of the Queen than of my subject, but was fascinating. Her theme was that Queen Victoria was not at all what people often thought nowadays – very obstinate through age, autocratic, but *kind* and *simple* and anxious to put the new Maid of Honour at her ease, pointing out the different kinds of trees at Osborne as Miss Baring 'trotted' beside her pony-carriage – drawn by a pony given by her

---

[*] Hon Harriet Phipps (1841–1922), daughter of Hon Sir Charles Phipps, Maid of Honour to Queen Victoria 1862–89, Bedchamber-Woman in Ordinary 1889–1901, acted as personal secretary to Queen Victoria, and was the go-between at the time of the engagement.

[†] Sir John Wheeler-Bennett (1902–75), official biographer of King George VI.

own uncle Lord Cromer.' These were the only times one was alone with her, and could speak of anything, but it was all rather breathless, 'keepin' up with the pony'.

Her first real outing with the Queen was soon after her arrival for first duty. Miss Phipps explained to her that the Queen liked to distribute her Christmas presents herself at Osborne, and off they set in a great high royal carriage, the Queen and Miss Phipps facing the horses, Miss Baring with her back to them and a pile of presents beside her. At the first cottage the woman came out and stood on the step of the carriage ('poor woman it was agonising for her to hold on'); Miss Baring took the appropriate parcel and handed it to the Queen:

'It's a rug, Your Majesty.'

The Queen said nothing and turned to Miss Phipps. 'What an odd thing to say, a *rug*, a r-r-rug! I have never heard it called that before. A rug is something which one stands on. It can be called a plaid, or a shawl, or even a wrap. But not a *rug*. And yet Susan calls it a *"r-r-rug"*. I have heard it called a plaid or a wrap, but never a rug.' This monologue went on for several minutes, over and over again, while the woman was clinging on to the steps; and Miss Baring overcome by it all, laughed and laughed and laughed till she nearly died. The Queen finally looked at her again and said: 'Her laugh is just like Bessie's' (an aunt, I think, of Miss B.).

At this late period, the Queen was always wheeled about indoors in her chair. No-one ever sat in her presence, none the less. One evening at Balmoral after dinner she had been wheeled into the centre of the room and Miss Baring was stationed beside her chair. Suddenly, Miss Baring, watching the men standing round the wall in a circle, saw Sir Douglas Powell,[†] the other royal physician, fall flat down on his face in a dead faint. Everyone gathered round and he was taken out. The Queen was thought not to have seen him faint as he was behind her; but she turned to Miss Baring and said 'And a doctor, too!'

The death of Queen Victoria was in a sense unexpected. She had seemed no worse than usual. King Edward (Prince of Wales) had planned a large Sandringham party, and asked the physicians in attendance whether he should put it off when she became slightly ill. They said no. He then said 'ask Reid' and Sir James Reid

---

[*] 1ˢᵗ Earl of Cromer (1841–1917).

[†] Sir Richard Douglas Powell, 1ˢᵗ Bt (1842–1925), Physician-in-Ordinary to Queen Victoria, and Edward VII. He fell down in a faint during one of the Queen's Drawing Rooms at Balmoral in the summer of 1899, bruising his face. His accident caused Sir James Reid to be called to Balmoral, which suited him, as he was missing Susan. But Powell made an all-too-speedy recovery.

advised him to cancel the party and hold himself in readiness in London. Only a week before her death Lady Reid saw the Queen for the last time, passing through the gates at Osborne in her carriage with the Duchess of Edinburgh* beside her.

Q.V.'s great objection to marriages in the Household was that married men tell their wives everything. The very idea of her doctor marrying was thus anathema to her, the worst of all.

Her letters at the end of her life were illegible. She would write to consult Sir James on all sorts of non-medical subjects. He couldn't read them and gave them to his wife, who put them on the floor and looked at them sideways, and when she had spelled out one word, built the rest up from there, often using her imagination.

All the household suffered dreadfully from the Munshi.† The Indian servants behind her chair were alright. 'We could take that, it all looked rather splendid'. But the Munshi was of such low caste, and so personally repulsive and disagreeable that he was impossible. He used to make endless trouble, and fuss and worry the Queen. Sir J. Reid was finally asked by the others to have a word with the Munshi, while at Windsor. He saw him and said 'Do you know what the people of Windsor will do if there is any suggestion or hint that you are causing any trouble to Her Majesty?' 'No' said the Munshi. 'They would roll you down the castle hill and kick you to pieces at the bottom.' After this the trouble lessened noticeably.

The Queen was quite unreasonable about the Munshi. When she was going to France on her last visit she was determined to take him with her. This would have involved his eating with the Household in the hotel; they all put their feet down at this and refused. Miss Phipps (I think) remonstrated with the Queen who was so angry she swept all the things off her table in a rage. The Household, fond though they were of the Queen, still held out and almost went on strike or threatened resignation *en masse*. Lord Salisbury‡ was coming down, and so he was appealed

---

* HR and IH Grand Duchess Marie of Russia (1853–1920), widow of Queen Victoria's second son, HRH The Duke of Coburg and Edinburgh (1844–1900).

† Abdul Karim (ca 1863–1909), brought from India to be Queen Victoria's Indian servant at the time of the Golden Jubilee in 1887, and styled Munshi Hafiz Abdul Karim (Official Indian Secretary) from 1889. The Queen favoured him and there were many tensions within the Household. After her death, Edward VII sent him back to India. His story inspired the film, *Victoria and Abdul* (2017).

‡ 3ʳᵈ Marquess of Salisbury (1830–1903), Prime Minister from 1885–7, and 1900–2. His visit to Queen Victoria was on 18 February 1898.

to. He was most reluctant to mention it, saying the Queen was now so old why not let her do as she liked; but in the end he solved the problem by saying to the Queen what odd people the French were and how funnily they might react if Her Majesty took the Munshi to France. 'What would they do, Lord Salisbury?' 'I am very much afraid they would laugh at Your Majesty.' The project was dropped.

~

Kind Edward had far more charm and real kindness of heart than any of the rest of the family. He was really *delightful* and trouble-taking; when the Reids in reply to his enquiries if they were comfortable at Abergeldie Mains* complained of the rats, he was dreadfully upset. 'There shall be no more *rats*' he said on leaving; and sure enough he kicked up such a row and had rat-people brought from Aberdeen that there were no more rats. Previously they kept one awake at night running in the walls, and Lady Reid used to lunch in the garden because rats would come out near a hole in the dining room sideboard.

~

Queen Alexandra had a spontaneity which Queen Mary never achieved or could emulate. Once they were all going on a picnic in the Balmoral woods in a waggonette, and Queen Alexandra and Sir James Reid were 'chaffing' and laughing, and she was so preoccupied that she had not seen the servants, who were playing cricket, all lined up as the carriage drove by, and bowing. In a trice she ordered the waggonette to stop, stood up there and then in her tweeds and shooting cap and bowed gracefully first to one side and then to the other with consummate grace and charm.

At the Edwardian court it was a custom, dropped by their successors, for the King and Queen to enter, and she would drop a low curtsey to the diplomatic corps on each side. This was a beautiful sight.

C. 1877: She was three years younger than Princess May, and one of her earliest memories is going to Taglioni's dancing classes at Kensington Palace. Taglioni, then a very small thin little old woman with grey side-curls (or coils?). On one

---

* The Reids stayed at Abergeldie Mains, in the grounds of Abergeldie Castle, very close to Balmoral in the autumns of 1906 and 1907.

occasion she was trying to teach the children the tarantella – 'we just stood around in a circle making hopeless gestures with our arms' – when the Duchess of Teck stepped in, and seizing Taglioni performed the tarantella with the utmost lightness and grace. At another dancing class (I think given by a man, a Mr D---- -, I couldn't quite gather from Lady Reid) one of the most embarrassing exercises was to go round the room alone in turn, making a curtsey. Princess May said 'Well, goodness, that's one thing *I* shall never have to do'. 'She was told to think again' remarked Lady Reid.

The Duke of Teck she occasionally saw and he seemed a nonentity. He 'went off his head' when Prince Eddy died, and kept going round and round in circles repeating 'It must be a Cesarewitch, it must be a Cesarewitch' – an untactful reference to the similar circumstance of Princess Dagmar's fiancé's death and her marriage to the brother.* 'He had to be told to shut up, and was put away somewhere.'

Prince Eddy's death, though a great mercy, created *at the time* widespread shock and surprise and grief.

Princess May held herself so well that she always stood out in any room.

Shyness due to the Duchess of Teck's ample manner. The Duchess would refer to this shyness in company, addressing remarks to her, and thus making her shyer and shyer still.

The Reids were one summer at Abergeldie Mains when the Yorks were at Abergeldie Castle. One night they dined alone with them. There was a ghillies ball – 'just a very small simple affair of the servants' – the Yorks told them they would all have to show themselves there and dance after dinner for a bit. Just as they entered the drawing room Princess May said in an undertone to Lady Reid – 'This is the sort of thing which makes me feel *so* shy.'

The Barings lived at Coombe Cottage,† and so her mother saw a lot of the Duchess of Teck and used to go with her – 'Princess Mary' – to the Cambridge Asylum every Wednesday. She was always tremendously jolly and would slap people on the back. They got deeply involved in the Guild Work.

---

* HRH Princess Dagmar of Denmark (1847–1928), Queen Alexandra's sister, was first engaged to Nicholas, Tsarevitch of Russia (1843–63), and then, after his death, married the future Tsar Alexander III (1845–94). She was the mother of the last Tsar, Nicholas II (1868–1918).

† This was in Coombe Wood, and the Cambridge Asylum was in Norbiton Road, both in Kingston, not far from White Lodge.

SIXTEEN

PRINCESS ALICE, COUNTESS OF ATHLONE

on the Württemberg Family and Hélène Bricka

29 April

HRH Princess Alice, Countess of Athlone (1883–1981), was a sprightly figure, destined to live into her late 90s and to hold the distinction of being the last surviving granddaughter of Queen Victoria. In her long life she attended every Jubilee from 1887 to 1977. She lived long enough to attend the christening of Peter Phillips, the son of Princess Anne, in 1977 and to be photographed with the infant Lord Frederick Windsor in 1979.

She was the only daughter of Prince Leopold, Duke of Albany, and his wife Princess Helen, 5ᵗʰ daughter of Georg Vicktor, Prince of Waldeck-Pyrmont. She was also Queen Mary's sister-in-law, having married Prince Alexander of Teck (1874–1957) in 1904. In 1917 he renounced his German titles and became 1ˢᵗ Earl of Athlone. Of all the Royal Family, it was to the Athlones that Queen Mary confided her thoughts and concerns. There exists a long correspondence between Queen Mary and the Athlones when they were in Canada, held in the Royal Archives.

Pope-Hennessy went to see her at 5pm.

'No my aunt was never Queen of Württemberg*, because she died before Uncle Willy, as we called him, came to the throne. She was called Mary.'

(P.A. displayed wild excitement and amusement at my account of her first cousin Pauline† – pronouncing Affy as though it were Effie).

---

*   HSH Princess Marie (1857–82), 3ʳᵈ daughter of Georg Viktor, Prince of Waldeck and Pyrmont. She married King Wilhelm II of Württemberg in 1877. He became King in 1891.

†   HRH Princess Pauline (1877–1965), daughter of King Wilhelm II of Württemberg. She married 1898, Friedrich, 6ᵗʰ Prince of Wied. Author of *Vom Leben Gelernt* (1953). J P.-H. interviewed her. See above.

PRINCESS ALICE, COUNTESS OF ATHLONE

(I told her she had pretended she couldn't speak English) 'Oh she did that to be tiresome, of course. Just like her. I think she became as she is because of Uncle Willy. He was very elegant and always arrangin' rooms and so on like the Duke of Teck. He made her learn the piano, and wanted her to be musical and so to annoy him she would play the piano with her fingers at meal-times on the dining room table. It was all a reaction against her father, do you see.' (This ties up with the Radowitz* story that Uncle Willy was notoriously homosexual and in his tastes effeminate?)

'No – it's too wonderful.' (Photo of Aunt Catherine[†] in *Vom Leben Gelernt*)[‡]. 'Tante Catherina – she had a huge red face and always dressed in purple and mauve. That's her.'

'My father-in-law[§] was really quite *distantly* connected with the King of Württemberg. He and Uncle Willy's grandfather were cousins.'

Princess Alice also spoke of Bricka:

Poor dear Hélène, she was a good old soul. She used to come and stay with us, and I always learnt a lot from her. She was a natural educationalist. But she became very tiresome towards the end – always asking one of us to help dear so-and-so – some bad singer or artist. People would ask her to bring the royal children out to tea – all that sort of thing. Queen Mary ended by being very angry with her. But she was a good old soul, and didn't mean any harm do you see.

She came to White Lodge after they got back from Italy because it was thought Princess May should have something to be doing during all the endless waitin' about. There was a family joke that she read the whole of Motley's *Dutch Republic*[¶] while waiting for her mother at various times.

---

* Carol von Radowitz, who took Pope-Hennessy to see the Fürstin zu Wied.

† HRH Princess Catherine (1821–98), third daughter of King Wilhelm I of Württemberg, married 1845, her first cousin, Prince Friedrich of Württemberg (1808–70). She was the mother of King Wilhelm II.

‡ *Vom Leben Gelernt*, p. 20.

§ The Duke of Teck (1837–1900) was a grandson of Duke Ludwig of Bavaria (1756–1817). King Wilhelm II was a grandson of Prince Paul of Württemberg, son of King Friedrich I of Württemberg, elder brother of Duke Ludwig.

¶ *The Rise of the Dutch Republic*, a popular but weighty history of the Netherlands, published in 1856 in three volumes, the work of John Lothrop Motley (1814–77).

James Pope-Hennessy, photographed by Cecil Beaton.
© The Cecil Beaton Studio Archive at Sotheby's.

Maud Russell described Pope-Hennessy as 'two characters lodged in one shell. The
serious, hardworking, self critical (so far as his writing was concerned) workmanlike
being, and that other self, wild, careless, unheeding. A person might easily have known
only one half of him and not had a clue to the other half.'

Queen Victoria in 1893 on the occasion of the wedding of Prince George, Duke of York (the future King George V) and Princess Victoria Mary of Teck

The Duchess of Teck and her children. Princess May is seated to the right.

Princess Mary Adelaide, Duchess of Teck, painted by Hermann Schmiechen.

Francis, Duke of Teck and the Duchess of Teck, with the infant Princess May.

Lord Hopetoun: 'Anyway I feel sure you will not
mention this 'tendresse' in the memoirs. It was only to
give an idea of her character & charm...'

Princess May as a young woman.

Prince Albert Victor, Duke of Clarence

Queen Alexandra

King Edward VII

Princess May and Prince George on their wedding day.

King George V and Queen Mary, dressed for their coronation.

The Royal Family at the Coronation of King George VI and Queen Elizabeth. From left to right: The Princess Royal; Princess Alice, Duchess of Gloucester; Prince Henry, Duke of Gloucester; Queen Mary; King George VI; Princess Margaret; Princess Elizabeth; Queen Elizabeth; Prince George, Duke of Kent; Princess Marina, Duchess of Kent; Queen Maud of Norway.

Sandringham

Balmoral

May Days at Barnwell Manor

Prince Henry, Duke of Gloucester

Barnwell Manor

Queen Mary and the Duke of Windsor in London.

The Queen Dowager

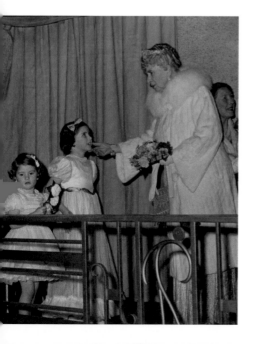

'In the midst of this shimmering Georgian enclave in bedraggled post-war London, visitors found Queen Mary herself, upright, distinguished, dressed perhaps in blue velvet or in pale grey, around her neck her ropes of matchless pearls. Awed strangers spoke of Queen Mary at Marlborough House as representative of another epoch, but this was a misjudgement, for the Queen Dowager was in no way isolated, a magnificent relic, in these eighteenth-century surroundings. She would sally forth from Marlborough House to listen to the proceedings at a court for juvenile delinquents – 'It was most interesting but I have never heard so many lies told in my life' – or to enjoy *Oklahoma* or *Annie Get Your Gun*.'

SEVENTEEN

A VISIT TO THE GRAND DUCHESS XENIA

'Artificial Respiration of a Memory'

14 May

HIH Grand Duchess Xenia of Russia (1875–1960) was the elder daughter of Tsar Alexander III, and the elder of the two sisters of Tsar Nicholas II. The assassination of her grandfather, Tsar Alexander II, in 1881 propelled the family into the centre of Imperial life in Russia. In 1894 she married her cousin, Grand Duke Alexander Mikhalovitch (1866–1933). She lived in St Petersburg until 1919. Following her father's death, she lived through the reign of her brother Tsar Nicholas II, during which her son-in-law, Prince Felix Yusupov, played a key role in the murder of the Mad Monk, Rasputin. During the First World War, she worked with the war wounded and arranged a hospital train to go to the Front.

After the Tsar abdicated in 1917, she was prevailed upon to leave Russia, and eventually departed with her mother, the Dowager Empress, and her children in 1919. She arrived in England, with no money, and George V (her first cousin; their mothers, Queen Alexandra and the Dowager Empress, being sisters) housed her, first at Frogmore Cottage in the grounds of Windsor Castle, and later at Wilderness House, a grace and favour house at Hampton Court. She occupied two rooms of a twenty-two-roomed house. The King gave her a pension of £2,400 a year.

Thus she lived in England throughout her later life, and was closely in touch with Queen Mary by letter. Queen Mary also visited her at Wilderness House. Apparently the Grand Duchess had not left the precincts of the house for ten years. A journalist, Francis Martin, who visited her in 1954, described her as 'small, frail, her clothes have no special distinction.' She would read until 2am or 3am and then sleep until 11am.[109]

Living with her there was the sinister Mother Martha (or Marfa), formerly known as Vera Maslenikoff. In her early life she had been betrothed to a Russian noble who had been killed fighting the Germans whilst serving with a

GRAND DUCHESS XENIA OF RUSSIA

MOTHER MARFA

crack Tsarist regiment. She then became a Greek Orthodox nun. She came into the Grand Duchess's life in the First World War, when she reorganised hospitals on the Front, and visited prisoner of war camps in Germany and Austria. In 1942 she came to look after the Grand Duchess, and was a fierce guardian of the gate, only admitting approved visitors. She was dietician, nurse and Lady-in-Waiting to the Grand Duchess. Francis Martin wrote of her:

At Wilderness House, Mother Martha, wearing the black habit of her order, wields quiet authority. Over gas-rings in an adjoining kitchen she cooks Russian dishes for the Grand Duchess.

After the Grand Duchess's death, Mother Martha attended her Memorial Service at the Russian Orthodox Church in Exile in Exhibition Road, standing a little apart from the family. At the end of the service they found she had disappeared, never to be seen by them again. Some members of the family later heard that she had gone to France, where she latched on to another royal exile.

Also lodging at Wilderness House was the Grand Duchess's young grandson, Prince Alexander Romanov (1929–2002).

Grand Duchess Xenia's younger sister, Olga (1882–1960), lived in Canada, and died a few months after her.

I had for some long time been wishing to go to see the Grand Duchess Xenia, sister of the last Czar and first cousin of King George V. This proved difficult to arrange, as although only 82, it was alleged by her entourage that her memory was bad, her health worse, and, of course that like all Royalty she was terribly, terribly shy. I finally asked the Princess Royal* to write to her, which did the trick. Negotiations continued however over three weeks between Irmgarde de Vaux,† on my side, and Prince Alexander Romanov,‡ a tall pallid gangling youth with

---

* HRH The Princess Mary (1897–1965), only daughter of King George V and Queen Mary. She told Pope-Hennessy she was writing to the Grand Duchess on 22 April 1957.

† Irmgard de Vaux (d. 1978), formerly Madame de Thun, later Mrs Ernest de Vaux. As a young widow she went to be chaperone-companion to Queen Helen of Romania's two elder daughters, and later sometimes represented Queen Helen of Romania at London memorial services.

‡ Prince Alexander Romanov (1929–2002), son of Prince Nikita, third son of the Grand Duchess.

a permanent smile, who lives with his grandmother at the Wilderness House, Hampton Court, on the other. The key person who seemed to be holding things up was the redoubtable Mother Marfa, an Orthodox nun who has been with the Grand Duchess 'night and day' for seventeen years. Just as it seemed that I should never see her, a peremptory message came through on Sunday 12 May that the Grand Duchess was expecting me at 3.30 the next day, Monday.

We accordingly set out after lunch on Monday, Irmgarde driving me in her little Ford. We drove up opposite the wall of Wilderness House and sat in the car, as we were 7 minutes too early which Irmgarde felt was wrong when visiting an Imperial Highness. At 3.29 we crossed the road, dodging heavy lorry traffic and approached the green door in the wall of the Wilderness.

'There's someone looking at us out of the top window,' I remarked to Irmgarde in the middle of the road.

'So there is, dear. Now I wonder whose face *that* is? That is *not* a face I know.'

The face, seeing itself caught in the act, quickly disappeared, and we opened the garden door.

The little Queen Anne house inside the walls, with a trim garden before it, seemed entirely remote, in another world, from the main road on to which it faced. It looked secret and quiet, like a house in a fairy story. We rang the bell and the door was at once opened by one of the Merry Wives of Windsor. This was Mother Marfa, behind whom stood Prince Alexander, smiling his meaningless smile.

Mother Marfa, a long and stout nun, wore a capacious robe of slate grey serge, and on her head a coif of unstarched, and indeed crumpled, linen of the tea-cloth variety, tied at the back of the head with two tapes. She has the face of a powerful elderly man, full-blooded and not at all severe, and eyes which gaze straight into yours. She puts her face very close to yours. In the little hall, as the others went upstairs, she caught my arm and leaning over me said:

'Her Imperial Highness expects you to ask her questions. Her Imperial Highness is very nervous and otherwise *she will not be able to speak*.'

On the way upstairs she stopped me again and skewed half round:

'What a wonderful work you are having. My life has never been the same since Queen Mary died. Always so kind and always *the* Queen.'

'Queen Mary came here often?'

'Oh constantly. And always so kind. But always *the* Queen. Nothing is the same since she died.'

On the threshold of a room on the first floor landing, at a door which Irmgarde had already entered, Mother Marfa stopped again.

'Now what is your name?'

'Pope-Hennessy'.

'What?'

'Pope-Hennessy'.

'Ah, yes. I remember.'

She entered the room and ushered me in:

'Mr Poke-Henderson, Your Imperial Highness.'

The room was small, pretty and light, facing on to the front garden and main road. It was very white, and full of photographs and one or two portraits. A long desk, covered with every sort of souvenir including a cheap china bust of King George, jutted out from one window into the middle of the room, and in the corner opposite the windows was a divan draped with shawls. The Grand Duchess, who rose to her feet, had been sitting (and did so during our talk) on a hard armchair at the end of this desk, so that she was in the dead centre of this little cluttered room. Mantelpiece and every available wall space were crammed with photographs, and a large group of the Czar, Czarina and their children, slightly tinted, stood on a small table by itself facing her chair.

The Grand Duchess is small and old, but one does not feel she has shrunk from age. She is beautifully made, like an exquisite little old doll. She was dressed in a dark dress, with a muslin at her neck, and ropes of big (I fancy artificial) pearls, and with an old-fashioned gesture she would constantly place her hand at her breast and finger the pearls. Her face was a synthesis, so to speak, of all the Danish Family's faces, with large slightly protuberant eyes, and the narrow heart-shape of Queen Alexandra. Her hair was grey and curled, with a centre parting. She smiled, waved Irmgarde and Mother Marfa out of the room and sank back, with her hand at her throat.

'It is so kind of Your Imperial Highness to let me come to see you.'

'Yes, Princess Mary wrote and I thought I must – I didn't want – I don't know how I can help you – now you must ask me questions – my poor old memory' (smiling like a girl and tapping her head) – 'I don't know.' She was like an exceedingly nervous wild bird, which felt trapped. Her voice and hands fluttered, and her remarks trailed nervously away. It was as if she had been too stringently protected from strangers for too long, as it were the member of an enclosed order suddenly brought face to face with a strange man. The charm and high spirits which had bewitched Prince George in Copenhagen in 1891[*] were quite apparent, though; but submerged and only evident in intermittent glimpses.

'What I really want to ask you about, Ma'am, is the *Danish* family. You see there is no-one to tell me about them, and when you are writing a book you can get all the facts together, but it's the atmosphere and how people *looked* that one wants to know, and that is what Your Imperial Highness could help me with. The Queen of Denmark, for instance, your grandmother.'[†]

'Oh,' She seemed startled and relieved. 'Oh yes I can tell you about *them*. We all used to go to Friedensborg and then – what is the name – the other place – you see I can't remember anything nowadays don't you – ah yes Bernsdorff – oh so charming' (she smiled) 'and so *simple*, the family life there. My grandmother was small and elegant. I remember her well although I was only a little thing.'

'I always imagined it was very simple, Danish court life.'

'Oh yes it was simple. They had grand dinners, of course, but they were happiest leading a simple life.'

'I have sometimes wondered if King George's love of York Cottage [Sandringham] and the simple life they led there came from his liking for the life he had seen in Denmark as a boy?'

'I think that is very possible. Oh you can't imagine how charming, how *cosy* York Cottage used to be. Oh it was delightful. It was very squashed being there, of course, but it was so charming when we were all there together.'

With the recollection of all this cosiness the Grand Duchess became gradually more animated and less intermittent, and we smiled at each other a great deal. She had at moments an innocent girlish charm which was very fetching.

She told me she had never met Queen Mary until 1910. 'We thought of coming over for King Edward's funeral[‡] but my husband said better not, so we came after it.' (I didn't get the meaning of this.) She had *not* been in Copenhagen when Queen Mary was there.

---

[*] Prince George and the Duchess of Fife were in Copenhagen in September 1891 with Tsar Alexander III of Russia, the Tsarevitch, the Kings of Denmark and Greece, and his mother, the Princess of Wales. Some of them were at a hunting party arranged by the King of Sweden on the island of Hveen.

[†] Princess Louise of Hesse-Cassel (1817–98), married 1842, King Christian IX of Denmark (1818–1906).

[‡] Edward VII died on 6 May 1910.

'In 1894, you mean, Ma'am'

'No, no, no later. In 1896 it was that they came' (quite abruptly).*

She said that Queen Mary was always so specially kind to her and agreed with me that she had much more warmth than anyone usually gave her credit for. I said this was a point I wished to make, to which she assented. She told me of the ivy-mania, and that one day arriving at someone's house in the country and finding them out Queen Mary set to work to strip the ivy off the walls – 'so bad for the stone, too absurd of them to leave it'. She agreed that the ivy-hatred was almost symbolic, the passion for order and tidiness being the dominant one. I told her about the papers at Windsor with their little labels which amused her. During King George's illness† she would lunch with Queen Mary and once said to her how deeply impressed she was by her calmness and absence of outward anxiety. 'George wouldn't like it,' Queen Mary replied, and the Grand Duchess felt this to be the key to the Queen's life and behaviour; she thought of nothing but him.

She became quite animated and almost governessy about Frogmore, as I asked her to clear up for me my present confusion about Frogmore House and Frogmore Cottage. 'The King and Queen *never* lived in Frogmore Cottage', she said, '*we* did.'

'But in 1910 Queen Mary refers to Frogmore as 'this dear little place' – this *must* have meant the cottage? I went to Frogmore last week and it is really quite a big house.'

'No, no, no, she meant the House, of course,' (leaning forwards) 'And then later Queen Mary made it into a museum – family, you know – Queen Alexandra – and...' (trailing away again). 'The little boy was born at Frogmore House, the first boy.'‡

'I think Your Imperial Highness is mistaken there. He was born at White Lodge.'

'White Lodge. Oh yes, of course.'

'Did Your Imperial Highness ever know the Duchess of Teck?'

'Never, but what a *charming person*' (she smiled and smiled). 'Everyone adored her. All the Wales cousins *adored her*.'

---

* The Grand Duchess was right. The Duke and Duchess of York attended the wedding of Princess Louise (1875–1906), daughter of King Frederik VIII of Denmark, to Prince Frederick of Schaumburg-Lippe in Copenhagen on 5 May 1896.

† King George V fell seriously ill in November 1928 and was still recuperating in August 1929.

‡ The future Edward VIII was born at White Lodge on 23 June 1894.

Queen Mary once told her that she owed her interest in art to a time she had spent with her parents in Florence. She had been so happy in Florence she said. It had been a beautiful time in Florence. The Gd. Dss. didn't know they had gone there because of the money trouble, and was simply *delighted* to hear it, and laughed and laughed. 'Oh she *never* told me that. That is *too* amusing.'*

By this time she was well under weigh, but switched back to her grandmother Queen Louise to say *en parenthèse* that she was deaf. 'Like Queen Alexandra.'

'Queen Alexandra's deafness must have been dreadful for her.'

'Oh poor thing she suffered so. Railway trains in her head. I can't stand this noise, I can't stand it, she used to say. That was in her later years.'

We seemed to be getting on so well that I ventured to ask:

'I suppose Your Royal Highness never knew the Duke of Clarence?'

'Of course I knew the Duke of Clarence. Very well. He was not *at all* like the other members of the family. He was quiet and he never seemed to mind what he did or what happened to him. I remember once we were all in a boat with the Wales cousins on that lake at Fredensborg (?or Bernsdorff, I forget: J.P.-H.) and his sisters had their little dog with them. And suddenly he just took this little dog and threw it into the lake. My grandfather was in the boat too and he said 'Why did you do that?' and he pushed Eddie into the water. He didn't seem at all surprised and just said 'I'm very wet'. 'Of course you're very wet,' said my grandfather 'you've been in the lake'. 'Why did you do that to me?' Eddie asked. 'Because you did it to the little dog,' my grandfather replied. He was like that, the Duke of Clarence. He never *minded* anything. Of course the Wales cousins were up to anything, always romping.'

She agreed with my delicate suggestion that it had been better for Queen Mary not to have married the Duke of Clarence and to have married King George.

Just at this point, when I had been there 20 minutes and everything was going better, and we seemed to have established contact and jokes, Mother Marfa blundered into the room.

'Mrs de Vaux says Mr Pope-Hennessy ought to be getting back to London.'

The Grand Duchess looked surprised and disappointed and fluttery again.

'Are you in a great hurry?'

'Not at all, Your Imperial Highness.'

---

* The Tecks lived in Florence (with certain breaks elsewhere) between September 1883 and May 1885.

Mother Marfa withdrew and Irmgarde came in, and was asked to be seated. But this intrusion had spoiled the whole atmosphere and broken the thread. We tried a few minutes more without any effect.

'It isn't that James is in a hurry, Your Imperial Highness,' said Irmgarde, 'it is only that one feels one must not *tire* Your Imperial Highness.'

Her Imperial Highness looked positively cross at this evidence of attention.

'And how are Your Imperial Highness's headaches?'

'Och, I have a headache all the time. It doesn't matter. It is the climate here – I don't mean the English climate' (smiling politely at me), 'the climate here by the river. My doctor says it is just the worst climate I could live in.'

'Has Your Imperial Highness never tried an osteopath?' I enquired (she had said it was fibrositis in the neck).

'Oh no, the whole thing is such a bore, I just don't think about it,' she said with a rather valiant sad smile.

Just as we got up to go, she said:

'But there is one thing I want to ask *you*. Dame – Dame – Dame – Dame …'

'Dame Una.'

'Yes Dame Una.'

'She was my mother.'

'Oh your mother. I am so glad. She came to see us years ago when we were at Frogmore. She wrote the Czarina's story.'[*]

We then withdrew, Irmgarde did her deepest obeisance (as to the Queen of Spain,[†] for minor German royalties she does what she calls 'the half-inch to an inch') kissed the Grand Duchess's thin, blotchy, old, beringed hand, rose and was kissed on the cheek, curtsied again and seized the hand, which the Grand Duchess withdrew.

'Och no! such nonsense!'

'But I will kiss it all the same, Your Imperial Highness.'

The Grand Duchess gave me a mischievous look, and when I said goodbye, said:

---

[*] Dame Una Pope-Hennessy translated *A Czarina's Story* (Nicholson & Watson, 1948), contributing a prologue and epilogue. This was the story of Princess Charlotte of Prussia's first three years of marriage to Tsar Nicholas I of Russia, from 1817 to 1820.

[†] HM Queen Victoria Eugenie of Spain (1887–1969), daughter of Princess Beatrice, and Prince Henry of Battenberg, a morganatic member of the Hesse family.

'You see, I haven't been able to tell you anything. You know so much already. Where's that boy?' she asked Mother Marfa.

'That boy is coming up to London with us, Your Imperial Highness,' interposed Irmgarde. 'He has to go to a dance.'

'Ah yes. A dance.'

She stood at the door of her room as we went downstairs.

'Her Imperial Highness's face is the image of that of King George the Fifth, especially here,' hissed Mother Marfa to me, drawing her hand across her chin. 'The image.'

On the way back to London Irmgarde and Prince Alexander indulged in Family small-talk. 'And have you seen Irina* yet' or 'Ah, you're going with Chips Channon† to Margarita's marriage'‡ 'Is Mother Marfa any happier?' Irmgarde asked at one point. 'Oh no, not at all.' 'She looked cheerful enough to me' I remarked. 'Oh no,' said Prince Alexander, in his sibilant voice with his eternal smile, 'Mother Marfa is never *cheerful*. She complains all the time. And she will never relax. Mother Marfa *simply can't relax*.'

~

I saw Irmgarde later that evening at Carmen Gronau's§ party.

'Jamesy, do you know *who* was that face at the window?'

'No of course I don't.'

'It was the Grand Duchess's daughter Princess Youssopoff. She knows *me*, of course, but she asked who *you* were. And when she knew we were coming to see the Grand Duchess she went away and hid herself. 'I can't see them' she said. 'I don't want to see *people*. *People* are such a bore.'

---

*   Princess Irina (1895–1970), the Grand Duchess's daughter, married 1914, Prince Felix Yusupov (1887–1967).

†   Sir Henry Channon (1897–1958), socialite MP, married to Lady Honor Guinness, later famous for his posthumously published diary, *Chips* (Weidenfeld & Nicolson, 1968).

‡   HRH Princess Margarita of Baden (1932–2013), a niece of the Duke of Edinburgh, was to marry Prince Tomislav of Yugoslavia at Salem on 6 June 1957.

§   Carmen von Wogau (1910–99), married Hans Gronau (1904–51). He was an art historian, and advisor to Sotheby's. She became the first woman director of Sotheby's and in 1958, head of their Old Masters department.

~

(I forgot to put in the curious effect of the Grand Duchess Xenia's voice. It is somehow a *floating* voice, vague and in some curious way outside herself. It is as if she is trying to catch it and bring it back again to say something else. You could almost see the sentences trailing like thin smoke round the room.)

Pope-Hennessy told Sir Owen Morshead about being introduced as Mr Poke-Henderson. Sir Owen duly addressed his next letter: 'My dear Poke-Henderson ...' and told him that he had been called every possible name, including 'Alan Horsehead'.[110]

EIGHTEEN

THE DUKE AND DUCHESS OF GLOUCESTER

May Days at Barnwell Manor *or* Never-be-frightened-again

25 – 27 May

On 12 May the Duchess of Gloucester wrote to Pope-Hennessy, inviting him to stay at Barnwell, their Northamptonshire home : 'Princess Alice is coming to us then & we would all love to hear how your book about Queen Mary is progressing & maybe between us might help with a few details in one way or another ...'[111]

HRH The Prince Henry, Duke of Gloucester (1900–74) was the third son of King George V and Queen Mary. The Duke was a dedicated soldier, whose wish to command his regiment had been frustrated by the Abdication. At this time he was one of the very few male members of the Royal Family undertaking public duties. One of his many duties was to visit numerous Imperial and Commonwealth war graves overseas.

The Duke has received poor treatment in the media, though in his youth, he had been what they would have called a kind of 'Action Man'. He was particularly respected in the army and the world of agriculture – in the 1950s, his farm was one of the leading farms in the country. He had a love of books, of which he assembled an important collection, including Edward Duke of York's The Master of Game, *and* The Kerdeston Hawking Book. *Some of his books were accepted by the British Museum in lieu of death duties in 2006.*

After his death, an official biography was written by Noble Frankland, Director of the Imperial War Musuem. It includes a line concerning his appointment to the position of Lord High Commissioner to the General Assembly of the Church of Scotland: 'But for a former cavalry officer who did not eschew a glass of whisky, or as Sir Henry Moore and a few others knew, the occasional blasphemous oath, the General Assembly of the Church of Scotland might not at once seem the ideal setting.'[112]

THE DUKE AND DUCHESS OF GLOUCESTER

In London the Gloucesters lived at York House, St James's Palace, and in the country (since 1938) at Barnwell Manor, near Oundle.

The Duchess of Gloucester was Lady Alice Montagu-Douglas-Scott (1901–2004), daughter of the 7ᵗʰ Duke of Buccleuch and Queensberry, and they had married in 1935. She had several sisters to whom she was close ; thus she did not feel the need to communicate her thoughts to a wider audience. She was reserved and shy, but in her book, The Memoirs of Princess Alice, Duchess of Gloucester *(1983), she revealed a dry sense of humour, which was most infectious.*

Like the Duke of Gloucester, the Duchess was an active member of the Royal Family in the 1950s. In 1965 the Duke was at the wheel of his Rolls Royce, driving back from the State Funeral of Sir Winston Churchill, when he lost control of the car. Though he was thrown free, the Duchess was badly hurt, but thanks to Arnica, she was soon in full health again. However, the Duke suffered a series of strokes, and in 1968 was no longer able to speak, and spent his last years confined to Barnwell.

After his death in 1974, Princess Alice, Duchess of Gloucester, continued to undertake engagements until in her 90s. She moved from Barnwell in 1994 and lived to celebrate her 100th birthday with a parade at Kensington Palace, where she died, aged 102, in October 2004.

Pope-Hennessy had a haircut in anticipation of his visit.

On 13ᵗʰ May I had a letter from the Duchess of Gloucester, asking me to stay at Barnwell from 25ᵗʰ to 27ᵗʰ May to discuss the book on Queen Mary with them; she added that Princess Alice* would be there. I had sat next to the Duchess at a Buckingham Palace luncheon in November, and the Duke I had seen early last year when I was beginning the book and when he was pretty fairly speechless. As the time to go to Barnwell grew inexorably nearer, my nerves went to pieces. The last day was spent being telephoned to by Ladies-in-Waiting about trains and arrangements, to such a degree that this mild expedition loomed formidable and alarming. I had forgotten the number one truth I had discovered last year in Stockholm, and which should be *axiomatic* for anyone having to interview

---

* Princess Alice, Countess of Athlone married the Duke's uncle, the Earl of Athlone, Queen Mary's younger brother. Lord Athlone had died on 16 January 1957, so she was in mourning. She stayed at Barnwell every summer.

or get tangled up with royal persons: it is *courtiers* who make royalty frightened and frightening; taken neat like whiskey they are perfectly all right. This does not mean that they are as others, but you can get on to plain terms with the species, like an ornithologist making friends with some rare wild duck.

As the tumbril-train drew out of St Pancras I felt as I hadn't since going to school from the holidays – an impulse to pull the communication cord, or get out at an early station. But there *were* no early stations, as it was an express; first stop Kettering, my destination. So I sat in my sunglasses intermittently reading Madame Maurois' book on Miss Howard[*], going in and out of the lavatory (five times), and then drinking large iced gins and dry ginger. With a palsied hand I gave the car attendant such large tips that he said: 'Are you coming back with me this evening, Sir?'

'No', I replied in the tones of Mrs Siddons, '*I am going to stay in the country*.'

At Kettering I got out of the train, passed through the tunnel beneath the platform, and then saw a very luxurious-looking chauffeur with beautifully cut silver hair, who took my bag and led me towards a brand-new green station wagon. The sight of the station wagon and the chauffeur was somehow reassuring, and as we whisked through the Northamptonshire villages my spirits began to rise, and I felt that one must pull oneself together. After half an hour's driving we turned off the main road towards some clumps of trees and a tiny yellow-grey village, crossed an old stone bridge over a stream, and turned into the gates of Barnwell Manor.

Barnwell Manor, as it was later explained to me, was built by a Montagu in the sixteenth century, apparently from the stones of Barnwell Castle, a square four-towered building, the walls of which, tufted with wallflower, stand across the lawn from the front of the house. Inside the castle is a tarmacadam tennis court. The house itself is what one would expect: L-shaped, grey-yellow, with a modern wing built of old stone. We drove up to the door and the chauffeur blew the horn. I got out and went into the hall. There was no-one about. A fire was burning in an iron basket in the fireplace. It was a low, panelled hall with some steps up into the passage and on to the big staircase. In a window embrasure stood a bearskin on a stand, complete with chinstrap. This empty threatening bearskin made me quail all over again.

---

[*] Simone André Maurois, *Miss Howard and The Emperor* (Collins, 1957), about Harriet Howard, mistress and financial backer of Emperor Napoleon III.

' 'Eres 'er Royal 'Ighness, now Sir', said the chauffeur from the door. I stepped quickly back on to the gravel, but could see no one. Then the Duchess popped out from behind the station wagon, dressed in jodhpurs, a hacking jacket and a headscarf of purple silk.

Like most royalties, (and although she was not born to the task) the Duchess of Gloucester looks much smaller than she is, or is much smaller than she looks in photographs. I think too that she belongs to the class of shy-ish person who literally shrinks from shyness; she seemed to get bigger, to expand, as the week-end went on though, on Sunday at Boughton, faced with twenty strangers on the terrace, she became rigid and tiny again. I had better say at once that she is an extraordinarily kind, and also clever, woman, towards whom I felt the greatest sympathy. Her *tension* is quite remarkable, and when shy she adds an extra sylla-ble to each vowel ending, rather as the musical-hall Italian ice-cream vendors do.

'Good morning, Ma'am. What a perfectly lovely day.'

'Yes, isn't it. Only-a it's rather-a windy-a, the poor lilacs'. Like that.

She seemed to come up to my shoulder and walked about very swiftly and abruptly (*vide* the Princess Royal's twinges of activity). When less shy she moves like anybody else; another speech element is a slow emphasis on odd syllables: 'What you call your ecce*ntric* Aunt at *Bigg*in' etc. She, like the Duke himself, in-spires one with a compassionate wish to help them face oneself or anyone else they are obliged to see; one wanted to look after her at Boughton for instance.

'Now, I don't know where they've gone. I think Prince Henry must have taken Princess Alice down to the farm.'

And she began rushing about the garden, through box hedges and past an empty swimming pool, under lilacs tossing like plumes in the high wind, over grass and down paths, with me like Alice in Wonderland at her heels.

I talked about various things such as Biggin and the Watts-Russells' and she seemed to calm down, and took me into the walled kitchen garden.

'If you'll just not mind coming to *help* me, I want to get a flower for the house. I know just where I want to put it.'

It was then that I detected that she had worked out a charming and mod-est plan to put *herself* at ease and make *me* feel at home. It was a clever and thoughtful plan, and consisted largely in getting me to do things myself, a kind

---

* Biggin was a nearby house in Northamptonshire, where Pope-Hennessy's mother had been raised. It belonged to her mother, Zephine Watts-Russell.

of physiotherapy. In this first case it was carrying a large perlagonium plant out of the greenhouse across the windy garden, discussing how to prevent the petals being blown off.

'I think, you see, if we can *egg* Prince Henry *on* to tell you about their childhood that may be useful. About the *tutor* and the *governesses* and Bal*mor*al and all that.'

'Yes, Ma'am, any detail or atmosphere is so useful. Princess Alice has been the greatest help.'

'She has a wonderful memory. Yes, atmosphere, that's it, atmosphere.'

Once we got into the house and were sitting on the arms of two armchairs in the large marmalade-coloured drawing room she became rigid again, and had to be coaxed to talk about the history of the house, why the oak panelling in this room had gone this '*hidjus* colour' and so on. After we had speculated for the fiftieth time on where Prince Henry and Princess Alice 'can have *got* to', the Duchess had the bright idea of leaving me alone in the room and going upstairs. The stout, black-haired butler came in; he, like the footman (a not wholly unattractive blonde batman-boy with large pink ears), was dressed in dark-blue battle-dress with embroidered epaulettes; it was made of a shiny cloth. I asked him if I could go and wash my hands and he took me up towards my bedroom. The Duchess of Gloucester was bounding nervously about on the landing, so I said soothingly, 'I'm just going to wash my hands before lunch, Ma'am.'

'Oh *yes*, and then I'll just go and change myself.'

She had already told me that her sister, Lady Margaret Hawkins ('Mida' to the family), and her husband, Admiral – or some such – Sir Geoffrey Hawkins*, were coming to lunch. This, also I think intended to alleviate, turned out badly, as they were both far more conscious of royalty than either I or the Gloucesters themselves.

I returned to the drawing room, having seen my very comfortable room, and observed with pleasure a small, framed notice on the dressing-table, a card with an 'H' and a Garter saying, 'Guests are particularly requested not to offer gratuities to the indoor or outdoor staff as they are NOT allowed to accept them.' I sat down, waiting for the next episode and looking at the drink tray, and smoking. There was a huge, high, Coromandel screen with six folds hiding the door, so

---

* Admiral Sir Geoffrey Hawkins (1895–1980) and his wife, Lady Margaret Montagu-Douglas-Scott (1893–1976).

that it was rather exciting, like a good play with new characters, waiting to see who was going to enter next. There was a good deal of heavy breathing and heavy martial shuffle, and the Duke of Gloucester, eyes bulging and his hair standing on end from the wind, entered, wearing corduroys, a jersey, a Guards tie and a tweed coat. His shoes were polished like mirrors, and were *black London shoes*. I jumped up and bowed and shook hands. He veered off like a tacking sailing-ship towards the drink tray and began delicately dropping angostura bitters out of a tiny silver-topped bottle into a large glass. He then took the gin bottle out of the three-bottle canister on the table and said:

'Haven't you had a drink?'

'No, Sir.'

'Well take what you like. Gin? What would you like with it?'

'Is that angostura, Sir?'

'Now' – he never says 'no' only 'now'; his other odd vowel is the 'o' of go, which is pronounced 'goa' – 'Now, it isn't. It's the other thing. I think it's got a better taste.'

He struggled to get the ice, which was a half-moon shape I have never seen anywhere before, out of the silver ice-pincers.

'Oh damn.'

There was a long silence while we stood by the window and he looked at the floor.

'I had a very quick journey down, Sir. It's much shorter than I expected.'

'What?'

'I had a good journey down.'

'On the train? Oh yes.'

The Duchess then came in, looking very neat and pretty in a light-violet colour-ed tweed, with a satin scarf and a large diamond-crowned 'A' on her shoulder.

I will here insert:

A GENERAL NOTE UPON THE DUKE OF GLOUCESTER

Prince Henry is one of the finest and most authentic specimens of the race availa-ble for study today. He is tall and bulky, and his head is wonderfully Hanoverian, flat at the back and rising to the real pineapple point of William the Fourth. He has protruding Guelph eyes. I could hardly take *my* eyes off him for the forty-eight hours I was there; he looked now like his father, now slightly like the Duke of Teck, occasionally glimpses even of Queen Mary. He is an immensely kind, potentially irritable man, whose chief aim in life is to laugh. This, as is well known, he does in his own manner: an hysterical piglet squeal which becomes uncontrollable and which I found very infectious. His face is all creased up with past laughter and hoping for future laughter. You could even say his laugh is orgasmic, so much pleasure does he get from it, so sudden and enjoyable does it seem.

He is not at all the stupid man he is thought to be. He simply works on quite a different system to ordinary people. He has, to begin with, the royal trait of expecting you to know what he is thinking about, and tosses out apparently irrelevant remarks at intervals which you have to catch and return like longstop at cricket. He treats himself as if he were somebody else, e.g. coming down to Sunday breakfast: 'I'm sorry to say this wind is going to make me very cwoss and irritable today, very cwoss and irritable I'm afraid'. A good deal of his time is spent *not listening*. After a long dinnertime conversation, with Princess Alice leading, about the controversial appointment of Lord Hailes* to be Governor-General of the West-Indian Federation, he asked me later that night what *I* thought about this appointment. I said I thought what Princess Alice had said was very sensible and well informed (which it was).

'Ah but you see I'm afraid I didn't listen to Princess Alice. Princess Alice is very prejudiced and so I decided "I won't listen to her", just like that. And so I'm afraid I *didn't* listen' (squeals of laughter).

He is also, but only *at times, incapable* of taking in a complex idea, or a statement in too lengthy a form. E.g.:

'I hate this bloody wind. It always makes me nervous. My mother hated the wind. She used to use the most bloody awful language in a wind, bloody awful.'

J. P.-H. (when the squeal had subsided) 'Byron was like that too, Sir, he built policies to protect himself from the wind at Newstead.'

'Huh?'

'I said: Byron *hated wind*, Sir.'

'Oh? Byron? Did'e? Now, I never knew that.'

I soon caught on to editing or reducing statements to their simplest proportions. He would then converse with great freedom and intelligence. What comes

---

* Patrick Buchan-Hepburn, 1st Lord Hailes (1901–74). In 1957 Harold Macmillan appointed him Governor-General of the newly-created Federation of the West Indies, an attempt to unite the larger British colonies in the Caribbean. Jamaica withdrew and became independent in 1962, and the Federation collapsed when Trinidad and Tobago left later that same year. As was said at the time: 'One from ten equals nought.'

out of his head is quite all right, but, possibly owing to its peculiar shape, too much cannot be inserted in one go.

He has charming manners, making one go out of the door in front of him, pushing cigarettes at one after tea, etc. but over *drink* you have to help yourself. This explains Wheeler-Bennett's mistaken view that he is either stingy or rude, because when he went to interview him Prince Henry poured himself out two whiskies without offering him any. Drink plays a *very great part* in his life, and he sort of guzzles it in a gluttonous way. A tumbler of whiskey and soda is drunk in two gulps – one gulp, then ten or twelve minutes and the rest of the glass is poured down the throat at one go.

He *says* he is very lazy and he related with peculiar glee and much squealing how, when we were all going round Boughton with Molly Buccleuch*, he had wandered off to the tennis-court ('looking at houses is bloody tiring') where he found a girl struggling with a wheel-deck-chair over some steps.

'I went up and pretended to help her, of course, but in fact I didn't do a bloody thing. I didn't even lift the thing. I don't believe in *doing things*. She had to do it all herself in the end!!'

The first night at Scrabble I had to play *his* hand as well as my own; the next night he suddenly played brilliantly and won hands down. He is liable to sit and say nothing, looking at the floor. Inaction is clearly a satisfaction in itself.

He has a strange trick I first observed at Buckingham Palace. He will be standing and then he will slowly advance, looking at the floor and putting one foot straight in front of the other, so that the shining black shoes are aligned; then the other foot; then the other and so on, like a child.

The not-listening system, which seemed to me wise and original, is allied to other private ideas, some of which are not at all bad. For example, he was very anxious for me to see his diary of his Japanese-Australian trip.† After much searching he produced it in his study late at night.

---

* Mary Lascelles (1900–93), wife of the Duchess of Gloucester's brother, Walter, 8th Duke of Buccleuch and Queensberry (1894–1973). The Duchess of Gloucester and the Duchess of Buccleuch were not in sympathy with each other, the former thinking the latter too worldly and no doubt immoral. In turn the Duchess of Buccleuch thought her sister-in-law unintellectual.

† The Duke was sent to Tokyo on a Garter Mission in 1929, to invest Emperor Hirohito of Japan with the Order of the Garter.

'Here's my diary I was telling you about. Well *I* call it my "diary" but of course it was kept by a clerk. All it really is, as you'll see, is my daily programme typed out and stuck in.'

'Did you never keep a diary yourself, Sir?'

'Oh I tried it once, but *God* I wrote such *bloody rubbish* I gave it up. Have you ever been to Australia?'

'No, Sir, but I always wanted to go.'

'Well they made me do too much.* All over the place, too many people.'

'And all that shaking hands too, Sir, must be dreadful.'

'Oh yes. It broke my father's hand once. *And* the Duke of Windsor's hand. Broke 'em.'

'I think Queen Mary got very tired shaking hands, too, on the Ophir cruise.'†

'Oh the Ophir cruise. I remember my mother was *furious* with me, perfectly furious. Before I went out you see she gave me all her books about Australia, all 1901, that sort of thing, to read. Well I never read 'em. So she asked me if I had read 'em so I said no I haven't read 'em and I'm not going to read 'em and I'm going to tell you WHY. She was FURIOUS. But I said to her, look here, if I read all about the places I can't ask the damn silly questions you have to ask when you meet all these people because I should know the answers. And I shouldn't have anything to say to them if I didn't ask 'em questions. And if I knew all the answers I wouldn't have anything to ask. She saw what I meant in the end.'

'That sounds a very sensible system, Sir.'

'Well, it's what *I* do anyway. But she – oh she was always swotting things up before she went anywhere, always swatting things up.' (All stories about his parents' anger are told with schoolboy gusto. They have much to answer for.)

Pope-Hennessy then resumed the narrative thread:

I made myself a strong pink gin. Princess Alice came in, dressed in neat black mourning‡ and pearls, a little black woolly over her shoulders, her hair

---

*   The Duke was Governor-General of Australia from 1945–7.

†   King George V and Queen Mary sailed to Australia and New Zealand, as Duke and Duchess of Cornwall, in the Orient liner, *Ophir*, in March 1901.

‡   For Lord Athlone.

marvellously silver and well arranged. Then the Hawkinses were announced and given drinks, during which I managed to snatch another glass of gin.

The Hawkinses were a mistake from the beginning. Lady Margaret Hawkins, a very tall weather-beaten woman with a closed mind, wearing a white, corded-silk tamoshanter like a dented puffball, introduced at once the element of fealty by deep curtseys to her brother-in-law and to Princess Alice. Her husband, a huge naval man now retired (and unable to work because it would increase his income tax), lives with her in a house about a quarter of an hour away towards Oundle. The Duke and Duchess had just been in Holland,* staying at Soestdijk with Queen Juliana,† and we had some chat about Holland, the Duke seated silently on the sofa by the window and breathing heavily as though he were asleep (which he wasn't). Sir Geoffrey was talking to me about what he called the 'Ricks' Gallery.

'What are you talking about, Geoffrey?' said the Duke suddenly from the sofa.
'About Holland, Sir.'

'Funny shape for a country, Holland. Damn funny shape', and the Duke relapsed into silence.

We went into lunch. The table was decorated with silver pheasants with sweeping tails, and there were napkins in polished napkin rings. The pats of deep-yellow butter were stamped with an 'H', inside a crowned Garter. The macaroni cheese had been in the oven too long, and there was Kia-ora for the ladies and beer for the gents.

It suddenly struck me like a thunderclap halfway through luncheon that I was not frightened but was terribly *terribly bored*. (This was the *only* moment of boredom I experienced and it was due to the Hawkinses' conventional minds.) Politics were discussed and the Duke said:

'What I can't stand about all these Labour politicians is that they're so damned insincere, every one of 'em.'

I had stood a good deal, but this seemed too much, so I spoke up politely.
'Do you think that's true of Bevan‡, Sir? I fancy he is quite sincere.'

---

* The Duke of Gloucester stayed in the Netherlands to visit war cemeteries. He was President of the Imperial War Graves Commission from 1937.

† HM Queen Juliana of the Netherlands (1909–2004). She abdicated in favour of her daughter, HM Queen Beatrix, in 1980.

‡ Aneurin Bevan (1897–1960), Welsh politician.

The Hawkinses looked at me menacingly.

'Never met the fellah.'

'Neither have I, Sir, but when you read what he says in the papers he sounds sincere and it's well argued. Gaitskell* is the only one I've met and I don't think *he* is very sincere.'

'Well, you may be right.'

'Bevan's got some pretty nasty evening habits', said Sir Geoffrey, glaring at me.

'Well, Mr Asquith† drank, too, didn't he?'

'And look what Asquith was', replied Sir Geoffrey. 'He wasn't much of an advertisement.'

After luncheon we went back to the drawing room where the Hawkinses remained till past three. The Duchess and her sister were having a conversation on the sofa about someone called Mabel. Princess Alice and I and Sir Geoffrey talked about Castellani‡, who used to treat him for malaria in his Putney nursing home. The Duchess suddenly began a long story told to her maid when she was in Germany the other day – 'Oh, you know, doing *WAAFS* or *some*thing or *other*'§ – by another German maid. It was good and pointful but not worth relating in detail. The Duke was entirely absorbed in talking to one of the three little dogs, which answered in squeals and pants:

'Oh you're a *very* talkative little dog, aren't you', etc. etc.

When the Hawkinses had at length gone, it was decided to garden.

'What do you want to do?' the Duchess asked me politely. 'Do you want to go and write?'

As the gardening was evidently part of her long-term assimilation plan, I naturally said I would like to garden but knew nothing about it.

'Oh well he can help me tidy up the irises', said Princess Alice genially. 'As long as he doesn't cut off the live heads instead of the dead ones.'

---

* Hugh Gaitskell (1906–63), Leader of the Labour Party.

† H.H. Asquith (1852–1928), Prime Minister in World War I, later 1st Earl of Oxford and Asquith.

‡ Marchese Conte Aldo Castellani (1877–1971), Italian doctor of questionable reputation and expert on tropical diseases. Author of *Microbes, Men and Monarchs* (1963). He escorted Queen Marie José of Italy into exile in 1946. He was the father of Jacqueline, Lady Killearn (1910–2015).

§ The Duchess joined the Duke in Germany on 17 May at the end of one of his war graves tours, and they stayed a night with Queen Juliana of the Netherlands.

They went up to put on headscarves against the hurricane wind raging outside. The Duke and I went into the garden room and he seized a short stick with a knife-edge blade at the end, placed sideways like a rake. 'You better take these', he said, thrusting at me a tremendously heavy pair of tree secateurs about as tall as myself (of which the Duchess later relieved me as useless).

We marched towards a tulip bed; and he began viciously jabbing upwards, cutting off the seed-pods where the petals had fallen. It was a *violent* energetic movement. I watched fascinated.

'What are you doing that for, Sir?'

'Stop 'em seeding' (jab, jab).

I cut off some pods with my secateurs but in a few minutes the Duke had disappeared and was wandering vaguely in the long grass under a tree.

The others came out and the Duchess, carrying some pieces of string, said to me:

'Would you mind helping me tie up the cotoneasters? They've come away from the wall.'

Had I known about gardening, I would have known that cotoneasters have thorns at least an inch long.

We marched down towards the farm. Here there is a long brand-new pig house ('pigs' palace I call it', said the Duchess) against the brick wall of which some cotoneasters had been planted but had never been tied up. They had grown forward and sideways, and an immense amount of cutting away was needed. The Duchess and I struggled with each bush in turn, our hands lacerated. We became very cosy over this. The Duke stood by watching and occasionally making suggestions.

'Couldn't you get a broom, darling?' The Duchess said to him, 'and then you could sweep away under*neath* while *we* hold them up.'

'You haven't got enough string, you haven't', the Duke replied – which turned out to be true, so we got some more off the pig-man. The Duke produced a broom and a wheelbarrow for the cut branches and again just stood watching. He then went off on his own, and *we* went and fetched a flat, rubber-wheeled barrow like a jaunting car and piled everything on to that and took it up to the incinerator.

'Where shall I tip it, Ma'am?'

'Do you know, I don't *think* we'll *do* any *more here*. We'll just *leave* it, and one of *them* can tip it up and put it away.'

On the way towards the iris border, which Princess Alice had finished in record time, I told her about the Grand Duchess Xenia*.

'Oh you *must* listen to this about that Orthodox nun', she said coming up to Princess Alice, stooping busily over the bed, and to the Duke standing by watching.

'An unorthodox nun?' said the Duke, and squealed.

'Oh *you* know', the Duchess said impatiently, 'the nun who looks after the Grand Duchess. Mother Marfa, the one who looks like a man.'

'Probably is a man', said the Duke thoughtfully.

'Anyway we are all *very* suspicious of Mother Marfa', said Princess Alice, knee-deep in the iris bed.

I related my anecdote, we had some more talk and went into tea.

By this time we had coagulated rather satisfactorily, and it was like tea with some *very* nice uncles and aunts. At this point they began seriously about the book and about Queen Mary. I said I had got to 1906.

'Oh, 1906?' said Princess Alice.

'Well I *had* got up to 1906, Ma'am, but all the letters you let me take away have sent me back to 1895. It's like snakes and ladders.'

'Dear, dear, dear. And are they useful?'

'Invaluable, Ma'am. And I also followed your advice and found the Cambridge letters at Windsor.'

We discussed the incompetence of the archives, about which they seemed to know, and I told Princess Alice how funny Prince Frank's† letters were.

'Oh Frank was perfectly *outrageous* – he was terribly funny but outrageous. And he did some very naughty things too. We were all very cross with him.'

We discussed his death – 'he never should have died' – his last visit to Balmoral‡, then to Balmoral itself.

J. P.-H. 'I get the impression, Sir, that Queen Mary didn't like Balmoral?'

---

* Pope-Hennessy had visited the Grand Duchess at Wilderness House but days before.

† HSH Prince Francis of Teck (1870–1910), Queen Mary's brother.

‡ On 17 September 1910 Prince Francis underwent a nasal operation at Welbeck Street nursing home for 'chronic disease of the antrum'. He went to recuperate at Balmoral with Sir James Reid in attendance, caught a chill which led to acute pleurisy, returned to London on 14 October and died at Welbeck Street on 22 October.

'Loathed it. Hated it. She had nothing to do in Scotland. How we hated it as children, too. Sunday lunch at Mar Lodge.* We used to go over in the motor all dressed up. Lunch began at one-thirty and we left the table after three. You can imagine what that meant for children. And we weren't allowed to speak and had to sit listening to conversation we didn't understand. And the food was much too rich – very good food but too rich. I was always sick.' (Squeals of laughter.) 'The motor made me feel sick to begin with, down all those twisty roads, and then the food and then directly after lunch what do you suppose they did with me? Took me out and put me on a swing – a swing I ask you – that settled it and I was always sick.'

(*Note*: In this and all other more intimate talks about his childhood, Prince Henry seemed to harbour a grievance against his parents and his whole upbringing. Sometimes he would make a joke of it, but sometimes he spoke with passion – as in the later conversation when he said 'my father was the most *terrible father*, most *terrible father* you can imagine').

Prince John† seems to have had the disconcerting habit of speaking out loud to himself. Princess Alice produced a good story that one day when the King was writing, Queen Mary came into the room and kissed him on the top of his head as she went by. Prince John was alone at the other end of the long room and they suddenly heard him say out loud: 'And she *kisses* him, ugly old man!' The parents could not control their laughter.

We talked till dinnertime (whiskey at 6.30) and they all told stories and seemed to enjoy themselves. E.g.:

'My father was indulging in one of his tirades one night at York Cottage. It was, as usual, about how he *hated* Harewood House.‡ He went on and on. So Uncle Alge [Earl of Athlone] said quietly to Queen Mary, "But what sort of house *does* he like, then?" To which my mother replied without blinking, "*This* damned house!" Or:

'My father was unlike any other man in the world. If you wanted to ask him anything awkward, ask it at breakfast. He'd always say yes. I found this out quite

---

* Mar Lodge, the home of HRH The Princess Louise, Duchess of Fife (1867–1931), sister of George V.
† Prince John was Prince Henry's youngest brother.
‡ Harewood House, home of the 6th Earl of Harewood, and Princess Mary, Queen Mary's only daughter.

soon, but my brothers never did. At breakfast it was always YES, the rest of the day it was invariably NO!'

The Duke said that when they first moved into the big house at Sandringham, he was given the room in which Uncle Eddie had died. It was still full of his things, his clothes, even his soap.

'I cleared it all out. It was horrible.'

'But what an extraordinary idea', said Princess Alice. 'Whatever was it kept like that for?'

'Waiting for him to come back, of course. My great-grandmother [Queen Victoria] always did that. She did the same with my grandfather's room. Just in case they came back, ye know.'

I remarked how crowded the death-chamber must have been with sixteen people. This fascinated them. How had I found that out? How dreadful.

The drawing room and other parts of the house, Barnwell, were, in places, cluttered with Princess Marie Louise's* books, watercolours etc. The conversation veered to the fact that she had made the Gloucester boys – the beautiful Prince William[†], who looks like Audrey Hepburn, and Prince Richard[‡], who has to wear spectacles – her heirs. Queen Mary had urged Prince Henry to ask the two old Holstein sisters to be godmothers to Prince William, but he had said 'one's enough' and had asked Princess Helena Victoria[§]. When Prince Richard was born, she again begged them to ask Princess Marie Louise which they did. 'Of course Mamma must have known Cousin Louie would leave them her things, that's why she suggested it'. The Napoleonic collection was rubbish and they have given it to a museum at Hove. 'The curator said he hadn't room for all the things, but I said, "you have 'em all or nothing" so he took 'em.'

'But what we didn't bargain for', said the Duke, squealing 'was that they had sold all the best stuff.'

'But surely not the tiara?' said Princess Alice.

---

*   HH Princess Marie Louise (1872–1956), daughter of HRH The Princess Helena and Prince Christian of Schleswig-Holstein. Author of *My Memories of Six Reigns* (1956).

†   HRH Prince William of Gloucester (1941–72). He was killed in a flying accident, while taking part in the Goodyear Air Race, near Wolverhampton.

‡   HRH Prince Richard of Gloucester (b. 1944), later 2nd Duke of Gloucester.

§   HH Princess Helena Victoria (1870–1948), elder sister of Princess Marie Louise.

'Oh the tiara!' the Duchess smiled. 'It's left to me for my life and then to Richard's wife. But I can't wear it, it's too big.'

'More like a mitre than a tiara, I remember', said Princess Alice.

'Oh *much too heavy*.'

J. P.-H. 'But couldn't you have it rearranged, Ma'am?'

'Well you know I've already got *two* tiaras – one Queen Mary gave me, and one he did when we married' (indicating Prince Henry). 'Sufficient unto the day, don't you know. And then having jewels arranged is *so expensive*.'

'And the worst of it is', resumed the Duke, 'that I've been stung for Louie's tombstone at Frogmore.* How much do you think it was?'

'I can't think, Harry'. (*Princess Alice*)

'Five hundred and fifty bloody quid. And *monstrous* at that.'

'Oh but Harry you shouldn't have paid that. If you'd left it, Lilibet [The Queen] would have paid, she'd have had to.'

'Well, I dunno, I thought I ought to pay. So I did. I say, Aunt Alice, I want to ask you a very rude question.'

'Yes?'

'Well it's damned rude. I nearly wrote to you and then I thought it was too rude. *What did they sting you for Uncle Alge's stone?*'

'My dear boy, how silly. I can tell you at once. They said to me at Frogmore…'

'When you went for Uncle Alge's – er – er – *interment*?'

'That's it. They said to me that Mr so-and-so at Slough would do it, but I said I've got my own arrangements. It's going to be a big slab for both of us, with armorial bearings on it. I don't know why but I rather like armorial bearings' (etc., gist being it is to be designed and executed by some school of stone craft). Further discussion of the will revealed that the only *real* value to come were the royalties from Cousin Louie's memoirs, which go to Prince Richard when he is twenty-one. I was talking quietly to the Duchess and said:

'But, Ma'am, I always thought no member of the royal family ever paid death-duties?'

'Oh no, oh no. That's only the monarch. And *that* is *why* Queen *Mary* left *every*thing to the *Queen*, because she knew this and she wanted to avoid

---

* Since the 1920s, most of the junior members of the Royal Family have been buried in the Royal Burial Ground at Frogmore, in the shadow of Queen Victoria's mausoleum. Princess Marie Louise had died the previous December.

death-duties.' (This is the first rational and convincing explanation I have heard of her will.)

We were talking of Queen Mary's never having been taught to ride.

Princess Alice: 'And she never had a dog. She didn't like dogs.'

'You're wrong there, Aunt Alice. When my mother and father married there was a collie called Heather. Wedding present to her from Henry Hervey Campbell it was.* Well my father stole it, of course.'

(I then contributed what I know of the exchange of Heather between husband and wife.)

'And then there was a dog called Happy†. And then another called...' (and so on).

'And then the parrot, Harry. Charlotte.'

Great talk about Charlotte, whom everyone had loved although she pecked.

J. P.-H. 'Oh I *am* glad, because that's cleared up something that was worrying me. In Queen Mary's letters after a certain date she said "I spent the evening alone with Charlotte". And I thought, well that is curious because I don't think she liked Charlotte Knollys. And then she says she has given Charlotte some bread crumbs so I realised it must be some sort of an animal, not a person.'

This brought the house down. When the hysteria had subsided, Princess Alice said:

'Funny old thing, Charlotte Knollys. I don't know why Dighton [Probyn] never married her.'

'Why who didn't marry who?' asked the Duke who was still squealing.

'Why Charlotte Knollys didn't marry Dighton Probyn.' Princess Alice then did a hilarious imitation of Sir Dighton after his stroke, his head held down horizontal with the floor. She is a good mimic.

'That wasn't a stroke Aunt Alice. It was when he was ill', he explained turning to me, 'and Sir Dighton, being a seek, wouldn't have a nurse and ...'

'I see, Sir', I said, very mystified.

Princess Alice asked what I had wanted to ask. I thought I had heard wrong.

---

*   Heather actually died in 1904, aged 11. Admiral Sir Henry Hervey Campbell (1865–1933) commanded HMS *Terrible*, when George V and Queen Mary visited India as Prince and Princess of Wales in 1905–6.

†   Happy (d. 1913) was a crossbreed terrier, to whom was attributed the book *If I were King George* (1911).

'What do you mean about Dighton being a seek?'

''Course he was a Sikh. Probyn's horse and all that. He swore to become an Indian so he became a Sikh. And instead of letting his hair grow he let his beard grow, right down to his stomach. I remember my brother John [Prince John] went up to him once and asked, "Is it real?" and he tugged at the beard and it *was* real' (squeals). 'The funniest thing of all was to see the poor old man at Farnborough air display – oh those bloody Farnborough air displays – well the old man could only have seen the aeroplanes if he'd been lying on his back. Well, anyhow, Probyn was a Sikh and he couldn't have a nurse when he was ill, so one day he was sitting up in bed and arranging his pillows himself, and his neck went wrong, a vertebra or something, and it never got right again.'

'D'you remember the bathroom he gave Charlotte?'

'Huh?'

'Harry, the bathroom Dighton gave Charlotte at Sandringham. All mirrors. Imagine endless Charlottes going away into the distance. It was a birthday present for her seventieth birthday.'

This led us on to birthday and Christmas presents, the number Queen Mary had to give, her bazaar rooms, her buying habits etc. etc. The Duchess asked if Princess Alice had noticed the drawing room doorstep.

'No. What is it?'

Duchess: 'It's what Mamma always had in her sitting room at Marlborough House. We never understood how she got it. It must have been a present. Our children always loved it.'

The Duchess got up and went and fetched a lead Punchinello doorstep painted garishly.

'Oh yes, of course. She can't have bought *that*, your mamma.'

'It was always in her room', said the Duke to me, 'and it swore with everything else in the room, too.'

Prince Henry then said that he had some of the hideous Maple furniture from York Cottage. The Duchess added that Queen Mary had given them the biggest and ugliest of the wardrobes and, knowing that they would hate it and want to get rid of it, said: 'I want it put in the bedroom I shall use when I come to see you', and there it still remains; she would enquire after it from time to time. (In a later, earnest and somewhat pathetic conversation the Duke related that the biggest compliment his mother had *ever* paid him, and which *delighted* him, was at her second tour of inspection of Barnwell Manor, after his alterations: she turned to him and said, 'Well, Harry, I should never have thought you could have made this house habitable, but you have'. High praise, he indicated.) The Duke said how furious Princess May had been to find York Cottage fully furnished and ready for her – 'furnished from Maple's at that'.

Amongst general anecdotes and reminiscences of this fruitful teatime I recollect:

Princess Alice saying King Edward's laugh was like tearing linen, linen being ripped (she is something of an actress and expresses herself with her hands, the act here of tearing up a cloth).

Queen Alexandra would *never* recognise that her grandsons were growing up. Her presents to them remained those for children of six to eight. Thus when the Duke was sixteen ('and I was a pretty tall sixteen at that') she gave him one of those cardboard boxes containing a miniature uniform for a child of five.

We talked of Bricka,* and Princess Alice repeated what she had told me before. Of Tatry† she did an excellent imitation, face all screwed up ('a yellow face') and almost blindly shortsighted. We talked of dressers and maids, and of Dunham's‡ cruelty towards the end of Queen Mary's life.

Princess Alice said that dear Aunt Mary Teck was such fun; they used as children to seat her on some velvet-covered scales to weigh her – 'and she would turn this way and that, so fat but so quick and graceful'. She was particularly popular with the crowd, who called her 'Fat Mary' because she had her own technique, or unconscious trick, when acknowledging cheers of leaning backwards smiling and waving so that the people in the windows and on the balconies saw her wide upturned cheerful face.

When we had sat down to tea Princess Alice remarked on a rather unpleasant Formica tea trolley which runs on rubber wheels and opens into a table.

'What a nice trolley *that* is, Alice.'

'Yes', smiling, 'it's the very latest thing. It won't burn or stain or scratch and it folds up. It was Lilibet's Christmas present to us. Wasn't it kind of her? Terribly expensive though.'

'How much?'

---

* Hélène Bricka, Queen Mary's governess.

† Queen Mary's maid.

‡ Miss Dunham evidently reduced Queen Mary to tears with her barbed comments, and used to pull her corsets in so that she could hardly breathe. She spent her last days in a flat at Kensington Palace. She was given no honour by the Royal Family.

'Seventeen pounds. It came from Fortnum and Mason.'

The Duke looked at it solemnly, and with the air of a man making a decisive announcement, the product of much thought, said:

'*Most* things that come from Fortnum and Mason are terribly expensive.'

I was beginning to feel *very* tired, and when the Duchess and their aunt went up to change at eight I tried to get away too. The Duke by this time had had his third whiskey and was at work sloshing back pink gins. He stopped me.

'Hadn't you better have a glass of sherry before you go up?'

He then told me with much giggling that he had been unable to remember whether it was I 'or that fellow who's writing about my brother, what's his name'* who had a stammer. He said his brother had never stammered to his knowledge before he was twenty-one or so. He told me of a Trooping of the Colour when his bearskin nearly blew off, the context being that he has to take a Troop rehearsal next week and was afraid of the gale.

J. P.-H. 'You know I've *always* wondered, Sir, in my ignorant way what's *inside* a bearskin – is there a little cap?'

'Well, do you see, it's all wicker inside and then you have a little cap over your head. But being made of solid skin, of course it resists the wind and that's where the danger comes from.'

'Doesn't the chin-strap help?'

'Now, it doesn't.'

He then told me about the kind of skins needed, how bad the new Scots Guards[†] ones are – 'dreadful rubbish, from Canada' – etc. I finally escaped at eight-twenty, with ten minutes for my bath and to change. Mr Maude[‡], the Duke's charming middle-aged valet with a kind nanny's face and periwinkle blue eyes, smiling all the time as if the whole thing were a great joke, came to ask me about breakfast and which kind of tea or whether I wanted coffee. I rushed down and had a sage glass of sherry.

By dinnertime Prince Henry was what is usually called merry and he talked a very great deal. As we sat down he said to me:

'Don't you think you'd better skip your church tomorrow? Don't you think so?'

'Well if it's outside the three-mile limit, Sir, and anyway if it's a nuisance.'

---

[*] The Duke was referring to John Wheeler-Bennett.

[†] The Duke was Colonel of the Scots Guards.

[‡] Maude does not seem to have remained long in the Duke's service.

'It's all a bit complicated.'

'But he could easily walk to Oundle across the fields', said Princess Alice mischievously, 'it's only a couple of miles. I've done it often.'

And so on.

At nine the wireless was switched on and we sat and listened to the news – Dulles* and so on. The announcer began pompously, 'At this moment Her Majesty the Queen and the Duke of Edinburgh are leaving Fredensborg Castle' etc. The Duke looked at his plate at this announcement and said simply: 'Bla, Bla, Bla'.

After dinner we played Scrabble. They had a very good turntable:

J. P.-H. 'What a nice turntable, Ma'am, it makes the whole thing so easy.'

'Yes, it comes from America.'

'My son made one for the Queen for a Christmas present, copy of this', remarked Prince Henry. 'Cost me two bloody quid though. Everything they do at that school costs money.'

(I forgot to say that over the port we had discussed farming, his overdraft, my overdraft, how to deal with bank managers, how essential it is never to open certain letters etc. I forget all the details of his finances, except that the farm – like, as I pointed out, all the farms I had ever heard of – was always going to pay next year and never this.)

Princess Alice didn't know the rules of Scrabble, but being clever very soon picked it up. The Duchess is an excellent player. The Duke that night was hopeless and I had to play his hand for him.

'Look here', said the Duke on seeing the Scrabble table, 'you won't catch me playing that damn game with this fellah. Knows all the words in the bloody dictionary.'

He was so hopeless that I made a few inane remarks and errors.

'Do you think there's a verb fease, as in feasible?'

'Now. I don't think your publisher would pass that. By the way I want to ask you a rude question.'

'Yes, Sir?'

'Are you, as a writer, allowed to make up new words?'

---

* John Foster Dulles (1888–1959), US Secretary of State 1953–9.

'Well, Sir, people like James Joyce* have done so, and there's nothing to prevent you. Only the reader wouldn't understand what you meant.'

'Huh.'

The game went on (punctuated by 'I *hate* this bloody game, *she* makes me play because she always wins'). Prince Henry keeping the score, on a long thin piece of paper headed: A. A., P. H., A. and S. [self].

(The next night he used the same piece of paper and somehow reversed the order so the scoring, I thought, went haywire. I had had sixty-three, won seven, then next turn won another seven:

'I don't think, Sir, if I may say so, that you've added my last score, seven.'

'Yes I have. Seven and sixty-three makes seventy.'

'But that was last time.'

'I suppose you're going to tell me I can't score next, eh?' smiling indulgently. 'Well, I'll believe you. Or rather I'll *give* you that extra seven.')

This second evening he played extremely well, scattering words like 'twinge' about the board and won.

'I think my twinge was pretty good, don't you' he remarked at intervals.

We looked at photograph albums of Princess Marie Louise, one containing a perfect, animated, laughing, charming photo of Princess May wearing a sailor hat on board the *Crescent*, 1898, which they want me to reproduce. He had also fetched down from his bedroom a little snapshot of Queen Mary, about 1912, in the biggest hat piled with roses I have ever seen, sitting on a fence with the children at Balmoral.

'I think you must put this in, doesn't she look *ludicrous*? Imagine walkin' about at Guisachan in a hat like that! Turning over the double frame: 'And here's my sister Mary after a May Sunday lunch, wearing an awful hat too. She always wore awful hats, my sister. Still does, as a matter of fact.'

After the Princesses had gone up to bed, we settled down for what I thought might be an hour's chat. It lasted till ten to two, punctuated by my saying 'It's awfully late, Sir. It's one o'clock', or whatever it was, to which he invariably answered, 'Good God, why so it is. How can it be? *I* know! It's that damned Scrabble game, it always lasts so long.'

He ranged widely that evening: Archbishop of Canterbury, Princess May going to mass in Florence, how he dislikes the local parson, how he won't read the

---

* James Joyce (1882–1941), Irish novelist, famed for his book, *Ulysses*.

lessons, how his father read them onboard ship etc. By this time he saw me as *a source of information* on matters which had been puzzling him *all* his life. This was when he told me what a terrible father they had had. He had no idea Princess May was so ill when pregnant.

'I hope you put that in, I think that's *very* important, put in every bloody thing you can'. (He agreed readily to read the typescript, which I think a good idea as well as a good move; he is a man who if treated as intelligent becomes so.) 'She never let on to me about that. We always thought we came out like a litter of puppies. Why when my wife had a Caesarean, I well remember her surprise and her sayin' to me: '*I* never had any trouble having children at all, never'.

He then edged towards the subject on which he really wanted to pump me: the Duke of Clarence.

'Now I want to ask you something. How much do you know about the Duke of Clarence?'

'Quite a lot, Sir. He will have to have a chapter to himself, although there's not much written material.'

'There isn't, eh? Well now I want to ask you – did Uncle Eddie *have ziph*?' (Pronounced *sic*).

'So I believe Sir.'

'But you haven't found anything about it?'

'It's not the sort of thing people keep evidence of, Sir.'

'Well I knew when we were children the first time we ever *heard* of ziph was when we were told Uncle Eddie had had it. Who told us, God knows. So I always wondered. Funny chap, Uncle Eddie. Don't you think so?'

'He was rather odd, Sir.'

'Was my mother fond of him?'

'I think he was very charming and she had led such a boring life as her mother's secretary that it was all very exciting and glamorous when they got engaged.'

'Now I suppose you can't put *that* in the book. How would you word it? About the ziph, I mean.'

'Well I don't think I could word it at all, Sir.'

'Seems a pity. I want you to put everything in. The more the better. I always think' – squeals of laughter – 'it was a damned good thing he died!' More squeals.

'Well I don't think he'd have made a good King, Sir.'

'And how awful for all of *us*. Why if my mother had married Uncle Eddie and he'd had ziph *I should never have been born*.'

'Or you'd have been born a monster, Sir.'

'That's it, that's it, born a monster.' He laughed till the tears came out of his eyes.

I told him of the unsubstantiated rumours that the Duke of Clarence was a drug-addict and bisexual. Neither seemed to surprise him.

'Now, I say, you just tell me how you'll put *that* in. It ought to go in, you know.'

'Well it all depends on the way it's written, Sir.'

'Yes but', (with an almost prurient gleam) 'you just describe to me the words you're going to use.'

'Well I never know till I sit down and write, Sir, how I'm going to word things.' We had both smoked ourselves out, but he had I thought some more in his little silver case: 'could Your Royal Highness *possibly* give me a cigarette. I've run out.' He opened his case and had only one, which he made me take. So ended the first day.

Sunday 26 May
(Queen Mary's birthday)

At eight-thirty Mr Maude came in.

'Will you be taking a bath this morning, Sir?'

'Yes, please.'

'A cold one, Sir?'

'No, no.'

'How cold, though? Tepid I expect, Sir.'

This seemed so much to be expected that I said yes. He came back in a few minutes:

'It doesn't look to me like nine-thirty breakfast Sir, more like ten I should say. I'll tell you what, you just lie in bed and I'll pop in and tell you how His Royal Highness is getting on.'

At twenty to ten came the news: 'His Royal Highness has just begun to shave', so I scampered into the by now stone-cold bath.

Breakfast I fancied would be a silent meal. Prince Henry came down in a tweed suit, remarking, 'aren't I terribly late', with a sort of satisfaction.

There was a silver tea-kettle and a good deal of messing about with china and tea and spirit lamps. 'Give yourself an egg.' The cups were so large they needed two hands to hold them, and he had filled mine to the brim with scalding tea.

'I'm afraid this wind is going to make me very cross and irritable', he said.

'There was quite a gale in the night, Sir.'

'Still is.'

After a long silence and at the marmalade stage he suddenly said:

'And you're *sure* there's no written evidence to show that the Duke of Clarence was a homosexualist?'

'Absolutely none, Sir, that I know of. It's pure hearsay from a generation ago, and may be quite untrue. It's the sort of thing people might say.'

'People don't say that sort of thing if there isn't something in it. Funny chap, Uncle Eddie. Neck like a swan.'

'Like a swan, Sir?'

'Yes, I saw his collars in his room at Sandringham. They were so high' (holding his hands ten inches apart). 'I always say, a bloody good thing he died when he did.' (Squeals of laughter.)

After breakfast he sauntered off towards a small room off the hall, so I vaguely followed him. It was a very nice workroom, with a desk covered with photographs, piles of books on every table and on the floor. Like all the rooms, full of flowers and plants.

'Is this Your Royal Highness's own room?'

'Yes, it is. Rather cosy I think.'

We looked at a gouache copy of a Winterhalter group of Queen Victoria, her husband and the children, trying to identify the children (which Princess Alice later did for me), and discussing whether it was water-colour or a print. I said it was clearly gouache. 'Well you may be right. I thought it might be a print. I thought I'd wet my finger and rub it along the edge to see if the colour came off.'

'But it's already come off on the mount, Sir, when the picture was first framed' (it was now unframed).

'So it has. Water-colour I suppose.'

'Or gouache, Sir.'

'Yes. Watercolour. Or gouache.'

He then told me that the secret about the Prince Consort was that he was very, very small. Once at Balmoral, King George V had said, 'I rather think Mackinnon* has the Prince Consort's stalking suit'. 'So I went off to see him and he had. So my father said, "Try it on". Well I'm not broad chested, I'm rather narrow up here,

---

* Possibly General Sir Henry Mackinnon (1852–1929), Commander-in-Chief, Western Command 1910–15.

and although I was only sixteen I couldn't get the bloody thing on. It was *tiny*.' Mackinnon, who remembered him as a boy, confirmed this.

The ladies came down, hatted for church. There was some waiting about, and Princess Alice identified the children in the picture. 'And *that* is Uncle Alfred'. He was beautiful when he grew up.'

'I always heard that, Ma'am.'

'Oh *beautiful*. So was Uncle Bertie [King Edward VII] for that matter. A beautiful old man – not down here of course' (patting her front), 'but head, a fine old man's head.'

The Duchess ferreted out a postcard of the vast palace of Soestdijk, where they had just been staying:

'Here's Soestdijk, Aunt Alice. Now *this* is where *Trixie*[†] lives at the moment' (running a polished fingernail along a complete wing of the building on the post-card); and so on.

'I think this might amuse you while we're out', said the Duke kindly, producing a typescript copy of the recollections of Prince Christian of Schleswig-Holstein[‡] (which did prove fascinating). 'The papers will be here in ten minutes.' And off they went, leaving me at last alone.

When they came back from church, he settled down to read the newspapers in the drawing room, they having gone upstairs. We sat on either side of the fireplace.

'Anything in the papers?'

'Nothing, Sir, except some nasty news about smoking and lung cancer.'

'That's all bosh. It's not going to affect me.'

And so we sat, silently reading until the butler brought in the drink tray.

At lunch he initiated rather an amusing conversation about phrases that catch on.

'My sons are always saying, "I haven't a clue", so I've caught it now. I used to say, "I haven't a notion".'

'And then before that, Sir, people used to say, "I haven't the foggiest".'

---

[*]   HRH The Prince Alfred, Duke of Edinburgh (1844–1900), second son of Queen Victoria. Later Duke of Coburg.

[†]   HRH Princess Beatrix of the Netherlands, later HM Queen Beatrix (b. 1938). Abdicated 2013.

[‡]   HRH Prince Christian (1831–1917), husband of Princess Helena (1846–1923).

We ranged on over 'couldn't care less' and 'did you or didn't you' and so on. The Duchess then talked about Biggin ('if you won't mind my saying so, your Biggin aunt is rather a bore'), and then to Aunt Susan.*

'Oh Susan, dear Susan, is she your aunt?' cried Princess Alice.

'Is Lady Susan still as big as ever?' asked the Duke. 'I sat next to her once and I said, "you're making a pig of yourself, if you don't mind my saying so." Never seen a woman shovel the stuff down so fast.'

'No, no, Harry, that wasn't it. It was somewhere else and Lady Susan was there and you had your little *dog* called *Susan* and you said to the little *dog*, "you're making a pig of yourself, Susan" and Lady Susan thought you were speaking to *her*', corrected the Duchess.

'Oh was it? Well, so it was.'

Before lunch the Duchess had arranged for us to go to Boughton to see Molly Buccleuch, her sister-in-law, at half past three. When she had come from the telephone, she had said:

'Molly says you'll find lots of your friends there. Alan Pryce-Jones and the Sitwells and Lord Kinross† and some people called Harrap – isn't it Harrap?'

'Harrod‡, Ma'am.'

'That's it, Harrod. Isn't he a publisher or something?'

'He's an eminent Oxford economist, Ma'am.'

'And who's Pryce-Jones?' asked Princess Alice.

'We-e-ell, he's a kind of relative of Molly's. And the current boyfriend, isn't he, Mr Pope-Hennessy?'

'Yes, Ma'am. They rely on the cousinship to make it sound respectable. But it's been going on some time.'

'At least three years', said the Duke in a bored voice.

'Oh and Harry, your favourite: Mark Bonham Carter.'§

---

* Lady Susan Yorke (1881–1965), married as her second husband Major Wyndham Birch, brother of Dame Una Pope-Hennessy, daughter of 7th Earl of Hardwicke.

† Alan Pryce-Jones (1908–2000), Editor of *The Times Literary Supplement* 1948–59, and close friend of the Duchess of Buccleuch from 1954 to 1993, though in the 1970s he left Britain to live in Newport, Rhode Island, some said to escape her; Sir Sacheverell Sitwell (1897–1988) and his wife, Georgia Doble (1905–80), and Patrick, Lord Kinross (1904–76), author and journalist.

‡ Sir Roy Harrod (1900–78), economist, and his wife, Wilhelmine (Billa) Cresswell (1911–2005).

§ Hon Mark Bonham-Carter (1922–94), later Lord Bonham-Carter, politician and publisher.

'Good God, not Carter? If Carter's there I shall stay in the car with the dogs. I can't bear that man. I have an indefinable dislike of him.'

'You're not alone in that, Sir. A lot of people don't like him.'

'Why the Queen and Princess Margaret* see him beats me.'

We piled into the station wagon, the Duke driving with Princess Alice beside him; the Duchess, I and the dogs in the back. The youngest dog, a bitch not yet mated, was sitting on the seat between us. I suddenly noticed some blood near my suit, so did the Duchess:

'Oh dear, oh dear, this little dog will have to be shut up.'

'What's that?' asked the Duke.

'I said this little dog will have to be shut up.'

We discussed the dog's marital plans and when it was to be mated.

At Boughton we found a huge party shambling and lounging on the terrace, out of the wind and in hot sun. Others were playing croquet in the middle distance; others were on the tennis court out of sight. Alan, Patrick Kinross, Mark Bonham Carter, etc., all wearing canvas shoes and striped London shirts with sleeves rolled up. Molly Buccleuch at her most simpering, in a grey silk dress and holding a picture hat of natural leghorn straw. As the Duke was stepping through the window on to the terrace there was a cry of 'Jamesy!' and Billa Harrod precipitated herself at me from one of the staterooms, like something rushing out of the undergrowth. She kissed me warmly. The Duke looked very startled and fixed her with the sort of unbelieving look Queen Mary could use, as though she couldn't be quite real; and I suddenly saw her through that blue Guelph eye looking incredibly untidy and shaggy, with her fluid figure and fat ankles. To my eternal discredit, I felt slightly ashamed of her. I presented her to the Duke.

We then began to go round the staterooms, the Duke dropping off in the second room and sauntering away by himself. The rooms I will not describe, nor Molly's incredible affectations and enthusiasms over the really wonderful contents, which she treated as though they were a series of *trouvailles*, constantly reminding the Duchess that this piece of Sèvres had, in her parents' days, been in the servants' hall, or how ugly this room was in the old Duke's time. It was a similar situation to that of Eva and Peggy† at Mentmore, only Peggy can cope and

---

* HRH The Princess Margaret, Countess of Snowdon (1930–2002).

† Hon Eva Bruce (1892–1987), married 1924, 6th Earl of Rosebery (1882–1974) ; and Lady Margaret (Peggy) Primrose (1882–1967), daughter of 5th Earl of Rosebery. She married 1st Marquess of Crewe.

the Duchess just suffered in silence – though as I afterwards discovered by asking her, she hadn't missed a trick, and had resented it as much as I supposed she had.

We left before tea, fortunately, and drove back the long way home to see the beautiful Eleanor Cross at Brigstock and through Benefield and past Biggin gates for my benefit, which I thought extraordinarily kind.

At tea they discussed Sandringham and how ugly it is. Princess Alice said that she had 'once asked Lilibet shall I burn the house down for you? I'm quite ready to. Would you mind?' To which the Queen had answered, 'I am not sure whether I should mind'. They said the Sandringham shooting lunches were so *terrible*, the vast tent put up in a different place each day, and if it had rained it took a great many men to move the saturated canvas with its poles; it finally wore out and there was then a lighter variety. The Duke showed me the book, which came out last year, *The King in His Country** about George VI at Sandringham and re-marked: 'you know I think it's extraordinarily clever to be able to write a readable book out of game-books – he had nothing else to go on. Don't you? You'd think it was the most resistant material in the world', with which I heartily agreed. They all said how simply enormous the Sandringham parties were in old days – forty sitting down to dinner a general rule.

After tea we went for a walk, past the cotoneasters and the pig-shed, along a cement path that winds uphill, round a pretty wood with long grass within it. Half way up the hill the Duke stopped.

Princess Alice: 'Oh Harry, you *are* idle. I wanted to walk up to the top of the hill.'

Duke: 'Can't go further, Aunt Alice. There's a house up at the top. And in that house lives a *talking man*. He *talks*. Can't get away from him. When you *do*, you can hear him talking to you all the time you're going away. We never go further than this.'

Duchess (sighing and smiling): 'Yes he *is* such a *bore*. He never stops talking.'

So we went back and looked at the garden and the Duchess's rock garden and the artichokes of which she promised us each some to take away.

When we came in there were drinks, and I managed to get upstairs just before eight. In my bedroom I found the poems of the Australian poet Paterson†, and I stood by the bathroom window, looking at the lilacs and reading these, forgetting the time. I then had a short bath and returned to my bedroom to find to my

---

*   By Aubrey Buxton (1955).

†   A.B. ('Banjo') Paterson (1864–1941), Australian poet. He wrote *Waltzing Matilda* in 1895.

horror that it was eight thirty-seven. I began rushing into my clothes when Mr Maude came in.

'Oh, I'm so late!' I panted.

'Don't worry Sir, His Royal Highness has only just gone down.'

I took the stairs at two leaps and landed up breathless in the Duke's study where he was pouring himself a drink. He looked at me with great amusement and smiled. The Duchess wasn't there, and came in a few minutes later.

At dinner the Duke said:

'Mr Maude came to me and said you weren't out of your bath yet. I said he must have drowned or gone down the plug!'

'I wasn't in my bath all that time, Sir. I was reading the poems of Paterson.'

This unleashed an interesting conversation on why there was so little Australian literature or painting, in which all joined and which lasted some time. Had Paterson written *Waltzing Mathilda* or hadn't he? Etc. etc. Then the nine o'clock news. After this the Duke quite suddenly said:

'Some horses *are* mad, though. I had one once at the Trooping of the Colour. It suddenly dashed ahead, past my brothers, past my father, and then when I got it to stop, do you know what the bloody animal did? Stood right up in the air. If I wasn't a good rider and hadn't got the big saddle on I should have fallen straight back on my head.'

'Ah, but Harry', said Princess Alice, 'I was there and it wasn't *your* head I was worried about. I was worried about Uncle Alge, poor old gentleman. Don't you remember *your* horse began making *his* horse prance, and I was terrified for him in all that armour plating he was wearing, too.'*

'Yes I remember. And then my father turned to me and said, "you'd better dismount". And I bloody well did dismount.'

Later in the meal Princess Alice began talking about oyster poisoning. The Duke said he had never tasted an oyster.

'When I was young the smell of an oyster made me sick. It's better now, I can just stand the smell but I never ate one. You see', he said to me, 'I never touch food I think I'm not going to like. Why should I? I'm sure I should dislike a mince pie, so I've never tried one. I don't know what's inside a mince pie. What is there?'

'Currants, Harry', said the Duchess, 'and peel and things.'

---

* Lord Athlone was Colonel of The Life Guards 1936–1957.

'I think the contrast between the pastry outside and the heavy things inside *is* rather unpleasant', I contributed.

'I wouldn't know', said the Duke (a favourite phrase), 'because d'you see I've never tried one and I'm not going to. Why should I?'

Before Scrabble I went up and fetched the Paterson volume, and it was proved the Duke was right and he *had* written *Waltzing Matilda*. The Scrabble was an excellent game, which I lost heavily and the Duke won. It was another good limbering-up idea of the Duchess's as one gets on to very easy terms: 'oh, isn't he a wretch' – 'he's an *impossible* person' – 'how *can* you do that, Ma'am, and ruin my whole plan' – 'Aunt Alice, you're not cheating by any chance?' etc. etc.

After this the Duke and I talked from eleven till three. We talked about betting, racing, why the Queen's horses are good now, Molly Buccleuch, availability of girls in London today, Duke of Windsor, Mrs Simpson, Queen Mary, [and] the problems of being a bachelor.

He seemed genuinely moved when I depicted Princess May's first heroic years of married life and begged me to emphasise this as it was so significant for her development and so unknown even inside the family. Had I seen their letters to each other? I said I had found they were at Windsor and had then asked the Princess Royal if she or he (the Duke) would mind my reading them and she had said if you're going to see anything you'd better see everything. He said he heartily agreed. The Duchess had written every week to Queen Mary from Australia and she replied every week. The Duchess had originally thought I ought not to see these letters which were private, but they had now agreed that I would come down again later on and work through them with her. (She confirmed this in the morning.)

DUKE OF WINDSOR

'My brother and I never got on, I'm afraid. We had one hell of a row in 1927. I'd said to someone I didn't think he'd ever be King, and it was repeated. He said to me, "Did you say it or didn't you?" So I said, "well I've either got to tell you a lie or tell you the truth and I'm going to tell you the truth. I did say it and I still think it." Then we had the row.

'The last time I saw him was when Queen Mary died. He rang up from Marlborough House the night she died and he said, 'can you put me up?' I'm not going to sleep in this mortuary. So we put him up for six days. It was so strange entertaining him at York House, where in old days I'd stayed with him when I came up to London on a Saturday and wanted to take somebody to bed with me after the theatre at York House.

'Mrs Simpson? Bloody bitch. I only saw her three times. We none of us ever thought he was going to marry the woman. He had always had such *nice* friends before. Mrs Dudley-Ward[*] was the best friend he ever had, only he didn't realise it. But that Simpson woman! No, I didn't read her book[†] and I'm not going to read it. Why would I waste eighteen shillings? Yes, maybe they are trying to come back with all these newspaper interviews; but they won't do it. Witchcraft? That's exactly what I've been wanting to say all these years. Yes they *did* say that about Anne Boleyn, only the difference was Henry VIII wanted to cut her head off and David didn't want to cut off Mrs Simpson's.'

Edward VIII had five private telephone lines, one direct to Lord Beaverbook.[‡] Nobody knew this until Queen Mary discovered it, poking about upstairs.

After a long sex conversation the clock struck three and I said with finality: 'Sir, I really do think we *must* go to bed.' I think he'd have sat up till five.

The next morning at breakfast we talked about helicopters, their expense and dangers and other similar oddments. The papers were full of the stabbing of the Countess Lubienska[§] on Gloucester Road station. His comment was:

'Stabbing an old lady of seventy-three. Seems a waste doesn't it?' (Squeals of laughter).

We then all four pottered about in his sitting room until the station wagon came at eleven, discussing domestic agencies, difficulties of getting housemaids or houseboys and so on.

At St Pancras, Princess Alice offered me a lift and then potluck. In the Euston Road she patted a basket of roses the Duchess had given her.

'Isn't she kind?'

---

[*]   Winfride (Freda) Birkin (1894–1983), married Rt Hon William Dudley Ward. Mistress of the Prince of Wales through most of the 1920s.

[†]   The Duchess of Windsor had published *The Heart has its Reasons* in 1956. It was priced at 12/6d.

[‡]   Max, 1st Lord Beaverbrook (1879–1964), founder of Express Newspapers, and a powerful figure at the time of the Abdication.

[§]   Countess Teresa Lubienska, an aristocrat from Eastern Poland, then living in Cornwall Gardens, was stabbed on the platform of Gloucester Road Underground Station on the night of 24 May 1957. She died soon after her arrival at St Mary Abbot's Hospital. 18,000 people were interviewed, but the murderer was never found.

'Yes, Ma'am. I had expected to feel so dreadfully shy and nervous, and I felt at home at once.'

'Of course you did. Dear little Duchess!'*

ADDENDA

The Lone Ranger

On books: 'I don't seem to read anything nowadays. I've got all those books there and I've never read one of 'em. Why I've only read five books since Christmas.' But he respects and likes books.

On foreigners: 'I sometimes think all foreigners are – well you know, aren't they?' 'I should like to send Monsieur Mollet† a telegram: «Congratulations on your length of tenure»!!' (squeals).

'There's only one thing worth seeing on television – the Childrens' Hour. I never miss 'The Lone Ranger' on Saturdays. I have a permanent date on Saturdays at a quarter to five.' (We all watched 'The Lone Ranger', which I greatly enjoyed.)

'I remember my father was bloody angry with me, when I was stationed at Canterbury (bloody awful little place Canterbury), because I told him there were more partridges in Kent than in Norfolk. He was *furious*. So I said well as you've never in my life asked me to shoot partridges in Norfolk, how would I know?'

FURTHER ADDENDA: INVASION OF PRIVACY

On Sunday evening, about six forty-five, the Duchess came scampering into the room like a frightened rabbit.

'There's some awful Americans with Kodaks driving up.'

'Huh?'

---

* Soon after this, James Pope-Hennessy wrote to his brother: 'And isn't Princess Alice most beguiling & somehow authentic? To think she is Pss. Mary Adelaide's daughter-in-law too!!' [Letter from Hagnau, 10 June 1958 – Getty].

† Guy Mollet (1905–75), Leader of SFIO party in France 1946–69, Prime Minister of France from January 1956 to June 1957.

'There are some awful *Americans* with *Ko*daks driving up. I'm going to escape this way', and she disappeared with the speed of someone escaping from a fire. She came back later. 'They've been told the garden is open for the hospital next week'.

Late on Sunday night Prince Henry was complaining, most legitimately, about the press, especially the Beaverbrook press. I think they feel genuinely persecuted, and with reason.

POST SCRIPTUM TO BARNWELL MANOR

Deep and lasting impression made by J. P.-H. on the Duke of Gloucester

(The following is a verbatim report by Sir Alan Lascelles on a conversation with H.R.H. at Barnwell Manor, 11 August 1958).

H.R.H.: Names? *I* can't remember anybody's name. There are those two chaps who are writing books – one about my brother, and one about my mother. They've both got double names, but I'm damned if I know what they are!!

Sir Alan Lascelles: Wheeler-Bennett and Pope-Hennessy, Sir.

H.R.H.: That's it. That's it. Wheeler-Bennett and Pope-Hennessy. One of them stammers and the other doesn't. Which is which?

Sir Alan Lascelles: As far as I know, Sir, Pope-Hennessy doesn't stammer.

NINETEEN

The Muddle Egg *or* A Visit to Lambeth Palace

11 July

The 99ᵗʰ Archbishop of Canterbury and Primate of All England was the Rt Hon and Most Rev Geoffrey Fisher (1887–1972). He was the youngest of ten children, and came from a family of Church of England rectors. Educated at Marlborough, he won a scholarship to Exeter College, Oxford, taking first classes in classical honours moderations, literae humaniores, and theology. He taught at Marlborough, was ordained in 1913, and became Headmaster of Repton in 1914.

In 1932 he was consecrated Bishop of Chester, and in 1939 he was enthroned as Bishop of London. William Temple, Archbishop of Canterbury, died suddenly in 1944, and early the following year he succeeded him. As Archbishop, he crowned The Queen at the Coronation in 1953. He was a widely-travelled Archbishop and became well-known to the general public through the medium of television. He resigned in 1961, was created Lord Fisher of Lambeth, and spent his last years at Trent Rectory, near Sherborne in Dorset.

After some correspondence with Dr Fisher, the present Archbishop of Canterbury, upon the absurd rumours of Queen Mary having died a Catholic and on the theory of her having frequented Our Lady of Victories, Warwick Street, it was arranged for me to visit the Archbishop for a 'brief talk'; the time given by his secretary being 11.40 a.m. to 12 a.m. [sic] on this Thursday.

I duly arrived at Lambeth, having been held up by the traffic and forced by an officious traffic police youth to go round by Vauxhall Bridge ('Buggers! Aren't they!' said the taxi-driver, quite rightly). The road outside Lambeth Palace is being taken up to make a suburban-looking freestone roundabout, and the noise, dust and mess is considerable. I rang a colossal bell pull, which operates a squealing electric bell, and the wicket-gate beside the carriage-entrance flew open.

GEOFFREY FISHER, ARCHBISHOP OF CANTERBURY

'Mr Pope-Hennessy?' asked a jovial old porter in a felt hat. 'Now come in.' He put his hand on my shoulder, and explained carefully, as though it were the most difficult project in the world: 'Now do you see that archway here on the right? Well you go through that, straight through. Then turn to the left – to the left at once – and then you will see the Palace door. Go up to the palace door and you will see the bell on the left – on the left of the door. Now you ring that. Have you got that clear, Sir?'

Having achieved this much, I waited at the great door on the top of a flight of steps; the façade of the palace, with angular bow-windows, is grey-yellow and looks about 1830 (?Wyattville or so?)*. The door was then opened by a rather luscious tall girl, heavily made up and wearing a Horrocks silk dress cut too loosely over her bosom, so that the front stuck out. I suppose she was a secretary of sorts.

'Mr - - -?'

'Pope-Hennessy. I have an appointment with the Archbishop for twenty to twelve.'

'Of course. Do come in.'

'The traffic seems rather bad outside' I said as we mounted a wide staircase covered in faded mole-coloured Wilton, to the mezzanine floor.

'Bad? It's *chaos*. Would you mind waiting here a minute. Do sit down.'

I sat in an alcove leading to a bay-window, and looked at my book. There was a high wide airy corridor, panelled in a kind of pitch-pine or lightly stained marmalade oak. Many lofty doorways led off it, with brass door furniture. Occasionally a secretary, or a young ecclesiastical person in dog-collar, spectacles and carrying a file or two hurried by. After two or three minutes a pallid youth with a pointed face, palely freckled and reddish hair kept close to the head appeared:

'I am the Archbishop's chaplain' he said in a sibilant tone. 'The Bishop of Fulham† is with the Archbishop at the moment. Would you mind waiting?'

I sat down for a few minutes more, when the sound of educated voices taking leave of each other rolled down the corridor:

'Oh yes, certainly, I *will* tell him.'

'Yes, do.'

'Goodmorning.'

---

*   In fact the work of Edward Blore (1787–1879) in 1834.

†   Rt Rev Roderic Coote (1915–2000), Bishop of Fulham 1957–66, Suffragan Bishop of Colchester 1966–87.

'Goodmorning.'

A door shut, and then opened suddenly again. I had been sitting there envisaging the bespectacled hard-faced man the newspapers make the archbishop; and was therefore unprepared.

'Mi-chael! Mi-chael!' cried a somewhat high-pitched voice.

'Mi-i-i-chael!' Down the corridor paddled a benign-looking egg in gaiters; the face and body making one form or cohesive element, the little gaitered legs somehow attached below; grey blowing-back hair, an expression of amusement and surprise. The egg pirouetted half into another room and in turning saw me:

'Now who is *this*?' The tone was that of the hostess at a children's' party welcoming a new face.

'My name is Pope-Hennessy.'

'Goodmorning, goodmorning. Come in, come in.'

'Goodmorning, Archbishop. It's so nice of your grace to let me come to see you.'

'Now just wait a minute. I'm trying to find one of my curates, to do a little telephone message for me. Mi-i-i-chael!'

'There seem to be several about – curates I mean.'

'I know, I know.' He propelled me into his capacious study and left by another door. 'Now just wait here. I do apologise.'

I stood on the hearth-rug and looked at the study. It is a very large fine room, again with a bay-window, again panelled in lightish orange oak or pine. A desk near to the window, two chairs in the bay, two by the fireplace, bookcases, no ashtrays, a Dictaphone, a telephone, on the mantelpiece a number of cheap plaster statuettes of the Virgin Mary and some saints, also some quaint and ambiguous African trophies and oddments; including a piece of mosaic with holy greetings from the Church of Malabar. Presently the Archbishop came paddling back, grinning and giggling. He ushered me into a comfortable armchair in the bay-window, taking himself a lower wood-and-stuffed-leather chair opposite me. We were both at right angles to his desk.

'Well' he said sinking back and crossing his hands on his corpulent stomach and apron, his buttoned frock coat falling back, and sticking out his little frog-legs 'I don't suppose I can help you. But here I am!'

'Well, Your Grace, before we begin discussing Queen Mary's religion, I should like to ask your opinion. I should like to insert a short historical note at some point in my book, about these alleged royal death-bed conversions. Knocking them on the head, so to speak, and beginning with the Jesuit sermons about Queen Victoria's mother, the Duchess of Kent.'*

'Did they say that about *her*? Well I never.'

'I thought, if you agreed of course, that it might be useful; It really is such rot, isn't it. And coming from me as a Catholic it might carry force.'

He squirmed with pleasure: 'Of course it would. From you – from *you* –' a pudgy finger with a big episcopal ring pointed full at me – 'from *you*, of course. And it would be the greatest relief to *me* to have it all shot down.'

We discussed this point thoroughly; and when we had finished I continued:

'What I should like to know is what your Grace thought of Queen Mary's religious views. I'm ashamed to say that having been brought up a Catholic I am disgracefully ignorant about the Church of England. I understand there is what is called a High Church and a Low Church. Now the Duchess of Teck was Low Church, and hated anything that "smacked of ritualism" and they all thought going to mass in Florence (which they often did to hear the singing) was mummery.'

'Do you know Lady Cynthia Colville?'

'I know her well. But *she* is very High Church I believe.'

'That's what I mean. *She* could tell you, because she isn't Low Church. Now let me see, yes, Queen Mary *was* what you could call Low Church, it's a tendency of all our royal family. They came from the continent, you see.'

'I see.'

'Now how can I explain it to you? Take the Queen Mother do you follow me? Now the Queen Mother's attitude to life is to make everything as easy as possible, do you see? It's all' he brandished his hands in a circular motion, indicative I gathered more of the Queen Mother's expansive all-embracing Christianity than of her physical appearance – 'well it's all like that. She's a profoundly religious woman, mind you, profoundly religious. But doctrinally shall we say there is little impact. When her niece married a Danish prince† – what was he called?'

---

* HSH Princess Victoria of Coburg (1786–1861), married 1818, HRH The Prince Edward, Duke of Kent (1767–1820).

† Anne Bowes-Lyon (1917–80), had married 1938, Viscount Anson, heir to the Earl of Lichfield. She had proved unfaithful, but Anson had been prevailed upon to be the 'guilty party' when they were divorced in 1945. In 1950 she married HH Prince George of Denmark (1920–86). Queen Elizabeth did not attend the wedding, which was the subject of some controversy, but she and Princess Margaret attended the luncheon at Glamis after the ceremony.

'Prince George of Denmark.'

'That's it. Prince George of Denmark. Well she didn't disapprove but she wouldn't go. Didn't want to get muddled up in it, if you see what I mean. Of course the papers made the most of it. Do you know what the papers, and particularly the Beaverbrook Press, hate most?'

'They seem to hate most things'

'Quite. Quite. But number one is the Archbishop of Canterbury. Number two is the Church of England. And number three – what they like, I mean here, – is Divorce. So they thought they could get us all at once over Prince George of Denmark – Queen Mother, myself, Church of England, marriage in Scotland of a divorced woman – the whole bag of tricks. And do you know what makes the Beaverbrook Press so hostile? Can you guess?'

'I should have thought it was the Abdication.'

'Exactly. Poor old Lang.[*] They always say *he* forced the Abdication. Actually between ourselves Lang felt *left out* – thought he ought to have been consulted more and been at the centre of things – he had nothing to do with it at all. Nothing at all. Well now to return to Queen Mary. What I have said about the Queen Mother applies equally to her – with of course many differences of character – but doctrine would have meant little. Take Princess Margaret now, she *understands doctrine* – knows what it's all about. In fact Princess Margaret is *a thoroughly good churchwoman.*[†]

'I have been impressed by two or three very simple and humble prayers which I have found in Queen Mary's diaries.'

'That's what I mean. *That* approach would be more important than the doctrinal one.'

'Queen Mary was always so open-minded. When one of her great-aunt's granddaughters made an unhappy marriage and divorced she was all for the divorce.'[‡]

'Of course. You see the Low Church attitude has always placed more emphasis on the spiritual content of a marriage than on its purely formal aspect. But I

---

[*]   Rt Hon and Most Rev Cosmo Gordon Lang (1864–1945), Archbishop of Canterbury 1928–43.

[†]   Princess Margaret preferred Holy Communion to Mattins, and frequently attended Sung Eucharist at St George's Chapel, Windsor.

[‡]   This is almost certainly a reference to Duchess Marie of Strelitz. The Grand Duchess of Mecklenburg-Strelitz was Queen Mary's aunt, not great-aunt. (see below in Württemberg chapter).

bet she wouldn't have wanted to get mixed up in that divorce. She would have thought it a bore.'

'That's just what she *did* think it. She wouldn't go to Germany while it was going on.'

'I remember the first time I went to Sandringham – I was Bishop of Chester then – the Duke of Westminster was there, and Queen Mary said to me: "Such a bore about all his wives"!!' That was her point of view.'

We then got on to doctrinal differences between our churches on re-marriage – 'Well since you have lured me into doctrine' he said with an expansive smile – and I learned much. According to the Archbishop his Church has developed over late years and is developing, under his tolerant guidance, all the time. The basis of this development is on the recognition of a dichotomy – on one hand the Church in its institutional capacity, on the other its sacramental role. Divorce is recognised by the institution as a fact, but sacramental remarriage in church is refused, except in rare cases. It is all a question of 'lee-way'.

'Had a case just now as a matter of fact sent to me by our naval man. High-up officer married during the war, his wife was unfaithful to him, but she wouldn't let him divorce her; as a matter of fact he couldn't collect the necessary evidence. So he goes and lives with another woman, and *then* she divorces him. Bad luck wasn't it? Anyway he marries the other woman and now they want to be married in church. It comes up to *me*, and *I* decide; – according to each case, if you follow me – I was a schoolmaster and I know you cannot run things on too many rules – individual cases must be treated individually. Well I said in this case – come back in five years. You see they've neither of them been confirmed. Well they must develop spiritually before they can be confirmed and they must be confirmed before they are married. Now what would *you* say?'

'I don't know, your Grace. But may I ask whether this spiritual development should not include regular confession?'

'*Ah.*' pointing again 'Now do you know you've said something very interesting there. I'm inclined to agree with you – but then does the Deity need an intermediary if the man repents? We do have confession but it's not obligatory like yours.'

---

* Bendor, 2nd Duke of Westminster (1879–1953), had three wives by 1930, and acquired a fourth in 1947.

'On my own experience, your grace, I don't think anyone would ever go to confession if it wasn't *slightly* obligatory. Nobody enjoys saying how beastly they are, even to a priest.'

'And yet as a schoolmaster I used to find little boys who loved coming to say how beastly they were. They had to be discouraged.'

'But *we* believe that confession is a sacrament and brings grace.'

'We too think it has its sacramental aspect.'

He then embarked, with charming apologies, on his difficulties with our hierarchy (including even David Mathew* whom he likes enormously, over the Alamein memorial). He said that all the little tags and leads towards the C. of E. carefully established by Cardinal Hinsley[†] had been systematically cut by Cardinal Griffin[‡] and his entourage. I spoke of the Maynooth grant[§] and the harm done by ignorant Irish priests; he said he had been disappointed in Douglas Woodruff[¶]. Had I seen that he himself had 'barked' about my church recently. I said that without impertinence I would like to ask him about that. I had never met these undermining hostile Roman Catholics.

'No, no, you wouldn't have, but believe me they exist, especially in the North. You can't expect *me* to like all this propaganda about "getting England back for the Faith"? How could I? At Westminster they always go on about *their* feelings being hurt, but I said to one of them (over the Hungarians at the Albert Hall) don't you suppose *I've* got any feelings to hurt? Here I am, in *my* country, head of my country's church, and you say I can't give a blessing because *the Archbishop of Liverpool* is present? They saw the point.'

I brought up the Malines conference**, and he said it was the climate he would wish to see restored if there was the slightest symptom of co-operation from our side. He told me several things in strict confidence. He ended by saying his dearest wish was to see a *very* small, equal-numbered group of laymen of both

---

* David Mathew (1902–75), Vicar-Apostolic of Great Britain 1954–63. Presumably this was the Alamein Memorial in Egypt.
† Cardinal Arthur Hinsley (1865–1943); Archbishop of Westminster 1935–43; Cardinal 1937.
‡ Cardinal Bernard Griffin (1899–1956); Archbishop of Westminster 1943–56; Cardinal 1946.
§ The Maynooth Grant was a major political fracas in the 1840s involving Sir Robert Peel.
¶ Douglas Woodruff (1897–1978), Editor of *The Tablet*, and a noted wit.
** The Malines Conference took place in Belgium in 1909, and marked the beginning of the popular liturgical movement in Europe.

sides (*me*, for instance!) who could meet and make friends, and be appealed to when difficulties occurred. He thought it might be called the Committee of St Augustine or some such. He had talked to Pakenham*, but Pakenham, we agreed, was too enthusiastic and silly and over-eager and a convert. The chaplain put his head round the door and said the Bishop of ----- had been waiting a long time. The archbishop pushed me back into my chair and continued. At the end he said: 'May I say quite frankly that I have derived more comfort from this conversation with you than from any I have had with any member of your hierarchy. I am really grateful to you.' This is only a potted version of a long and interesting talk. He is a good, urbane, friendly man; not a great spiritual force but evidently meaning extremely well and mercifully un-naïf. He again said there was a great hostile body of Roman Catholic opinion:

'Not anyone you know, of course, or that I know personally. All the Roman Catholics I've known have been – well – don't you know – such *fun!*'

He took me out into the passage and promised to read the doctrinal passages in my proofs.

---

* Frank Pakenham, 7th Earl of Longford (1905–2001), converted to Catholicisim in 1940.

TWENTY

MR JOHN WILSON

A bookseller's verdict

1 August

John & Edward Bumpus Ltd was the bookshop most favoured by the Royal Family. Situated at 350 and then at 447 Oxford Street, London W1, it became the most fashionable bookshop in the capital. Its Chairman and Managing Director from 1941 to 1959 was John Gideon Wilson (1876–1968). He was bookseller to King George V, whose reading list in the last years of his life was published in John Gore's memoir of him.

Wilson was the son of a husband and wife team of bookbinders in Glasgow, James and Margaret Wilson. He worked there as a bookseller with John Smith & Son. He moved to London and worked for Constable, and then Jones & Evans, before joining J. & E. Bumpus.

He was famous as having assisted T.E. Lawrence when he failed to find enough subscribers for a fine-press edition of The Seven Pillars of Wisdom. *Wilson was considered the most influential bookseller in London in his day. He was awarded the CBE in 1948.*

On 1 August 1957 I went to have a talk with Mr Wilson of Bumpus, in his little book-loaded den at the back of the shop, as I sometimes do. On this occasion I wanted to ask him about Queen Mary. Mr Wilson is eighty-two but looks sixty-five.

He protested that he did not have an anecdotal mind, nor could he throw light on her reading habits. Her ladies, and especially Miss Wyndham with her incisive mind, could do that for me. He then spoke of Q.M. with great objectivity and – rare indeed – with genuine affection.

Mr Wilson, being a simple Scotsman, had never made a fuss and called her Your Majesty etc. He would speak directly to her and she to him. The *directness of communication* was the characteristic that seemed to him the salient one. She would give you information, never pretend to know anything she did not, and accept information in return; a positive unaffected conversation. Her communication or questions always required a *point d'appui* – herself, her memories of her youth, some person she had met; outside this she did not stray. She would come into the shop, make the rounds of the personnel she had always known, look at the books, talk to Mr Wilson and leave again. In contrast to the aristocratic clients, who flung orders or information at you, or else were maddeningly vague, she was precise and concentrated and knew exactly what she was about. He also believed that she had influence in stopping the bad old habits of the aristocracy of letting huge bills run on; she always wanted the bill, and her attitude to accounts was prompt and correct. Anything outside her (long and fairly wide) experience was of *no* interest. Everything turned on what she, Queen Mary, had done or seen or heard or read or been told. Everything in fact radiated outwards from one centre – herself.

Sometimes she would come in to look through a famous book of flower-prints (?Thornton?): 'Ah yes and *there* is the tulip' (her favourite illustration in this volume). Latterly she would select books for children, have them sent to Marlborough House, peruse them, and send back the rejects she did not want as presents. She seemed to like children. Once she was standing looking at some books in a shelf and a child in a perambulator was crowing and holding out its arms. Scarcely looking she handed it her umbrella to play with. When Miss Rose Fyleman[*] opened the first exhibition of Titania's Palace in the old shop in Oxford Street, Mr Wilson had asked some children to a party; when it was under way, Queen Mary suddenly and unexpectedly appeared and enjoyed herself hugely. On the whole she did not notice what was going on in the shop, confining herself to a round of the assistants she had always known.

He says I should see Mary, Countess Howe[†], to whom he is writing on my behalf.

---

[*] Rose Fyleman (1877–1957), writer and poet, author of *There are Fairies at the Bottom of my Garden* (1917).

[†] Mary Curzon (1887–1962), married 1907, 5th Earl Howe (1884–1964), Co-Founder of the British Racing Drivers' Association. Divorced 1937.

TWENTY-ONE

August Depressions

19 – 26 August

James Pope-Hennessy then went to stay with his aunt, Lady Susan Birch, at Clunie Mill, Braemar, Aberdeenshire, in order to visit Mar Lodge, Balmoral, and Abergeldie Castle, and to interview certain survivors. He found himself unexpectedly invited to lunch with the Queen, an event which took place on 23 August.

He had hoped to be able to visit Balmoral without seeing any members of the Royal Family:

> I seem to have won the battle for Balmoral, as Patrick Plunket answers my note that the Queen would like me to go and see it whenever I like, just telephone the Equerry, which I much prefer from the book point of view; and they are so dreadfully anti-historical. Even Judy Montagu was shocked, staying at Windsor last weekend, by the fact that they treat visits to the Mausoleum at Frogmore as a kind of music hall joke or knock-about-turn – 'Now let's go into the Mausoleum and have a good laugh' – such lack of *pietas* can bring no luck ... Queen Mary, at least, was not vulgar – tho' Queen Alexandra was.[113]

On 19 August 1957 I went up with my Aunt Susan* to stay at Braemar, in Jack Gordon's little converted mill-house, so as to see the country and Balmoral, Abergeldie and Mar Lodge.†

---

* Lady Susan Birch, his maternal aunt.

† Balmoral was the Scottish home of the Queen; Abergeldie Castle was a mile or so away on the road to Birkhall; and Mar Lodge (home of Princess Arthur of Connaught) was five miles west of Braemar. One of the few mistakes Pope-Hennessy made in his biography was to place it south of the River Dee, when it is in fact on the north side.

It rained a good deal of the time.

I returned to London 26/27 August.

MAR LODGE AND MRS CUMMINGS

After lunch on Thursday afternoon, 22 August 1957, we drove from Braemar to the Quoich, or Devil's Cauldron, to a place where a tributary of the Dee rushes over curious flat rocks, one of which has a smooth egg-shaped hole in it. Here, when the river is in spate, the water boils and thrashes. This afternoon, which was sunny and mild, the river was low, slipping over the flat rocks and plunging through a ravine over which is a stone bridge. Not far from the bridge, on the side of the brae, is a small stone cottage built for Queen Victoria by the Duke of Fife.* The ground beneath the birch and pine trees is peppered with miniature fir cones, and grey-green with moss-lichen and twigs.

After leaving Braemar the whole valley of the Dee lies below you, very wide and shallow-looking, like a map on a coloured postcard. The hills rise in the distance and more sharply on each side, and as your eye follows the ribbon of the river, it encounters a group of red roofs and black and white eaves – this is Mar Lodge, which, when you drive above it (the road turns like a hairpin at the Lin of Dee) shows itself as a Sunningdale-type mansion in a trim garden, with verandas supported on black-painted tree trunks. The old Mar Lodge was situated on high ground just across the Victoria Bridge, a scarlet iron suspension bridge on the Braemar side of the property. Queen Victoria laid the foundation stone of the new Mar Lodge in 1895.

We sat beside the Quoich for some twenty minutes; it is a place of singular melancholy, very shut in by the trees, and with an alien atmosphere but not an attractive one. I found a rounded pebble, like a golf ball, of the ugly reddish granite which abounds in this countryside. You can also find cairngorms, if you dig for them and know what to look for.

Mar Lodge is kept up, as its owner Princess Arthur told me earlier this year, as though it was to be inhabited next week.† The Queen later told me that P.A. allows

---

* 1st Duke of Fife (1849–1912) had owned the land on which Balmoral was built. He loaned it to Queen Victoria in 1848, and she purchased it from him in 1852 and built a new castle there. The Duke of Fife married her granddaughter, Princess Louise, daughter of the future Edward VII.

† Princess Arthur was confined to her home in London.

no-one to live there or use it. The neighbours say the property itself is going to seed and that the keepers have become understandably slack.

On the way back we gave a lift to a talkative and sweating hiker, who had just walked twenty miles from Aviemore, over the pass (2,000 ft) into Inverness-shire. To me there is nothing romantic about the word 'pass' in connection with this lamentable, blunt scenery. The hills all along to Mar are denuded of trees, greyish stumps everywhere; which makes me think that in Queen Victoria's day it must have all been heavily forested and thus much more German. (I asked the Queen what she thought about this and she said after some cogitation: 'Perhaps'.)

When we got back at five, Jack telephoned to Mrs Cummings and I set off to see her. Mrs Cummings is the daughter of Fraser, one of the Mar keepers, and in a vitrine in her living-room she has many silver souvenirs given by King Edward (1884), King George and the Duke of Windsor to Fraser. Mrs Cummings lives in a nice tidy little house on the outskirts of Braemar, up a precipitous garden filled with very bright and flourishing sweet-peas, geraniums and so on. Her house is let 'to some people from Singapore' for the season, and she and her husband live in a wooden house at the back of it. She is a very short old lady with whitish-yellow hair, dressed in a loose pink cardigan and colourless skirt; a long sensible intelligent face, very well-educated and outspoken. 'But you're a very young mun, aren't ye, and here am I expecting an older person' she said as she came to the door.

She was, as usual, afraid she could tell me nothing of much use to me. As the conversation got going it became clear that all her loyalties were with Mar against Balmoral; some illustrated paper had actually published a photograph of a shooting party leaving the Derry with the caption 'a lodge on the Balmoral estate' whereas of course it was the Mar estate. Her father, Fraser, lived at the Derry and there she was brought up; it is now the Cairngorm Clubhouse, whatever this may mean. From childhood she remembers royal parties coming to the Derry for tea or for a walk. She feels a feudal admiration and affection for Princess Arthur, enhanced and strengthened by the fact that she too has bad arthritis and cannot write any more.

Her chief theme was that 'they' were all 'just like other folks' up here. The Balmoral party would come over of a Sunday and on alternate weeks the Mar family would drive along the winding roads to Balmoral: 'You come to us this week and we'll come to you next, sort of thing just like any other folk'. The royal ladies never really walked – 'You used to wonder what their legs were for' – they would just get out of a carriage or pony-trap and wander by the Quoich: 'Although of course Queen Mary was a big, hefty person and could have walked'. Princess Maud* was startlingly beautiful – 'if she'd never been princess or queen you'd have remarked her'; Princess Victoria very easy, and the tallest; Princess Louise 'very nervous, a very shy person'† who kept her children far too much with her.‡ Queen Mary would never 'go out on the hill' and so it was King George they chiefly saw. 'Why he'd discuss anything with my father. I remember one day he was wearing some new garters and my father commented on them, and the King took them off and said "My wife made these for me, Fraser, you ought to get your wife to do the same" and Queen Mary explained just how they were knitted; but nothing came of it, for my mother didn't take to the idea.' Queen Mary was taller than King George, but 'managed it very well' – 'if she'd worn flat hats instead of the toques she would have looked taller, you understand'. The Wales sisters would drop in for tea with Mrs Fraser – 'we do so much enjoy having jam, we never have jam, neither a dish nor pot of jam, at home; everything is made into sandwiches, and there's never enough jam in the sandwiches' etc. etc.

Her father knew the Duke of Clarence and liked him, but he was so delicate he could never go out on the hill much, and they had always to see he didn't get wet.

She showed me a nice photo of Q.M., arms linked with Duchess of Fife and the Fife girls, standing on a veranda at Mar Lodge. At the Derry groups [group photos] were often taken of them, standing after a shooting party.

The Mar Lodge footmen would often come up of an evening after their work to chat with the Fraser family and have tea: 'great strupping young luds, with nought to do' – too many of them. One of them, a certain Marriner, accompanied the Fifes to Sandringham on his first Christmas in the royal service. He was standing one evening, after duty, gazing out at the snow in the park and thinking how beautiful it was. He heard no-one coming up behind him ('it was the thick carpets, do you see') and suddenly on looking down found Queen Alexandra standing by his side. 'Are you lonely?' she asked, 'for you look lonely, and I should

---

*   HM Queen Maud of Norway.

†   As we know these were the three daughters of Edward VII.

‡   Princess Louise had two daughters : Princess Arthur of Connaught, and her younger sister, Princess Maud (1893–1945). Lord Farquhar helped Princess Maud escape from her mother by offering to leave £50,000 to her or her groom. The 11th Earl of Southesk (1893–1992) took the bait and married her in 1923, but Farquhar's estate was proved to be bankrupt so he never got the money.

hate anyone to be lonely at my house at Christmas time'. He assured her he was not, and they had a long conversation – 'for by luck he had the tone of voice the Queen could hear'. She asked his name and said 'but I expect you come from my country originally, there are many Marriners in my country'; and then she told him to wait there and she went away. She came back with a beautiful pair of gold cuff-links and said to him 'these are my own present to you; you'll get your other presents from the tree tonight'.

At the Derry 'the others' were always trying to speak for Queen Alexandra because of her deafness – 'but she would always slip away round the corner for a word with my mother, for she didn't like them speaking up for her at all, she wanted to talk herself'.

Mrs Cummings was a small child when Queen Victoria laid the foundation stone of Mar Lodge. She was very much disappointed by the Queen – 'just a little old body in a black bonnet, no better than my own mother' – but has never forgotten the Indian attendant* with a flashing jewel in his turban which twinkled in the sun every time he moved.

Mrs Cummings thinks I should try to see Miss Jessie Black, the old retired Mar Lodge housekeeper who knew Queen Mary well.

AN INTRUDER AT BALMORAL

On Friday 23 August I went to lunch at Balmoral. This was something I had privately tried or wished to avoid, since I am not made for court life, and having already lunched last winter at Buckingham Palace my curiosity was amply assuaged. Patrick Plunket†, who was out of waiting, had told me to ring up the current Equerry, Sqn Leader Blount‡, who first arranged for me to go over in the afternoon and be shown round by the Queen's Page. However, after 'a word with Her Majesty' this was altered to an invitation to lunch, and the odd hour of 12.15

---

* The Munshi.

† Patrick, 7th Lord Plunket (1923–75). His parents had been killed when he was young, and he was the nearest thing to a brother to The Queen. He was then a temporary Equerry and later Master of the Household.

‡ Squadron-Leader Christopher Blount (b. 1925), Equerry to The Queen 1954–7. He married (1957) Hon Susan Cobbold, daughter of Lord Cobbold, later Lord Chamberlain.

appointed. I was much ashamed of feeling nervous that morning, as Jack Gordon drove me towards my goal, but this was nothing to the state into which I had got after a few minutes inside Balmoral.

Both outside and inside, this house is far lighter, whiter, prettier and more spacious than I had imagined. It is in many ways similar to Osborne* in atmosphere, with many large windows and well-proportioned rooms; all of which leads me to think the Prince Consort had very good, *gemütlich* architectural ideas. The panelling, which in Queen Victoria's day was covered with a thick brown-orange varnish (still to be seen in the back passages) was stripped by Queen Mary, and is in consequence a pale natural pine-wood, solid and well carved over the doorways and so on. There are very long narrow passages, papered in a grey-cream-coloured flock paper with VRI in a lozenge all over it.

The policeman in the drive told us, by a confusion, to go to 'the Tower door', which is by the Equerries' room (the household is lodged in the Tower). Here a cheeky looking young footman in the ugly blue cloth battledress with epaulettes and monogram, seemed much surprised to see me, and telephoned to the Queen's page, a tall and as it later transpired extremely friendly man called Childs[†] who seemed more surprised still. The latter led me along a corridor of great length to the hall, where two other footmen were waiting on the open front door for me to arrive by that way. 'I suppose you'll be lunching on the hill, Sir?' he asked. I said I had no idea. He then led me back again and consulted in the passage, at my elbow, with two more footmen: 'But do either of you know *who this gentleman is*?' 'I rather think he's the gentleman who's writing about Queen Mary' said one of them: 'That is correct' I said tersely. I was then led back again to the Tower door where they telephoned to Sqn Leader Blount who was changing in his bedroom. 'But we can't put him in the Equerries' room, because Sir Michael and Colonel Agnew[‡] are working in there'. I was then sat down in the little hall, with the younger footman staring at me. Presently the Sqn Leader came bounding downstairs: a smooth, blonde, tight-skinned face with mildly protuberant blue

---

* Osborne was Queen Victoria's home on the Isle of Wight.
† Stanley Childs, Page of the Backstairs to The Queen.
‡ Sir Michael (later Lord) Adeane (1910–84), Private Secretary to The Queen 1953–72 ; and Sir Godfrey Agnew (1913–95), Clerk to the Privy Council 1953–74.

eyes, which looked at me askance as though I might have been Lord Altrincham* in disguise. He was excessively shy and awkward; I felt more than ever like a Christian traveller who has blundered into the wrong part of a mosque.

We finally went into the Equerries' room; the door opens on to a short flight of steps, and the room itself, once used before Crathie church was rebuilt as a chapel, is vaulted and panelled, with two fireplaces, a huge window and many royal engravings and lithographs on the wall; until recently it had a billiard table in it, on which King George V would play. Here was Sir Michael Adeane whom I know and like and who is very easy, and a smallish man with a white face, dark brown hair, moustache and tweed suit, who was Agnew, Clerk to the Council. They gave me some sherry, and then Sir Reginald Manningham-Buller†, a great ugly hulk of a man with a contused face and thick black eyebrows and strong spectacles, lumbered into the room. He was dressed in a very new-looking grey and blue tweed suit of large squares and held a small cardboard box of fishing flies upon which he began to discourse. The Secretary of State for Scotland‡ was also there, with curly yellow-grey hair and a long pink Scots face. It was all very sticky, and reminded me of the Equerry to the King of Sweden. They talked fishing, shooting and stalking while I watched.

After a nervous 25 minutes we adjourned to the drawing room. This is a fine light room, with white-on-white striped wallpaper, a great bank of red geraniums in a corner by the piano (which was literally covered with boxes of chocolates) and gladioli in big urn-like vases. The carpet, a slightly virulent jade-green, is stained here and there by the yellow marks of dogs' mess. There are two doors either end, one leading into a small library in which King George and Queen Mary would breakfast, the other into a small sitting room in which King George and Queen Mary would take tea; beyond this sitting room there is a dark slip room with marble busts, and then the dining room.

---

* John Grigg (1924–2001), then 2nd Lord Altrincham. That very month he had created a major stir with an article in *The National and Evening Review,* in which he disparaged the Queen's education and attacked some of the more outdated customs attached to the monarchy, such as presentation parties.
† Sir Reginald Manningham-Buller (1905–80), later 1st Viscount Dilhorne, controversial Conservative Attorney-General 1954–62. Later Lord Chancellor 1962–4.
‡ Rt Hon John Maclay (1905–92), later 1st Viscount Muirshiel, Secretary of State for Scotland 1957–62.

It now transpired that there was to be a Privy Council before lunch, which explained the sheaf of stiff typewritten papers laced with emerald green ribbon which Adeane was carrying in his hand. The library door was suddenly opened by an elderly footman, who said, very loudly: 'The Acting Lord President' whereupon Mr Maclay went in, bowing his head at the door as he entered. There was the burble of a high-pitched female voice and the door closed. All this was rather mysterious and exciting and one could imagine Queen Victoria behind the door. Presently a bell rang in a passage, the footman came in again, and everyone but Blount went into the council room. He and I were left sipping sherry and smoking. Near the bow-window (in which is a satinwood desk with oval miniature photographs of the Duke of Clarence and, I think, of the Duke of Albany* on it) is a small low carved armchair covered with tartan cotton or cloth; here Queen Victoria always sat, back to the light and no-one is allowed to use it. On the walls are what the Queen calls 'those glorious Landseer heads' of ghillies, two other Landseers of the Queen and the Prince Consort at Osborne, and a very long picture on slate of the P.C. and his eldest daughter† returning, on horse and pony, from stalking: this I gathered was found by Queen Mary in one of the little houses and brought here. An untidy-looking sealyham pottered into the room, and went to sleep in front of the electric fire.

'Hello, Jon-Jon' said Squadron-Leader Blount brightly. 'Jon-Jon belongs to Princess Margaret. Don't you Jon-Jon?'

Jon-Jon made no reply, and we continued our nervous, patchy conversation about the passage wallpaper.

The library door flew open, and the Queen marched in accompanied by several dogs. She walked briskly across the room and held out her hand.

'You're staying up here, I understand?' she said with a curt smile, taking cover behind the long brocaded stool which was standing in front of the fire.

'Yes Ma'am, at a mill-house belonging to the Farquarsons'‡ etc. etc. etc.

---

* HRH The Prince Leopold, Duke of Albany, son of Queen Victoria, and father of Princess Alice, Countess of Athlone.

† HRH The Princess Victoria, later Empress Frederick.

‡ Captain Alwyne Farquharson, 16th of Invercauld (b. 1919), and his American wife, Madam (Frances) Farquharson of Invercauld (1903–91), formerly wife of Captain James Gordon, and widow of Hon James Rodney.

She lapsed into dead silence, so I tried again, standing near her behind the stool.

'I've never been in this part of Scotland before.'

There was a three minute silence, during which she looked at the lowering sky out of the window. I thought she hadn't heard; but as it seemed a new technique of conversation I remained silent too.

'It's rather beautiful, isn't it?' she remarked still looking at the sky. I then remembered Tommy Lascelles telling me she always looks out of the window before making a decision. At this point Mr Maclay ambled up to speak to her, and the Queen Mother came into the room, dressed in a grey and pale pinkish red tartan, beautifully scented.* The Queen, who was wearing no scent, was dressed in a (?Stuart) tartan skirt, a little olive green tweed jacket and a complicated raspberry-coloured blouse; on her left lapel was a large thistle in diamonds, the flower being a mauve cairngorm. Her brogues were brilliantly polished and reflected the light.

Adeane came up with two sheets of typed paper and handed them to her. She seized them firmly, glanced at them and gave them back with the nod of a head-girl checking the afternoon's hockey team.

A SLIGHT NOTE ON THE QUEEN

By no stretch of the imagination can this Queen be called an historical figure. About the lower part of the face, which juts out more than one expects, she has a slight look of Queen Mary or Queen Charlotte†, but that is all. She looks a little careworn, with lines from nose to mouth, and could easily arouse one's compassion were it not for some element which is hard to define – smugness would be too crude and unkind a word – it is rather that she clearly does not *feel* inadequate. She is not shy, but she is clearly living at great tension, and does not give an impression of happiness. Her hands are thin and worried-looking. She is extremely animated, gesticulates when telling anecdotes, makes comic or pathetic faces, and simply cannot remain still. One feels that the spring is wound up very tight. She is brisk, jerky and a little ungraceful. She mimes stories – e.g. telling Mr Maclay and me about a certain keeper '*our* MacCardie' (as against one of Mr M's in Renfrewshire I gathered) who puts live frogs into your hands,

---

* The Duke of Edinburgh was at Balmoral at this time, but not present at lunch.

† Queen Charlotte (1744–1818), wife of George III.

THE QUEEN & PRINCESS MARGARET ON DEESIDE

she went through all the motions of holding a frog, and then flung up her arms and squeaked to show how one felt on receiving this frog from MacCardie's closed hands, with shut eyes. She suddenly knelt down on the stool in front of her and kicked up her heels. She is kind and business-like, and somewhat impersonal; her mother is far more feminine and knows how to simulate an interest in whoever she is talking to, whereas the Queen just talks, and sometimes is too busy trying to listen in to what her mother is saying across the table to catch on. Certain subjects – the removal of the Aberdeen sleeping train, which in despair I brought up at lunch – she pounces upon, because they interest her personally; but on the whole it is clockwork conversation, not at all difficult on either side, but not, on the other hand, memorable, interesting, or worth the paper it could be typed upon.

At lunch Queen Elizabeth made general conversation across her part of the table; but the Queen spent the cold beef course talking to Mr Maclay on her right and then turned to me, with perfect debutante manners for the next course: 'How are you getting on with the book?' etc. I mentioned a wish to see Abergeldie and before one could turn round she had sent the Equerry to telephone and arrange it; in these ways she seems efficient and helpful. Abergeldie has dry rot and may be pulled down: just before leaving the drawing room after lunch, (to gallop helter-skelter, head scarf and all, into the rain) she said to me with an almost maternal earnestness: 'Now please be careful at Abergeldie, and see you don't fall through the floor'.

Lunch over we returned to the drawing room, and Queen Elizabeth came over to talk to me. She has the very feminine gift of making one feel interesting and feel oneself. By some inflection in my voice when I said I hadn't been up before and was staying in a mill-house belonging to the Farquharsons etc. etc. etc. she gathered I didn't like Scotland and gleamed at me:

'We all have rather *fun* up here, you know, we do really.'

Of Queen Mary she said, in a mock whisper, finger on lips: 'Shshsh, the truth was she *didn't like Scotland*':

'When I first married,' continued the Queen Mother 'it was nothing but expeditions, expeditions, expeditions every single day. Of course Queen Mary had one of the most interesting minds I ever knew. *Everything* interested her – *Dior* or *whatever* it was – isn't that so?' turning to the Queen who was switched off on to stalking talk, and tapping her shoulder:

'I was saying, darling, that Granny was interested in everything, wasn't she?'

There was again a silence, while a curious furtive train of thought passed over the Queen['s] features.

'Well almost everything' she replied.

It had seemed to me earlier, at luncheon, (but this may be wishful thinking) that Queen Mary meant in some way nothing to the Queen; either as a person or a concept. It was almost as if she had never seen her, but why this should be so I cannot assess.

After lunch when they had dispersed Childs, the Queen's Page, who first came as a footman in 1927 showed me over the ground-floor and back premises of the house, including the rooms, most meticulously, in which I had already been: 'And this, Sir, is the drawing room. And this, Sir, is the dining room'. He was particularly anxious that I should know what forethought Queen Mary had shown about the servants: we went up a spiral staircase to a big attic room, in which were three cubicles and a drying-cupboard; also there was the young footman from the Tower door, nude with a towel round his waist:

'Now go back to your box, John, would you' said the Queen's page kindly. 'When I first came there was no drying cupboard and no bath up here. Queen Mary had them put in. We were six up here, in the boxes. A very jolly little community, I must say' he explained.

I asked him what uniforms they used to wear etc. He said that in those days you were chosen on height. (General gist was what a come down these dwarfs in battle-dress were.)

He then telephoned for a car to take me to Abergeldie (for which see separate sheet).

A CRATHIE SCHOOLMASTER: MR JOHN BROWN

On Saturday 24 August we drove out again in the direction of Mar and the Linn of Dee, for me to see Mr John Brown, for 30 years schoolmaster at Crathie, and now eighty-five years old. He lives in a cottage at Inverie. On the way I was more struck than before by the silver-birch-woods on either side of the road: the bark very white against the heather, which grows thickly on the hillsides beneath them, and is at this time of year of a very virulent puce colour, almost glazed, like a pattern on a chintz. The river Dee was rather more full and more brown, owing to the perpetual storms of rain, I presume.

Mr Brown came as schoolmaster to Crathie in 1901. He is a small old man with spectacles and an apple face, very tidy in brown tweed, and settled into the corner of the sofa of his snug little sitting room, dominated by a vast sideboard down one wall and an upright piano, with scottish reel-music open upon it, down another. He was a little wary, quite amusing, and very Scots in speech.

Queen Mary used to come to the school from time to time, often with Princess Mary, and ask the children to sing to her. He didn't know 'how much she really liked Scotland'; she would attend sales of work, and even sell at stalls. She would make expeditions to Mar Lodge. Mr Brown's great friend Arthur Grant, the ghillie, told him that one day the King had said 'we are going away next week, Arthur'; Grant replied what a pity it was, and the King said: 'Oh if I had anything to do with it I would never go south, but it's the Queen'; whereupon Grant remarked 'Then next time why don't you leave her at home??' Mr Brown's other bosom friend was Dr Stourton, the Minister: he looked after the books in the Balmoral library and used to discuss rare books with Queen Mary, and on one occasion had to give her a bible she said they hadn't got at Windsor but which Dr Stourton possessed and, unluckily for himself, showed her. After the children grew up she seemed to like Scotland less and less.

The Glassalt Shiel house, built by Queen Victoria, was not a cottage at all but quite a big house; by accident it had been built on Abergeldie land, where the boundary was vague, and so the Laird claimed it. It was full of 'beautiful crockery' (like the Quoich!) and there was an old resident housekeeper, an old body named Maisie Anderson. One day Queen Mary sorted out all the china there, locked it into a room and said: 'Now Maisie, I'm taking all this down to Windsor. It's no use here at all. But don't tell the King anything about it.'

'Mrs Simon' was the widow of Simon the merchant near Balmoral. The shop now belongs to Strachan, the Braemar grocer, who also owns shops in Ballater and in Aboyne. The Simons' shop in his day was run by the two old spinster Misses Simon, whom Queen Mary had known as a young woman and whom she would go and see when there. They sold everything and if they hadn't got what you wanted they got it for you; their prices were very high, and the Misses Simon retired with £22,000. The Balmoral household, under Queen Mary, finally decided that they were exorbitant: they even made the keepers' and ghillies' suits, but these never fitted well and were very expensive. The tailor was called Blake and couldn't make a coat to fit.

Mr Brown used to go to the dances in the castle, for the ghillies. Queen Mary danced beautifully and 'very queenly': she would send to ask you to dance with her; the King never danced, and at 12.00 he would appear at the top of the stair-case, which was the signal for the court to go to bed, but not the dancers who kept it up, till almost any hour.

He had never seen the Duke of Clarence but from what people said he would *not* have made as good a king as his brother.

He told me about the cairn on Craigowan, put for the fall of Sebastopol; and a good deal about the Presbyterian church and how Queen Victoria would com-municate in it, but her successors could not or would not – which was embar-rassing as the sequence of the services had to be re-arranged to give them time to make an exit.

In Crathie Church, before it was rebuilt (the old building being larger than the new one, apparently) there was a stained glass window put up by Queen Victoria to the memory of Dr Macleod.* His nephew Dr Norman Macleod, preaching there one day, had asked what had happened to this window, and talked of it at dinner at Balmoral. It transpired that it had been taken out and never put into the new building. Queen Mary came to see Mr Brown the next morning, 'very put about that anyone should have moved a royal gift, do you see', and asked him to find out where the window was. There was a rumour it was in the Manse, but Dr Stourton, as a real antiquarian, had been right through the manse and never seen it, and it turned out to be in a church in Glasgow, Dr Macleod's birthplace.

Mr Brown remembered Canon Dalton and Archbishop Lang† staying at the Castle. I had the impression he was holding out on one, and probably had a lot of local gossip, but he was very set on not getting his name into print, and was being shrewd and wary, and I was rather tired. Queen Mary was very good at putting people in their place; on some occasion when pictures were being moved in Balmoral, and the Queen was superintending this, some visitor arrived and put out his hand. This was not taken, as it was for the Queen to put out hers first. This seemed to please Mr Brown, as being very right and proper.

---

* Rev Norman Macleod (1812–1872), theologian, author, and social reformer, Moderator of the General Assembly of the Church in 1869; Queen Victoria placed two windows in Crathie Church in his memory.

† Canon John Dalton (1839–1931), tutor to George V and Canon of Windsor ; and Most Rev Cosmo Gordon Lang (1864–1945), Archbishop of Canterbury. Both stayed for some days each summer with George V.

*The meeting between James Pope-Hennessy and The Queen had been an un-
comfortable one. The following April Sir Alan Lascelles had dinner with her,
and told Pope-Hennessy what she said:*

> Then she asked, Did I think that J P.-H. would make a good job of
> Granny? To which I answered Yes, I was quite sure he would make
> a first-class job of it. Then she said that J P.-H. was difficult to know
> – he was so *cold*. (That's a good one, I thought). And I said he wasn't
> cold when you really got to know him, & that I liked him very much.
>
> You have to try again there. There must have been something
> superficially wrong for her to think that of you.[114]

*On 13 November Pope-Hennessy had a meeting with the Queen Mother at
Clarence House, but this was not recorded in the diary.*

TWENTY-TWO

LADY CYNTHIA COLVILLE

8 December

Pope-Hennessy now had a further interview with Lady Cynthia Colville. He had in fact noted some of her thoughts at the very beginning of his work, in 1955.

I seem to have made no notes of my previous talks with Cynthia, perhaps because nothing very sensational transpired.

I lunched with her again yesterday, 8 December 1957, and asked questions about routine. She told me:

1. The Women of the Bedchamber, of whom she was one (also Lady B. Dawkins etc.)* were always there; Ladies-in-Waiting as Lady Shaftesbury told me, were more ornamental and for big occasions. Women were fetched and carried by one-horse broughams, Ladies by two-horse broughams, the Mistress of the Robes† by an altogether more pompous vehicle.

2. Household prayers at 8.45. King and Queen breakfasted at 9.00. At 9.30 the Queen's bell went in the sitting room of the current Woman, who then went in with all her letters in her hand. She would find the Queen seated at her desk, having opened, as she always did, every letter addressed to herself no matter who from. Very few lunatics, many begging letters (these she would initial for the alternative charities to deal with); marvellous memory 'I thought I knew that handwriting' and it would be some woman who had written from Australia eleven years before. The Queen would deal efficiently and quickly with these and with those brought her by her Lady – 'Say

---

* Lady Bertha Dawkins (1866–1943), third daughter of 1st Earl of Lathom, married 1903, Major Arthur Dawkins (1865–1905). A Woman of the Bedchamber to Queen Mary as Princess of Wales from 1907–10, and as Queen from 1910–35. Extra Woman 1935–43.

† Evelyn, Duchess of Devonshire.

yes', 'say no' etc. The Lady would take everything away after the business was finished (seldom more than ½ hour), and then settle down to the work of answering, which often took hours. Household lunch of ten or twelve. The Queen would sometimes say that she wished to go out at 12.00 to the dentist or to a gallery at 2.45 and one always had to be there a few minutes before as she was very punctual, and if not she would have said 'about a quarter to three' and then arrive about eleven minutes to. King and Queen lunched alone. In the evening the Lady would often dine alone with the current Equerry, but if she had not too much work could slip off to dine at her own house. The King's Equerry could never never do that as the King or the Sovereign must always be provided with an educated person to hand to whom he can say 'ring up the Prime Minister at once' or some such.

This was the B.P. routine. In the country things were easier and one might sit with her in the afternoon under the awning at Sandringham; indeed at B.P. one did sit in the tent with 'that horrid parrot, a ferocious bird' and read to her. The tent was very comfortable with chaises-longues etc. At Marlborough House one ate with the Queen in the evening and talked or read to her. She was never idle, even if she was only stitching.

3. *Pages.* These stood one outside the door of the Queen's sitting room, one outside that of the (adjacent) King's study. If you wanted to see the Queen about a telephone message or some such you would go to the page at her door and he would go in and ask her if she could see you. You would then go in, and there she would be at her desk. Conversely she would ask the page to send for somebody she wanted to see.

4. There *was* a lot of standing but on the whole Q. Mary was very considerate.

5. Q. Mary used to speak of her mother's unpunctuality and tactlessness; several hours for the children in the carriage outside the Duchess of Cambridge's* apartments, late back to find the Duke fuming†, then wandering up to spend three quarters of an hour changing till he was almost *mad* with rage. She told Lady Cynthia that she well remembered when very young seeing her father throw a plate at her mother across the dining table. Always, Cynthia thinks, afraid of both parents in different

---

* HSH Princess Augusta of Hesse-Cassel (1797–1889), married 1818, HRH The Prince Adolphus, 1st Duke of Cambridge (1774–1850). She was Queen Mary's grandmother.

† Presumably the Duke of Teck.

ways. Duchess of Teck so proud of her 'Beauty Boys' as perhaps to make Princess May feel unwanted?

6. *Duke of Kent and Poppy Baring*[*]. Various people, including Cynthia, whose cousin in some way she was, were consulted about this. Peggy Crewe helped to stop it. The reason was that it was felt the public would not accept her as a queen or her child as a sovereign should the older sons be wiped out. She had had several love-affairs and was 'living with' the Duke of Kent out of sympathy for him. Lady Elizabeth Bowes-Lyon was alright because she did descend from the old Kings of Scotland and one of them had even been murdered at Glamis. Princess Marina[†] such a relief.

---

[*] Prince George (Duke of Kent) had been in love with Helen 'Poppy' Baring (1901–79), elder daughter of Sir Godfrey Baring, Bt, for some years. In 1928 she married William 'Peter' Thursby.

[†] Princess Marina of Greece married the Duke of Kent in 1934.

1958

TWENTY-THREE

HON DAISY BIGGE

Connaught Square *or* 'Between Ourselves'

February

Pope-Hennessy visited the Hon Margaret 'Daisy' Bigge (1885–1977). She was the younger daughter of Lord Stamfordham (1849–1931), who had been in royal service since 1880, and had served as Private Secretary to Queen Victoria from 1895, and to Edward VII and George V until his death in office in 1931.

On the advice of Tommy Lascelles I wrote, in January 1958, to Miss Daisy Bigge (Hon: Margaret Bigge), who lives at 25 Connaught Square. Miss Bigge is the (?) elder [in fact younger] of the two daughters of Lord Stamfordham, and during the last year of her father's life is believed to have worked so closely with him as to have been virtually the Private Secretary herself.

I went to see her at six o'clock on a misty February evening and stayed with her for precisely an hour, and very interesting it was. Miss Bigge lives in a comfortable, newly painted house in Connaught Square, an old parlourmaid opening the door; she herself at that moment occupying the L-shaped drawing room on the first floor, the door of which on to the staircase was kept permanently open during our talk – perhaps because of her eyesight. It was a cheerfully light room, with a blazing fire, a sherry decanter and a glass on a small occasional table, armchairs, a desk, books etc. Miss Bigge would seem to be about 70: a shortish, stalwart old woman, with angular firm movements (sitting with a hand on each knee, or twisted round raising her head to peer at one); dressed in black, with fuzzy grey hair twisted into a bun at the nape of the neck. Her face that of an intelligent man with a strong profile; her eyes, poor thing, veiled in cataract for which she has just had an unsuccessful operation. They look glaucous and grey, like cods' eyes and she says she can see almost nothing with them. Her attitude was welcoming and genial.

'Well, *you've* got a difficult task haven't you? Impossible I should say.'

She settled me down in a chair with sherry, seating herself near the fire, and looking now into the fire itself, now round at me. We had a little desultory conversation and then I asked her whether she could help me to assess how much or how little Queen Mary knew of what was going on politically. Did the King tell her everything, or nothing? What had Lord Stamfordham thought of the scope or range of her knowledge of contemporary affairs?

'Well she certainly didn't know everything. In fact she was not told much. But she would always be sending my father little notes, you know, saying "do ask the King to do this or that, but don't say it came from me". She was terrified of the King you know, whatever people tell you to the contrary. They used to say *he* was hen-picked but it wasn't true. She was frightened to death of him.'

We talked of how she would never stand up to him over his shouting at the children: 'And if she had done it once, he would have given it up. He just didn't know it upset them, but *she* did.'

I mentioned that the Duke of Windsor had called her a moral coward:

'How extraordinary. I wasn't goin' to say it, but it's true. I well remember my father used to say to me: "The Queen is the biggest moral coward I've ever met in the whole of my life".'

I suggested that all royalties dislike awkward situations and shovel them off on to others, to which she assented.

'But with the Queen it was worse than that. Once somebody had retired, she never went near them again.'

'Well, you know, she did go to see Lady Bertha [Dawkins] when she moved into Kensington Palace on her retirement.' I ventured loyally;

'I've no doubt why she went there, once – just to see how the rooms had been arranged' Miss Bigge answered tartly. 'Her behaviour to poor Derek Keppel* was dreadful. Do you know that when he was dying she never enquired or sent a message; Bridget had to write to her herself to ask her to send a message. And Derek had idolised the King and Queen – oh to a maddening extent we all thought – ye know if one said "look the Queen's got her hat on crooked" or something of that sort he would be horrified and say we were incredibly fortunate to have the

---

* Hon Sir Derek Keppel (1863–1944), Equerry-in-Waiting to George V as Duke of York 1893–1901, Equerry-in-Ordinary to him as Prince of Wales 1901–10, and as King 1910–12, Master of the Household 1912–36. He married 1898, Hon Bridget Harbord (1870–1951), seventh daughter of 5th Lord Suffield. She was an Extra Lady-in-Waiting to the then Duchess of Cornwall and York on the Colonial Tour of 1901.

privilege of being near Her Majesty at all – that sort of stuff – drove us all mad, poor Derek; but there it was and when he got ill – nothing.'

She was warming to her theme and I mentioned Bricka and 'another milestone gone'.

'Typical, typical. I don't believe she was ever fond of any human being in the whole of her life. She wasn't capable of it. The King was very warm-hearted.'

We talked a little of the Duke of Windsor, of his intelligence and the waste of his life. Of the Duke of Kent, too: 'I always said what luck he died a hero's death, otherwise …' We brushed lightly on his drug-addiction.[*] She then mentioned that, 'romancer' though he was, the Duke of Gloucester *had* had an awful time as a boy, being sent down to Broadstairs in the house of Sir Francis Laking[†], to go to a day school as he was delicate; Sir F. Laking being a notorious drug addict, like many doctors.

Of doctors:

'You never saw Sir Stanley Hewlitt [in fact Hewett][‡]? Yes, he's dead. Well he'd have told you no end, old Stanley. He used to say "Queen Mary is a *real tough guy*". And whenever he came to tell her one of the children was ill all she would say was "Tiresome! tiresome!".'

We also spoke – nothing new here – of Princess Victoria's intimacy with the King and the daily telephone conversations which Queen Mary so much resented.[§]

Of Prince John she said he was a very bad case, and that she was certain Princess Alice had tried to minimise it to me by saying he was a harmless epileptic who

---

[*] In the 1920s the Duke of Kent became a drug addict due to the attentions of 'Kiki' Preston, known as 'the girl with the silver syringe'. His elder brother, the Prince of Wales, rescued him, an act of kindness never forgotten by Queen Mary. This was not mentioned in *Queen Mary*.

[†] Sir Francis Laking (1847–1914). In 1912 Prince Henry was sent to live at Laking's home in Broadstairs, York Gate House, Laking giving his opinion that Broadstairs was a health-giving place. In those days he had to wear splints on his legs, and in the summer of 1911, Laking allowed him to give up wearing them at night. Prince Henry went to school at St Peter's Court.

[‡] Sir Stanley Hewett (1880–1954), Deputy-Surgeon Apothecary to George V 1911, then Surgeon Apothecary to George V, Queen Mary, Queen Alexandra and the Prince of Wales. He retired in 1949. He was one of the doctors in charge during the long illness of George V in 1928/9.

[§] The story is told that Princess Victoria thought she had been connected to the King, and said, 'Hallo, you old trout!' The telephonist was forced to say, 'I am sorry, Your Royal Highness, His Majesty is not yet on the line.'

had been treated wrong. We spoke of his 'dear little home' in Wolferton Wood, and I had said that Queen Mary had taken such trouble, choosing wall papers. 'But that was exactly the part of it she enjoyed, choosing wallpapers. She'd have loved that.'

'The Queen got much better looking as she got older. When I first remember her she could only be described as – well, really, as frumpish.'

'Rather German-looking, you mean?'

'Very German-looking. And *frumpish*.'

Meals at Balmoral were often very uncomfortable, if you happened to be (as Miss Bigge often was) seated next to the man who was seated next to the Queen. 'He'd be holding himself ready to answer her when she spoke to him, so he couldn't speak to you. And then very often she wouldn't turn to him at all during the whole meal, if she'd nothing she wanted to say'.

'But then, of course, she *did* very well, didn't she? The public all loved her. They thought and they still think her wonderful. That's going to make it difficult for you, because you don't want to debunk her completely.'

'Of course not, but I want to present a faithful portrait.'

At another point in the conversation she declared vehemently: 'Queen Mary was the greatest *pincher* I ever knew. She was always pinching and screwing. The Prince of Wales, though, was tremendously generous, until Mrs Simpson turned *him* into a pincher, too.'

Princess Louise, Duchess of Fife, was really a mental deficient. Her daughter the present Duchess* – 'oh you've seen her?' – is chiefly animated by a hatred of the *whole* Royal Family past and present – 'she just hates 'em all'. 'Nice lot, aren't they, when you come to think about it? Nice family!'

'Some of them loved her though' (referring to the *suite*) 'Claud did, for one. Have you seen Claud?'†

'I have, but Lord Claud didn't strike me as really *loving* Queen Mary. He said she was very parsimonious about the food at Marlborough House.'

'So she was, as I say, a terrible *pincher*.'

At several points in the conversation Miss Bigge emphasised that it was all 'between ourselves'. 'I shouldn't like to be quoted, you know.'

---

*   HRH Princess Arthur of Connaught (see above).

†   Lord Claud Hamilton (see above).

I finished my sherry and we talked of cataract, Williamson Noble[*] and so on, and tried vainly to telephone a radio-taxi. I began to go downstairs and we stood for moment on the first-floor landing outside the drawing room door.

'I'll be awfully interested to know how you're going to deal with it all. It's an almost impossible task, I'd say. How well Harold Nicolson did though, because he didn't conceal anything. But then the King was a really *loveable* man.'

'Which you feel couldn't be said of *my* subject?'

'No. I was very *proud* to know Queen Mary, I *admired* her; but I wasn't *fond* of her. No, I didn't love her.'

She lent over the banisters as I walked downstairs, smiling:

'You see – she *wouldn't let you.*'

On this authentic note I unlatched the front door and let myself out into the glimmering street.

---

[*] Frederick Williamson-Noble (1889–1969), an ophthalmic surgeon, who described a practical bifocal contact lens in 1950, and was fitted with a pair three years later.

TWENTY-FOUR

THE MARQUESS AND MARCHIONESS OF CAMBRIDGE

'But oh those poor poor eyes a piteous sight'

12 February

George, 2ⁿᵈ Marquess of Cambridge (1895–1981), was Queen Mary's nephew, the elder son of Prince Adolphus, Duke of Teck. He became 1ˢᵗ Marquess of Cambridge when those of George V's royal relations who still had German titles renounced them. These included Tecks, Schleswig-Holsteins and Battenbergs. In 1923 he married Dorothy Hastings (1899–1988), second daughter of Hon Osmond Hastings, and they had one daughter.

The Cambridges lived at Little Abington, near Cambridge, but also had a London flat, and spent quite a lot of time in London in those days.

Pope-Hennessy chose the title for this interview from an extract from the letters of Empress Frederick:

> *I went down to pay Aunt Mary Teck a visit who was staying with the young Tecks and I saw the poor Baby – it's such a sweet little thing ... but oh those poor poor eyes a piteous sight! I think it sees a little with one eye, but they are all scarred and disfigured! I really felt inclined to cry!*[115]

In February 1958 I wrote to Lord Cambridge, the son of Queen Mary's eldest brother Prince Dolly, to ask whether I could see him. He very courteously made a special journey to London and gave me a rendezvous at Dolphin Square at 3.00 p.m. on Wednesday 12 February.

Born with the eye affliction to which the Empress Frederick refers in the above letter [*now in the Kronberg Archives*], the 2ⁿᵈ Marquess of Cambridge would, but for the 1917 change of royal titles, be third Duke of Teck. Both these facts are very evident when one sees him for the first time: for his eyes and eyelids look mutilated, while the whole head and bearing is very reminiscent of the Teck/ Württemberg line, as we know it from pictures and photographs.

Lord Cambridge was seated on a bench or sofa in the dingy hall of Keyes House, Dolphin Square. He took me up in the lift, and along the really squalid corridors of that building to a small lock-up flat. We sat down on either side of an electric fire, in armchairs; there was a low bookcase (out of which he later took and lent me Sir George Arthur's sketch of Q. Mary's life*) some of the military prints which he has collected all his life ('uniforms are my line o' country') and a table.

At sixty-two Ld Cambridge is spare, military looking and erect, leaning slightly forward and with his head a little cocked to one side, apparently so as to see better. He has an eagle head and face, though in a very gentle version; he is light-coloured, pinkish, with balding hair and a little moustache; dressed in a neat brown small patterned tweed. He is a man of the greatest straightforwardness, with a charming courteous manner and a low heavy voice. When I made to go after an hour and a half he detained me; at 5.00 Lady Cambridge† came bustling in, and we stayed talking altogether some three hours.

Like his wife, Lord Cambridge was evidently devoted to Queen Mary, and took her more naturally than either her children or the remnants of her entourage seem to me to have done. The nearest equivalent would be the attitude of Mrs Bill, Prince John's nurse (*see Sandringham account*). He called her quite simply 'my aunt' throughout our conversation. I remembered that, in Oslo, the Crown Prince had said how much easier she was with nephews than with her own children, and here was clearly a case in point. The only awkwardness during this very enjoyable talk was that caused by one's uncertainty as to where or at what Lord Cambridge was looking; and with which eye if either. The right eye is pale blue, the left squinting and cloudy like a cold poached egg; the eyelids and skin along the top of the cheek bones looks scalded and inflamed, even orange in places. However he reads a great deal and seemed to see all that was necessary.

The conversation did not proceed from topic to topic but wove its way back and forth, so that it will be easiest to summarise the points:

---

* *Queen Mary* by Sir George Arthur (Thornton Butterworth, 1935). Sir George Arthur, 4th Bt (1860–1946), had been Personal Private Secretary to Lord Kitchener. He penned a number of contemporary royal biographies, of figures such as Queen Victoria, Queen Alexandra and George V.

† Dorothy Hastings (see main note).

THE MARQUESS OF CAMBRIDGE

1. *The Duchess of Teck*, 'my grandmother'. Usual comments on her extravagance and improvidence – 'She'd take money from anybody at any time.
Why Grand-Daddy – my Westminster grandfather* – was always slipping
her a thousand or two.' His father had told him that as boys travelling with
her on the train from Mortlake to London they were always obsessed with
the worry of how to get her out of the carriage if there was an accident. He
thought the Duke of Teck had no money and was very tactless with the
English royalties. There was 'no love lost' between Queen Victoria and the
Duchess of Teck.

2. *The Duchess of Cambridge*†. 'My father and all of them *hated* her.' Her
teas were very stingy. *Aunt Augusta*‡ was a great figure but exceedingly
mean, and when the young Tecks went to stay with her at Strelitz from
Vienna [where Pce Dolly was en poste] Princess Dolly would take enough
supplies of food to last the visit out. Lord Cambridge remembers her in
Mecklenburg House.§

3. *Florence.* The one thing Princess May hated about Florence were the funer-
als going through the dark streets at night-time. They frightened her.

4. *Q. Mary and the past.* Neither Queen Mary 'nor any of 'em' talked much
about their childhood, their parents or the past. It had been a happy
childhood, but they never referred to it. He thought the reason was 'she
had no time'. 'Far too busy, don't you see, doing things – duties; shopping,
moving furniture.'

5. *Q. Mary and friends.* From this last remark he led on to ask if I had noticed that 'my aunt *had no friends*'. Again she had no time to have personal

---

* Lord Cambridge's mother was Lady Margaret Grosvenor, 4th daughter of 1st Duke of Westminster.

† HRH Princess Augusta of Hesse-Cassel (1797–1889), married in 1818, HRH Prince Adolphus,
Duke of Cambridge (1774–1850), 7th son of King George III; mother of Princess Augusta.

‡ HRH Princess Augusta of Cambridge (1822–1916), daughter of the Duke and Duchess of
Cambridge. She married 1843, HRH Grand Duke Friedrich Wilhelm of Mecklenburg-Strelitz
(1819–1904). She and Queen Mary carried on a spirited correspondence. The Grand Duchess
was wildly reactionary in her views on most subjects. Pope-Hennessy wrote: 'Aunt Augusta,
we may recall, did not share Queen Victoria's sane views on the subject of morganatic blood.'
[*Queen Mary*, p. 401].

§ After the Duchess of Cambridge's death, in 1889, the Grand Duchess took an 18th century
London home in Buckingham Gate and called it Mecklenburg House.

friends, nor did she feel the need of them. All her acquaintanceships could be traced to some logical purpose – common interest in collecting jade etc.

6.   *Prince Dolly* was by far her favourite brother. He thinks it was Dolly, not as I have been told Frank*, who started her off collecting. They looked rather alike and were very close.

7.   *The brothers.* The two elder loathed and bullied Prince Alge – it was alright when he grew up. They thought him rather fat and that, as the youngest, his mother spoiled him. He had a different nurse to the others and the servants put them against each other.

8.   *Prince Frank* was great fun and like his mother very extravagant. He was perfectly dressed, like a tailor's dummy. When he came to call, even when almost bankrupt he always had a very smart electric brougham, or, failing that, the taxi he would hire for a whole day, waiting outside the door. Ld Cambridge told me the same as Pss. Alice about Lady Kilmorey[†] and the jewels[‡] – most of which she kept. Prince Frank was entirely unrepentant and always began betting and running debts all over again as soon as his previous commitments had been paid. It was an age in which such people expected their debts to be paid for them. Even Prince Dolly would send his father-in-law his bills.

9.   'Duty' was in his view the whole mainspring of his aunt's life. Included in this was devotion to the monarchy. This sense of duty precluded her from understanding the Abdication: 'Had she fallen in love with a barman she might have suffered but she would never have given way or abdicated her position'.

10. He supposed his aunt and uncle were *not* good parents, nor did the children have a happy childhood. They were horribly rough children, always fighting and squabbling amongst themselves.

---

*   Queen Mary's brother, Prince Francis of Teck.
†   Ellen Constance Baldock (1858–1920), daughter of Edward Baldock, MP for Shrewsbury. Married 1881, 3rd Earl of Kilmorey (1842–1915). She was Prince Frank's mistress, and had been the mistress of Edward VII. Her 2nd son, Hon Francis Needham (1886–1955), was ADC to HRH The Duke of Connaught from 1919–21. He rose to be a Major-General in the Grenadier Guards.
‡   These were the Cambridge emeralds, consisting of eight large cabochon emeralds.

11. His mother used to say the smell of cooking in *York Cottage* was perfectly revolting, it pervaded all the rooms. Also the discomfort of having to race, or to wait, for the few bathrooms, made staying there thoroughly uncomfortable.

12. *Duke of Clarence.* None of them ever mentioned the Duke of Clarence or the first engagement [see (4) above].

13. There is a book by an ex-butler who was White Lodge footman which he is going to send me.* He lent me Sir G. Arthur's book on Q. Mary and a book called *The Land of Teck*†. He thinks that if one reads around in the Arthur book it might yield oddments, since he knew her so early; he believes that it was Arthur who would take the boys out to Florence from school [I don't – J.P.-H.].

14. I shall have difficulty dealing with the subject of Queen Mary's relations with her mother-and-sisters-in-law. Princess Victoria was a dreadful trouble-maker etc.

15. I am *wrong* in thinking his grandfather Teck had good taste. They had a lot of White Lodge furniture and it was dreadful stuff: Maples mostly. The Duke would buy Chinese pots and vases which were now worthless. The photos of White Lodge show how perfectly ghastly the interior was.

16. *Queen Alexandra* also had abominable taste – Maples again – lots of little white painted shelves and alcoves covered with oddments were *her* ideal. The bank sent her new batches of £5 notes every month, and when she died about £2,000 was found in various hatboxes. She would send them out indiscriminately in answer to appeals, but never quite finish one bundle, and when the new one came would chuck the old one aside and start afresh.

---

* John James, *Memoirs of a House Steward* (Bury, 1949). In 1943 James was in touch with Lord Wigram about the possibility of including conversations he claimed to have had with the spirits of Queen Alexandra, George V, Princess Louise, Duchess of Argyll and others. As the King's Assistant Private Secretary, Alan Lascelles, put it: 'I've no idea if the law gives one any protection against spiritualists publishing the alleged utterances of the ghosts of one's departed relatives, … I am quite sure the King would [resent it], especially as many of the *obiter dicta* attributed to his father, grandmother and great-aunt are damned nonsense.' [Duff Hart-Davis (ed.), *King's Counsellor* (Weidenfeld & Nicolson, 2006), p. 122].

† S. Baring-Gould, *The Land of Teck and Its Neighbours* (John Lane, 1911).

17. I ought to see old Walker*, of the Walker Galleries in Bond Street. He is 93 and Q. Mary had been there all her life.

18. She enjoyed *Badminton*; no, she was *not* bored there. She went through everything in the house, labelling it and reading family papers. She made it her business when there to visit personally every factory [connected with the war effort] which was too small for the King to visit. Her servants behaved abominably there and they were very difficult, greedy and spoiled. It drove his sister [the Duchess of Beaufort] almost mad when the Marlborough House party first arrived.

19. *The Ophir cruise*. I should try to unearth and read Prince Dolly's letters to his wife reporting on this. They would almost certainly be useful to me. He deposited them with Morshead† himself.

20. She never appeared frightened during air-raid alerts or when the bomb fell near Badminton. She would descend to the shelter holding King George's barometer, which she clutched throughout a raid as a kind of talisman. Also other little private possessions would be brought down with her.

21. In her reticent, indeed secretive, way she would correspond with many foreign royal relatives and never tell any of the family here about it at all.

22. He had been at Rumpenheim‡ as a boy. It was a 'strange place', all divided into apartments, and then you would all meet for meals in the central block.

23. She was extremely kind, and very thorough in her kindness and charities and ways of helping people.

24. Of *Prince Frank* again: 'My father used to say he dreaded doing Christmas shopping with Uncle Frank. He'd say "come on we'll buy the children some presents" and he'd get us beautiful things and then it would all be found on my father's account afterwards. And when Uncle Frank gave presents he *did* give presents.'

25. 'My grandmother, I always think, would have given away somebody else's last shilling in charity.'

---

* Augustus Walker (1868–1965) of Walker's Gallery (picture dealers), of 118 New Bond Street, London, which he founded in about 1890. The son of a tailor, he ended with a fortune.

† Sir Owen Morshead (1893–1977), Librarian at Windsor Castle 1926–58.

‡ Schloss Rumpenheim, near Offenbach, summer residence of Landgrave Wilhelm of Hesse-Cassel, where royalty gathered *en masse*.

Following this meeting Lord Cambridge was in touch with Pope-Hennessy about military prints: 'It is not a very scientific form of study but it gives me a lot of amusement, and doubtless keeps one from other vices.'[116]

LADY CAMBRIDGE

The Marchioness of Cambridge was the wife of the Marquess (see above).

Lady Cambridge rang the door bell, and came bustling into the little room – longish waved grey hair, maroon velvet hat, fur coat neckerchief tightly twisted. 'Being a loving wife I've got an egg and two rashers for yr breakfast' she announced flinging a paper bag on to the table and herself into a chair. 'I say he's awfully young isn't he?' she asked, looking quizzical and began to chain-smoke Craven A cigarettes. She is a highly amusing, histrionic woman, a good mimic and with a warm easy manner. She also loved Queen Mary and spoke in a cataract of affectionate enthusiasm about her, but always seeing the comic or odd aspect. *Her chief points:*

1. Queen Mary had the supreme advantage over all other members of the Family of having been poor and understanding what having no money meant. Hence her presents were always carefully thought out, very personal, very practical. She knew exactly what you were liable to need.

2. She and Queen Mary used to sit and talk in the garden at Badminton; she would read to Queen Mary (but read so badly she wasn't often asked to do so). Her choice of books was often surprising: e.g. absorbed by the *History of the Rifle Brigade* written by Lady C's brother*, which Lady C herself 'wouldn't dream of reading though I believe he wrote it quite well considering'.

3. 'This you mustn't put in the book – but I loved the way that when she sent or brought you flowers they always came from her own vases. She never bought flowers at the florist. She'd go round picking them out of the vases in her rooms, so that often they were dead the day after she brought them.'

---

* *The Rifle Brigade in the Second World War, 1939–45* (Gale & Polden, 1950), by Lt-Colonel Robin Hastings (1917–90).

4. The present Queen has certain similarities with Q.M. – jaw, look of her, manner of concentrating on the person she talks to, love of acquiring information, phenomenal memory.

These, I think, were the main points, but it was the general attitude of affection which made it important. She ended by saying would I come and stay whenever I liked, if it would be a help, although their house is small.

TWENTY-FIVE

Pension Iris *or* 'Why aren't you taking notes ?'

7 March

In March 1958 Pope-Hennessy went to visit Miss Mary L. Chromy (b. 1866), who had been governess to Lady Glenconner. Elizabeth Glenconner was the second wife of 2ⁿᵈ Lord Glenconner (1899–1983). She was the daughter of Lt-Colonel Evelyn Powell, Grenadier Guards, and married Lord Glenconner in 1935.

Miss Chromy was then living at the Pension Iris, Bergmannstrasse 10, Graz, in Austria.

Having reached Graz in heavy snow at midnight, Friday 7 March, and stayed at the old Erzherzog Johann, I set off with Rudolf in the Volkswagon to find the Pension Iris, to call on Elizabeth Glenconner's old governess, Miss Chromy.

The Pension Iris is situated on the ground floor of a grim-looking residential building, reared presumably in the '70's at the corner of two wide, mild streets near the Park to the north of the centre of Graz. Behind the high front door, which is kept on the latch, is a stone entrance hall which manages to be at once dank and musty. To the left of this a chipped enamel plate announces PENSION IRIS. We rang the bell and an oldish skivvy with a broom snatched my visiting card and hurried off, after ushering me into the parlour:

'Die Frau Professor *Chromy*? Ja, ja! Kommen sie herein.'

The parlour – which it transpired is the dining room of the establishment – was rather like a convent parlour, with a long central table covered in rust-coloured velour, chairs along the wall, some engravings, and a tin stove. Near the window, sagging slightly on a chair, was a very old gentleman with a white beard, who was wearing a little grey-and-green Austrian jacket. He said 'Goodmorning' very politely to which I replied. Presently there was a sound of shuffling feet, the door opened, and Miss Chromy advanced, holding my visiting card in her left hand, with some flat, illustrated literature about Queen Mary under her arm.

Miss Chromy, who later told me she was born in 1866 and is thus 91 years old, shows astoundingly few signs of age. She is short and soft and squat-looking, with horn glasses which she takes off when she does not need them, and grey hair. She wore a dark red woollen dress and matching cardigan. Her eyes are extremely shrewd, rather like a clever vole or field-mouse. The only real symptom of her considerable age is the puffiness which the very old get about the face – those very old I mean who do not go very thin: the quality of a windfall apple that has lain for some time in the grass.

'Mr Pope-Hennessy?'

'Yes, did Elizabeth write to you to say I was coming?'

'What?' I repeated my remark louder thinking she was deaf; I afterwards discovered she is no more deaf than I am but simply wanted to talk and not to be interrupted or thrown off her selected track; she had prepared a talk about Queen Mary which was as lucid and well-planned as a history lesson.

'Of course Lady Glenconner wrote to me' she replied almost snubbingly. 'Now let us sit down (she took the head of the table with me on her left). Lady Glenconner tells me you are writing about Queen Mary? Well I thought you might like to know there is this book about her' (spreading out the illustrated Peacocke brochure* on the table). 'Oh you know it already? I thought you would, but all the same I want you to look at the pictures with me' and so on. Her comments on the illustrations were admirable. 'I knew Queen Mary first in Budapest' she said unexpectedly, and went on to explain how she had nursed there after (I gathered) the First War. 'Hungarian ladies of the best families in Budapest used to come and help. They knew nothing about nursing of course. They just would put something white over their heads and come and wash the patients. But they meant well.'

At this point we were interrupted by the voice of the old gentleman by the window, saying in cultivated tones:

'Am I in the way, sitting here? If you'd rather I was not listening I can return to my room.'

I looked over and began to say: 'of course not', whereupon Miss Chromy's eye flashed: 'Don't get involved with *him*' she said at the top of her voice: 'he's a dreadful BORE.' This not unnaturally wounded the old gentleman who began muttering: 'She calls me a bore, she calls me a bore' and then left the room. Miss Chromy afterwards said he was a *particularly* nice man, who had been Hungarian

---

*   *Queen Mary – A Pictorial Biography* by Marguerite D. Peacocke (Pitkin, 1948).

ambassador in Rome, lost all his estates to the communists and was kept in the Pension Iris by his five daughters: 'he never had a son, you see.'

Miss Chromy then told me that when Q.M. was in Budapest she had had several chats with her, and that she (Q.M.) had summoned or had had summoned all the representatives of her morganatic grandmother's family of Rhedey.

'The Queen's grandmother was Hungarian*, you know. Oh you do know that?'

She then told me that Q. Mary had inherited from a German business man the house at Petersham which she turned into a summer holiday place for 'twelve professional ladies' (this was what Q.M. herself called 'my governess's home': J.P.-H.). She had had the pleasure and the honour of going there three summers running, introduced by Mrs Leo Rothschild†. When Queen Mary visited it the first time she had come straight up to Miss Chromy, who was standing in the drawing room in a semi-circle with the other professional ladies, and said 'Ah but I know you already, from Budapest'. This made the other ladies very jealous of Miss Chromy, but Miss Chromy didn't mind *that*. The drawing room was beautifully furnished with gilt chairs upholstered in pink brocade with roses on it, and the pictures were all full-lengths of members of the Royal Family, the biggest one on a wall by itself being the portrait of Queen Mary as Duchess of York. 'She was an angel of goodness' Miss Chromy continued. 'Once, when I was at Petersham again, and the Queen was at Balmoral, a cardboard box arrived at the house. And what do you think was in it? Twelve little bunches of white heather, with a card in her own handwriting saying 'for My Guests'. Wasn't that sweet? Oh but she was like that, an angel of goodness and kindness. Well, now, there's Queen Mary for you. Now Lady Glenconner tells me you are also interested in the von Hügel family. Why?'

I explained that Q.M.'s aunt was a Baroness von Hügel‡ of Schloss Reinthal, which I had come to Graz to see.

'I have never heard of those von Hügels. But they must have been related to *my* von Hügels in England – I call them mine because they were almost like a family to me do you see?' She then outlined the family briefly, including Baron

---

* Claudine, Countess Rhédey (1814–41), married 1835, Alexander, Duke of Württemberg (1804–85).

† Marie Perugia (1862–1937), daughter of Achille Perugia, a Trieste merchant. Married 1881, Leopold de Rothschild (1845–1917), English banker and racehorse-trainer.

‡ HSH Princess Amalie of Teck (1838–93), married Paul, Baron von Hügel (1835–97). She was the younger sister of the Duke of Teck.

von Hügel's three daughters Gertrude, Thekla and (?) Ursula*. 'The father was very deaf' she continued 'and I had a particular aversion to him. I always found myself sitting next to him at meals, and having to shout into a very large, white, *bloodless* ear – I can see it now' she chuckled, 'large, white and bloodless. I can see everything in the past *perfectly*.' She then made me guess her age. 'I have it all up here in my head' tapping her forehead 'everything I have ever seen, and believe me I have had a wonderful life, and I bless God for it. Of course Queen Mary had a wonderful memory herself. Are they trained to it do you think, or do they train each other? Now I wonder what *your* memory is like?' She looked sharply at me as though it was obviously unlikely to be very good. 'I notice you don't take notes of what I'm saying. But I hope you're going to write it all down. It's all very interesting, what I'm telling you.'

This approach, so diametrically opposed to any of my previous experiences of such interviews ('between ourselves I always thought', 'I don't want to be quoted, but' 'I may as well tell you but please don't' etc. etc.) startled me very much; it was her good historical sense, the pedagogic note, I supposed, coming out.

When we had dealt at some considerable length with the von Hügels I said (which was true) that I must reluctantly go as I had to find Reinthal† and get to Vienna that night. But first I had promised Elizabeth to find out just how Miss Chromy was.

'You can tell her that I am getting rather shaky and that I'm getting old. But I'm quite alright. This place isn't bad, some very nice people here, and I go to Vienna for Christmas and from time to time to see my brother; he's 82. That's why I left England, to be near him; but Vienna is much too noisy. I couldn't possibly live *there*. So I live here and make the effort of the journey to Vienna. Elizabeth is an angel, she writes to me so much and she sends me tea; Austrian tea is disgusting, undrinkable.'

'Is the food here alright, Miss Chromy?'

---

* Perhaps Miss Chromy was right and Pope-Hennessy should have taken notes. This was Friedrich von Hügel (1852–1925), the Austrian Catholic lay philosopher and writer. He moved to England in 1867, and in 1873 married Lady Mary Herbert, daughter of Sidney, 1st Baron Herbert of Lea, the eminent politician. They lived at Vicarage Gate in London, and the daughters were Gertrude (1877–1915), Hildegarde (1879–1926), and Thekla (1886–1970).

† Schloss Reinthal, home of the von Hügel family, in the Styrian Hills, near Graz.

'Oh it isn't bad. We have three meatless days a week, just vegetables. But it isn't at all bad. Now come and see my room, I'm just through here next to the dining room.'

Miss Chromy's bed-sitting room was as touching as her whole personality itself. It is on the ground-floor, looking out into the wide snowy street. In the corner beneath the window is a very white bed with a white cotton bedspread, and pinned against the wall all round it a wide strip of peasant embroidery – white with crimson horses and figures in a kind of peasant cross-stitch. On another wall is a tall white painted wardrobe with a row of apples sitting along the top; on another a bookcase; and so on. In the centre of the room a small deal table covered with papers and notes and books, and a little hard chair with a cushion where she sits by preference to work and read. Until very recently she gave English lessons, and she still corrects a University professor's English articles:

'A very cultivated man, Professor Christian*. Oh he comes here often and often to talk with me, I see him nearly every day.'

I had been there some eighty minutes, and though I longed to stay I really had to try to leave. This was rather agonising, as she so obviously enjoyed talking about England and her English pupils and dead friends. She showed me a photo of Emma and Sebastian Yorke† on the bookcase, and then burrowed into the wardrobe.

'I want to give you something' she said very sweetly, retrieving a black wine bottle from among several on the bottom shelf. 'I don't think you'll have ever had it before. Now drink it up, it can't hurt you. It's beer-liquor, I make it myself. Rather delicious, don't you think. Have some more.'

The liqueur was in fact awfully good, very sweet; made of pure water, black beer and some wine substance and something else I forget what.

'Now here is something *else* that might interest you' she said coaxingly.

This proved to be a very large photo of Oswald Birley's portrait of Mary Roxburgh[e]‡, looking more like a simpering Snow Goose than ever, with an affectionate inscription on it. 'Her father was ambassador in Paris, you know.'

---

*   Professor Christian, of the University of Graz.
†   Hon Emma Tennant (1937–2017), novelist, daughter of 2nd Lord Glenconner and his wife Elizabeth; married 1957, Sebastian Yorke (b. 1934); divorced 1962.
‡   Lady Mary Crewe-Milnes (1915–2014), daughter of 1st Marquess of Crewe. Married 1935, 9th Duke of Roxburghe (1913–74). Divorced 1953. Painted by Sir Oswald Birley (1880–1952).

I explained I had written his life and wd. send her a copy.* This seemed to give pleasure, and she again urged me to make notes about Q. Mary's heather and about the von Hügels, whom everyone had forgotten but her. I asked her if on the whole she had happy days in the Pension and she said yes she read a lot and then there were these very nice people like that old gentleman who was so distinguished but had no son.

It was really horrid saying goodbye to this perfectly charming old lady, who held my hand for five minutes in both of hers, and treated me as if I were the last link she had with England and the past. She thanked me again and again for coming until I nearly broke down and cried. It is clearly a very lonely life, and a terrible contrast to the past – travelling with 'three or four girls of good family – all rich, of course, money was no object' all over Europe, or any of her other activities in a full long life. I asked her whether Graz was not rather a nice place to live in. 'Oh Graz' she replied, 'Graz is alright, but I find the people a bit dull, I'm afraid.'

The Pension Iris is not exactly like the pension in Père Goriot, but it is not so very, very far removed from it: sad, somewhat frugal and not, in spite of Miss Chromy's good spirits, the most cheerful place in the world.

Pope-Hennessy settled in Hagnau to write his book, remaining there until 13 August, but there were two expeditions to visit royal sources.

---

*   *Lord Crewe 1858–1945 – The Likeness of a Liberal* by James Pope-Hennessy (Constable, 1955).

TWENTY-SIX

'Lilac-Time in Württemberg'

27 May

Queen Mary's family was, as we have seen, a morganatic branch of the Royal Family of Württemberg. Pope-Hennessy now visited the current head of the family, Duke Philipp, and his brother, Dom Odo of Württemberg, OSB, first mentioned by Lady Cynthia Colville at the outset of his research.

Württemberg had first become a kingdom in 1806. The first King of Württemberg was Friedrich II, Duke of Württemberg (1754–1816), eldest son of Friedrich Eugen, Duke of Württemberg (1732–97). He became King Friedrich I and his first wife was Princess Auguste of Brunswick (1764–88). (His second wife was HRH The Princess Charlotte (1766–1828), eldest daughter of King George III.)

Queen Mary descended from the King's younger brother, Duke Ludwig (1756–1817). He was the father of her grandfather, Duke Alexander of Württemberg, who made the morganatic marriage with Pauline, Countess Rhédey.

Duke Philipp (1893–1975) was Head of the Royal House. He was the son of Duke Albrecht (1865–1939), who succeeded King Wilhelm II as Head of the Royal House in 1921. Duke Philipp was a grandson of Duke Alexander of Württemberg, 7ᵗʰ son of Friedrich Eugen, Duke of Württemberg, and a brother of Duke Ludwig (Queen Mary's great-grandfather). He lived at Schloss Altshausen, in Upper Swabia. This castle was given to Duke Albrecht by King Wilhelm II in 1919, when Albrecht was forced to leave Stuttgart. It is still in the possession of the family.

Dom Odo was an interesting figure. Formerly known as Prince Carl Alexander of Württemberg (1896–1964), he had become a Benedictine monk. He also lived at Alsthausen. Shortly before the visit, he wrote to Pope-Hennessy, telling him that he had sadly lost nearly all Queen Mary's letters to him in enemy bombing during the war. In hesitant English he wrote concerning von

DUKE PHILIPP OF WÜRTTEMBERG

Ribbentrop, Mrs Simpson, and how the Duke of Windsor had supposedly demanded to be made Commander-in-Chief of the British Expeditionary Force, and to be made a Field Marshal, as he had been when King, and that the Duchess be made a Royal Highness and 'the First Princess of Great Britain'.

Dom Odo went on to speculate about the Duchess 'being the only woman who had been able to satisfactorily gratify the Duke's sexual desires'. In his poor English, Dom Odo said that Queen Mary had said to him, 'I don't know more this son.'[117]

Shortly before his visit, Dom Odo wrote again:

> The Duke of Clarence in his agony called always Hélène*. It was most embarrassing for Queen Mary!!!! Queen Alexandra brought her therefore out of the death room. Clarence died with the word Hélène on his lips.[118]

Pope-Hennessy wrote to his brother John from the castle:

> Duke Philipp I adore. I told you that he wears 9 baroque rings (heavy, jewelled, knobbly over) and has long yellow teeth like a beaver? Dom Odo a globule – Benedictine – knows Downside well etc.[119]

He also described Alsthausen, mentioning 'the perfection of this vast schloss in which an old-fashioned, simple comfort reigns':

> A corridor some 300 yards long, chock-a-block with Spanish & Italian Renaissance cabinets, portraits too – & a truly marvellous Gainsborough of Queen Charlotte, which Hitler wanted but couldn't have! My room all blue-and-white toile de Jouy – with curtains that let down on strings – & all the china (wash-basin, sponge-dish, etc:) in white with crimson crowned in initials – Köninglich – blazon! Two kinds of cigarettes in one's bedroom.

---

* HRH Princess Hélène d'Orléans (1871-1951), Catholic love of the Duke of Clarence in 1890. She married the 2nd Duke of Aosta in 1895.

The Duke (= King of Württ) met one on the perron. He's not unlike
Gerry ([Duke of] Wellington) in physique – chatters away in English/
French/Deutsch: 'Hier ist auch ein meuble Français you see.'[120]

On Tuesday 27 May 1958 I was fetched by Duke Philip of Württemberg's chauffeur (in grey serge uniform with black felt collar) and taken to stay with the Württemberg family at Schloss Altshausen. Kreis Saulgau – behind Friedrichshafen, through Ravensburg and past the vast Benedictine monastery of Weingarten.

I had already met Duke Philip and his bother Dom Odo, a Benedictine priest, head of all the Catholic youth, one of Hitler's most prominent opponents whom the Gestapo tried to assassinate in Switzerland and America during the war. They had both come here one morning to take me to see the desolate schloss at Friedrichshafen*, looted and smashed up by the French occupation troops who seem to have behaved like wild animals and made themselves as hated here as the Germans did in France.

Duke Philip is the eldest son of the late Duke Albrecht of Württemberg, head of the Catholic branch and so, after the death of the last King of Württemberg Wilhelm II, the head of the whole house of Württ: and heir to the throne if such continued to exist. He is a man of nearly seventy,[†] I should think, rather short, with a soft somewhat ovoid face, a rather prominent moustache, long teeth, pale blue eyes full of good humour and kindliness; he wears nine baroque rings on his fingers, and suits of English-looking tweed or of palest grey flannel.

Dom Odo is purely 15th century Burgundian: very tall, immensely fat with a stomach like a ten-gallon barrel beneath his habit, held in place by a huge leather belt. His face is perched upon three chins or so, he is almost entirely bald, with a circular head and wonderful comic eyes – circular too, like bright blue pebbles, and with a histrionic sense he is always throwing his glance towards the ceiling before embarking on some new scandal or piece of family gossip. I liked them both immensely the first time, and still more this time. Pater Odo speaks English, at times with an American accent of which he is ashamed as he loathes Americans and the USA. The Duke can also speak English but prefers French – which he speaks with the rapidity of a machine-gun, never drawing breath. He is a little deaf but says he won't use 'electric nonsenses' in his ears.

---

*   Schloss Friedrichshafen was previously a Benedictine Priory, and until 1918 was the summer residence of the Kings of Württemberg. It is now a school.

†   In fact he was sixty-five.

Altshausen, the only house they have left, and filled with all the family things from Stuttgart, Friedrichshafen, Ludwigsburg and Bebenhausen, was built by the Knights of some Order I couldn't make out which*. The little town stands 600 metres high, and the Schloss is in the midst of it, with a colossal gabled gatehouse. Through this one enters a kind of garden-courtyard, absolutely alive with clumps of purple and white lilac blowing in the wind – too beautiful – all planted by the present Herzog. At the door of the main building the Duke was waiting. He took me up one of the two main staircases: 'D'abord on voit le Gainsborough' he said and there sure enough was a very fine Gainsborough of Queen Charlotte, with a copy of the George III opposite it. This was brought over by Queen Charlotte Matilda (1766–1828), first Queen of Württemberg, and the eldest daughter (Pss. Royal) of Great Britain: she also brought wedgewood, many Cosway miniatures and so on; all through the afternoon when they were so kindly and thoroughly showing me the Schloss the words 'Queen Charlotte Matilda' kept cropping up every few moments.

The Duke then took me to the second floor, where runs the main corridor; a passage of almost incredible length, with windows down one side and some forty doors of bedrooms opposite; the rooms of the Knights of the Order originally; between the doors 17th century cabinets – German, Spanish, Italian – lacquer – with stiff portraits above them – in the window embrasures great cloisonné vases and bells and plates on stands. The dallage of the corridor is loose and clatters as one walks along, which the Duke said he hoped wdnt. wake me up in the morning. My bedroom large, airy, with white linen stores ruched above the windows, blue and white toile de jouy furniture (French?), a gaming table, a big brass bed, a charming old bureau with veneer coming off. He apologised for the lustre – 'épouvantable mais je n'ai pas pu tout faire en même temps'. Also for the fact that there had been 2 maids in the corridor – 'terrible for an Englishman – servants must never be seen'. He said they had great domestic problems, but as the luncheon (delicious) was served by 4 footmen in the black-and-scarlet royal livery of Württemberg I feel their troubles must be comparative only.

We then went down to the main drawing room to wait for 12.30 lunch. Here was Dom Odo; the Duchess†, a pleasant quiet woman with grey hair and a certain

---

* It was built by a Teutonic Order.

† HI & RH Archduchess Rosa (1906–83), younger daughter of Archduke Peter of Austria, and younger sister of the Duke's first wife, Hélène (1903–24).

embonpoint; one of their daughters*, rather pretty in a very traditionally royal German way – puffy cheeks and golden hair, pretty teeth and smile; their second (I think) son†, tall, thin, charming manner, blue eyes, constantly amused, about 25, looking like his grandfather D. Albrecht; and a very fascinating very aged (80 looks more) Aunt, the Duchess Robert of Württemberg, born an Archduchess of Austria‡: bent, with a bloodless fine old face and beautiful skin, white-silk hair dressed high, a black ribbon round her throat, a very shrewd mind and eye, and a little fluted die-away voice. At lunch, in a very big dining room, I sat at one end of the table between this old lady and the son: the old Archduchess talking about French politics – 'mais vous devriez acheter les journaux anglais à Ravensburg – librarie Dorf – il faut sa-voir ce qui se passe, je ne l'aime pas *du tout, du tout*'. (Next day on leaving I found she had ordered me a bundle of newspapers to be put in the motor-car.)

We had terribly good venison and then asparagus and so on, really good cui-sine. At lunch the Duke talked a good deal, warming up until the afternoon when he never drew breath and always very fast. After lunch the Duke and Dom Odo took me round the whole place; we identified an early George in turquoises which I suggested they should have photographed and looked at everything. Much very pretty Viennese china with views, Sèvres from the Orléans gt.-grandmother, the sculptress of Joan of Arc etc. (they have many maquettes); portraits, miniatures, bibelots, they know exactly what everything is and Duke Philip is a real connois-seur – so different to our ignorant Royalties! It made me think that perhaps the Württemberg influence or heredity in Q. Mary helped her in her interests.

Would I like to see the family tombs? they asked, after we had been through the Library (full of armour from Benehausen) and looked at the newspaper reports of Louis XVI's trial. I said I would. We went first into the Chapel which is very gemütlich and pretty, baroque but not excessive, and then the Duke unlocked a door at the west end of the church. We went down a few steps into an intensely light chapel with big white glass windows, bathed in sunlight. A narrow black altar was built against the west wall, with a line of prie-dieux in front of it. The rest

---

* They had four daughters between them, Hélène (b. 1929), Elisabeth (b. 1933), Marie-Thérèse (b. 1934), and Marie Antoinette (1937–2004).

† The second son was Duke Carl (b. 1936), the present Head of the Royal House of Württemberg.

‡ HI & RH Archduchess Maria Immaculata (1878–1968), daughter of Archduke Karl Salvator of Austria; married 1900, Duke Robert of Württemberg (1873–1947). She lived at Schloss Althausen, and died there on 25 November 1968.

DOM ODO

of the chapel was occupied by 14–20 or so *immense* scarlet and gold objects: enormous coffers, they seemed, covered in scarlet velvet stamped with gilt studs and with gold braid cross and edgings – they might have been giants' chocolate boxes – the tops domed, sloping downward to the narrower end. Each of these caskets stood on claw-feet, and these feet rested on four stone capitals or pillars with cherubims' heads and wings. 'N'est-ce pas que c'est *charmant* ici? Ça ne ressemble en rien du tout aux autres tombeaux de Famille – on peut y venir quand on veut – voici mon père [pointing] voilà ma mère* – ma soeur etcetera†; tous ensemble. Charmant, n'est-ce pas?' 'Mais oui, Monseigneur' I replied somewhat stunned. It was one of the strangest places I have ever seen – these coffins standing side by side and one behind the other, all upholstered in scarlet and gold, with detachable domed lids. After this visit, we each went 'pour un *nap*', Dom Odo calling me at 4 while I was still dozing heavily on my bed: – 'Oh my dear: I am too urrrly – I will wait outside'. We then adjourned to *his* room for tea, before which I went to confession: astoundingly wise and clever man *most* helpful and sophisticated.

The Duke came in for tea and talk began again – family talk – Father Odo contributing many stories – mostly infinitely exaggerated – e.g. Marie Strelitz, her mother and her sister Jutta‡ *all* had children by Hecht the footman ('All?' 'Yes, yes, my mother told me so herself') which were then taken to an institution and killed. Marie used to wear the footman's livery button on a chain round her neck etc. After some hour and ½ of this, during which we had drunk tea and good Cognac, we went to the Duke's room ('tout en désordre' – which indeed it was) and began talking again. They told me a great deal about the Nazi times, the occupation troops, Nuremberg trials having disillusioned Germans, and so on. I had little chance to

---

* The Duke's mother was Archduchess Margarete Sophia (1870–1929), daughter of Archduke Karl Ludwig of Austria.

† The Duke had four sisters : Maria Amélie (1897–1923), Maria Theresia (1898–1928), Marie Elisabeth (1899–1900), and Margarethe Maria (1902–45). They all died unmarried, the eldest and youngest at Altshausen.

‡ HSH Duchess Marie of Mecklenburg-Strelitz (1878–1948), and her sister, HRH Duchess Jutta (1880–1946). The latter married 1899, HM King Danilo of Montenegro 1871–1939). They were the daughters of HRH Duke Adolf Friedrich V of Mecklenburg-Strelitz (1857–1914) (son of HRH Princess Augusta, and thus a first cousin of Queen Mary), and his wife, Princess Elisabeth (1857–1933), daughter of HH Friedrich I, Duke of Anhalt.

contribute much, save: 'Ah, vous croyez, Monseigneur, que ...' or 'Votre Altesse Royale pense-t'elle alors ...?' Anyway it was all very deeply interesting to me.

Dinner was at 7.30 and we again met in the big salon, with fine big windows at either end, great porcelain stove, fine Louis XV cartel hanging on the mirror above the fireplace, silk-seated chairs in a cirlce, little tables with cloisonné ash-trays, aubusson carpet, portraits of Louis Philippe and so on. After this meal we sat for 20 minutes in the drawing room and then at 8.25 we all went to bed: I had nothing to read, and slept for 2 hours, to awake to total insomnia till 6 am.

At nine my breakfast was brought in and I was seated at the old French gam-ing-table pouring coffee from a white *cafetière* with the Württemberg monogram on it, dressed in a clean white shirt, trousers and slippers (rather Byronic I thought, looking in the smoky old glass) when a tap at the door and in came the Duke, very brisk and matinal. He sat down in the chair at the other end of the table lit a cigarette and began to talk about how badly Italian noblemen ran their estates; it was if he had been wound up in the night for he talked faster and more intelligently even than before. From this we passed to Spanish estates, then Portugal, Salazar* and back to one of his favourite topics: Free Masonry. Both he and Dom Odo see the whole of Europe riddled in 1788-fashion with Free Masons, anarchists, servants of the devil and atheist Jews. After five hours with them I believe it too.

The speed of this morning conversation was amazing. Halfway through the valet brought in my cleaned shoes. 'Et-quant-à-Salazar,-voyez-vous,-c'est-un-grand-homme,-un-homme-simple,–qu'est-que-c'est? – ah on vous apporte vos souliers – qui n'a ni palais ni château de campagne – ça va comme ça? voulez-vous que je vous cherche a Shoe Horn? Non – et qui-a-chassé-la-Franc-Maçonnerie de là-bas' etc. I munched my brioche and listened. When I had finished my break-fast – 'ah! mais je vous dérange à votre petit déjeuner' – so I said no, no, I'd loved it all (true). 'Et maintenant nous allons rejoindre le Pater Odo pour un peu de bavardage si ça ne vous ennuie pas?'

This peu de bavardage, which occurred with us three seated round a small Empire table with a top of black marble and mounds of cigarettes in open boxes, lasted 3 ½ hours, until lunch. They ranged over every topic they thought would interest me – working backwards from the Duke of Windsor – 'il ne faut jamais s'encanailler comme il l'a fait' said D. Odo: 'Jamais' replied the Duke: 'mais aussi

---

*   António de Oliveira Salazar (1889–1970), Prime Minister, and effectively dictator of Portugal 1932–68.

il ne faut jamais non plus se mettre sur un piédestal.' They worked backwards to range over all the eccentricities, the insanities, the crimes of every Royal family in Germany and Austria – a Wittelsbach princess who lived with a goat, some prince who lived w. his own daughter – and so on – would I could remember them all – 'Ah King Gustaf* was a *very peculiar gentleman*!!' It gave one an extraordinary panorama of the last century seen through royal eyes – and both these are such intelligent, Christian and cultivated men – it must have been exactly the kind of conversation the Duchess of Teck most adored. They have a very sensible assessment of the present Queen Mother who doesn't answer telegrams or letters from them on family occasions etc. – nor had latterly the Queen. This seems very bad, part of the Kensington-girl policy of non-attachment to German-relations I suppose, or just ignorance, laziness and sloth.

After lunch we sat in the drawing room again, reduced to the Duke, his brother, daughter, son and governess, and Dom Odo then took over and kept us in hysterics with stories of Catholicism in the USA for 1 ½ hours – I hadn't laughed so much for months. As I took my leave, the Duke said, going downstairs that he believed in 'des contactes personnels' and how much he had enjoyed my visit (v. polite I thought as I had contributed little save a sympathetic expression of phiz.) 'Mais je crains que vous n'ayez pas été *trop serré* – on ne vous a pas laissé un instant seul!!!'

So ended an absorbing expedition backwards in time.

---

* HM King Gustaf V of Sweden (1858–1950). He was implicated in a homosexual love affair, the Haijby Affair.

TWENTY-SEVEN

PRINCE AND PRINCESS AXEL OF DENMARK

A Glimpse of the 'Danish Family' *or* 'Oh, for God's sake, yes.'

15 June

Pope-Hennessy went to Copenhagen to see Prince Axel of Denmark on the recommendation of Sir John Wheeler-Bennett, who told him the Prince's address was simply 'Copenhagen, Denmark'.

Prince Axel (1888–1964) was the second son of Prince Valdemar of Denmark (1858–1939), brother of Queen Alexandra. He had been a member of the International Olympic Committee since 1932. He was the father of Prince George of Denmark, who had married the Queen Mother's niece, Viscountess Anson, in 1950. His wife, Princess Margaretha (1899–1977), whom he had married in 1919, was the eldest daughter of Prince Oscar of Sweden (1861–1951). She was the sister of Crown Princess Märtha of Norway (1901–54), and Queen Astrid of the Belgians (1905–35). She was a first cousin of King Gustaf VI Adolf of Sweden.

To a friend, Pope-Hennessy wrote, 'I went to Copenhagen … horrid, dank, dreary, drinky city – but was a smash-hit with Queen Mary's cousin, Prince Axel, who showed me all the palaces and filled me up with alcohol to the eyelids – a stiff, genial, jolly, elderly Admiral he is …'[121]

On 15 June 1958 I left the rural peace of Hagnau for Copenhagen, where I had a rendezvous with Prince Axel of Denmark at 11.00 a.m. the next morning, June 16th. I went from Hagnau to Konstanz by boat, to Zurich by train, from Zurich to Copenhagen by air. The journey was uneventful; Zurich was hot and dull, the aeroplane, as usual, over-full and sordid; nasty hot food dished up at 5 p.m. In the bus from the airport to the centre of Copenhagen I got conversationally entangled with an old lady from New York, who was doing a 'package trip' round Europe. 'Now, I wonder, am I going to like Copenhagen?' she said gazing out of the bus window: 'They've given me three days here, but what am I goin' to do??' I felt rather the same when I looked out on the Tottenham-Court Road main street of the city. That evening I went to the Tivoli Gardens and hated it. There is a determined gaiety about the Paris of the North which is tiring and unvigorous. The streets were filled with sailors looking like drenched herons. All the Danes seem to crane forward, as though they had dislocated necks.

Prince Axel, whom I saw the next morning, also seems to have a dislocated neck, and carried his head well to the fore. The second son of Queen Alexandra's youngest brother Waldemar and his wife a daughter of the Duc de Chartres*. Prince Axel is, as he kept on telling me, six weeks short of 70. He is married to a stiff Princess of Sweden and has two sons, the elder of whom is married to the Queen Mother's divorced niece†. He is thus, unlike the dear Württemberg dukes, right in the middle of things, and more informative than enquiring.

Prince Axel is a very tall rather wooden-looking naval man; he has grey hair, and his face is laced with purple veins, his eyes marbled yellow and crimson, due I can only fancy to alcohol and nicotine. His favourite expression and expletive is 'Oh for God's sake' – with 'yes' or 'no' added as may be – pronounced all in one: 'Offergotseck!!' When I reached the floor of his office in the East Asiatic Company's building near the Grand Hotel (where *I* was currently perched) he stepped through his door most welcomingly. 'Haf you a lunch engagement?' 'I have no engagements, Sir.' 'Good, we are now going to lunch with my sister‡. It is better than an interview, we will talk.' We scampered down the stairs and into a large Bentley, occupied by a gigantic Alsatian dog called 'Gin'. 'I only wonder my brother didn't call him 'Whiskey', Princess René of Bourbon-Parma later remarked to me. 'Offerfgotseck, Mag, no dog can have a double name' replied Prince Axel.

It was a delicious morning of hot sun and slight sea-breeze. As we bowled out towards Bernstorff along the road beside the sea and the harbour ('there is Sweden right over there', Prince Axel explained waving a beringed finger at the horizon) we came upon a scene of great animation. 'There He is, there They are, get out of the car, you sure do have damn luck!' cried Prince Axel. What was happening was the return of the King and Queen of Denmark§ from a state visit to Finland. The

---

*   Prince Axel's mother was Princess Marie (1865–1909), daughter of Prince Robert, Duc de Chartres (1840–1910). She had been born at Morgan House, Ham, Surrey.

†   HH Prince George (1920–86), and Count Flemming af Rosenborg (1922–2002).

‡   HRH Princess Margarethe (1895–1992), married 1921, HRH Prince René of Bourbon-Parma (1894–1962). She was the mother of Queen Anne of Romania (1923–2016).

§   HM King Frederik IX (1899–1972), and his wife, Princess Ingrid of Sweden (1910–2001).

PRINCE AXEL OF DENMARK

Royal yacht, escorted by two cruisers lay in the bay; guns were firing, sounding like bursting paper-bags in the clear air; the sailors lined the decks like little dolls, cheering and waving their hats, while a launch flying two royal pennants scudded round the cruisers, the King a tall thin figure in the prow. 'He's thanking them, you see' explained Prince Axel, who had tears in his eyes. The launch returned to its mother-yacht, and the flag on this was changed: 'Ah yes this is the incognito flag – they wish to live quietly on the yacht'. Next morning Prince Axel told me he had telephoned to the Queen of Denmark about my seeing Fredensborg*. 'He can see anything he likes' she had replied: 'but do ask him *why Aunt May was never Princess of Wales*.'† Prince Axel told me They like living on the yacht, which is very luxurious he assured me, because it is more 'private' than any of Their palaces.

This loyal little scene brought forth a cataract of reminiscence of English royal yachts, of how far back Prince Axel's memory went, and so on. Soon we passed a hideous villa with caryatids supporting a positive froth of little balconies – it faced the sea – 'This was the house which Queen Alexandra and the Dowager Empress lived in‡. They would pick up shells on the sea-shore. It isn't pretty as you can see but those old ladies loved it.' 'Now *Your* Royal Highness can tell me …' (this is my stale technique with each of Them, to make Them feel oracular) – 'did Queen Alexandra speak German' (this was to see the reaction, I knew the answer): 'Offergotseck NO!' Prince Axel almost screamed: 'The Family *hated* the Germans – the Schleswig-Holstein duchies do you see.' He then talked of Queen Mary, calling her 'May' which thrilled me – no-one but Princess Alice can do this today and she wouldn't to *me*. Prince Axel's entrance line or theme song is the sentence: – 'As May said to me the day that Bertie died'. The story of that is this: on the morning of the late King's sudden death at Sandringham§, Prince Axel, being in London at the Savoy Hotel on East Asiatic business, had an appointment with Queen Mary at Marlborough House for the early afternoon. A Lady-in-Waiting rang him up, and said 'Her Majesty wishes you to know that *whatever rumours* you may hear this morning in London, she is still expecting

---

*   Fredensborg Palace, the main residence of the Danish Royal Family, used in spring and autumn. It stands on the Eastern shore of Lake Esrum.

†   Queen Mary became Princess of Wales on 9 November 1901, and was so styled until the death of Edward VII in May 1910.

‡   Villa Hvidore, not far from Copenhagen.

§   King George VI died on 6 February 1952.

you.' 'Well, I never ask questions, so I just said yes of course I quite understand – (I didn't understand at all matterofact).' During the board meeting the news of the King's death was released. Prince Axel repaired to Marlborough House at 2.45 p.m. 'And there was May, just sitting there, like *this*' (folding hands in lap for a moment, off the wheel). 'Well there was May, quite calm and natural. And do you know what she said? She said: "Axel – this is the third time this has happened to me – the third of my sons to die unexpectedly – curious, isn't it?".' This sangfroid greatly impressed Prince Axel.

We stopped for a moment at Prince Axel's own villa in what was once the grounds of Droning Louise's favourite residence, Bernstorff, now all building lots except for the immense park-like garden of Prince Axel's capacious modern villa, next door to that of his sister Princess René of Bourbon-Parma. He has a charming library, books to the ceiling and many more strewn about the floor – a big drawing room hung round with family pictures – a terrace with canvas chairs – flowers everywhere, huge windows, jalousies, shadow and sunlight. 'Now, how about a glass of sherry?' 'That would be wonderful, Sir, but may I wash first?' 'I was just going to suggest it. Either here or here' – indicating two doors. The loo was spectacularly agreeable, filled with coloured guest-towels (vide Wallis of Windsor), silver-backed hairbrushes and fascinating bottles labelled *Eau de Waldemar*. We had three tumblers of sherry in quick succession and then drifted across the garden, between the lilac bushes, to Princess René's smaller abode. There was nobody in, it seemed; but soon Princess René bustled in – a really charming human being, with robin's eyes, an easy roundabout figure and delightful manner. More sherry, more cigarettes. 'I am afraid you are having a Danish lunch' she said, leading the way to the circular dining room table which was not laden but cluttered with cold things – laks, ham, sausage slices and so on – mauve sweetpeas and some silver saltcellars shaped like toadstools helped fill up the few gaps between the plates. On a side-table was a hot dish with chicken on it. We began with the chicken, then moved on to the colder elements. 'Red wine or white? 'And now you *must* have schnapps!!' 'Oh no, Sir, thank you!' replied the unusually sage J.P.-H., remembering Stockholm. He kept on replenishing my glass of claret, and at the end of the meal I said 'May I bring this glass in with me' (back to salon): 'My dear,' said Princess René, 'in this house you can do just anything you want – in this house – well *everything goes!!*'

I gave them *Grüsse von Altshausen*, which delighted them. 'Oh! Fergotseck that Dom Odo, that *is* a sweet thing!' cried Prince Axel with enthusiasm: 'I met him first at the wedding at Drouz [Dreux]* last summer – and I said to my sister, who is that *sweet thing* over there?' 'I knew him well in New York during the war,' Princess René explained[†]. We agreed on what fun he was as a confessor.

Before, during and after lunch we spoke intermittently of 'May', her relations with her mother-in-law (who was their Aunt Alix) and so on. Nothing very new, but confirmed all I already supposed to be true, and somehow vivifying to talk about her. They said Aunt Alix's deafness was a dreadful trial. They said above all she (May) was 'such a *darling*' – such fun – so unstiff, so much the opposite of what most people thought. I said this was one of the *clous* of my book and this pleased them greatly. They talked very frankly ('between you and I and my sister and the gatepost' said Prince Axel in his best English) and so did I, and it was all *most* useful to me. Coffee was followed by a *sea* of cognac – 'not Hennessy, I'm afraid, Ho! ho!' – and this by Prince Axel suddenly standing up like a jack in the box and saying: 'Now I am going to be lazy. I shall not drive you home. I shall get you a taxi and I shall then have a *nap*' (vide Altshausen naps). 'When Queen Mary died,' remarked Princess René, to wind up our conference, 'something went out of the world – something that has never been replaced – it was the end of the Empire'. 'As May said to me on the day that Bertie died – that I shall never forget, never' added Prince Axel a little alcoholically. He dated me up for 10.30 the next morning at the hotel, promising to arrange for everything to be opened for me to see. It was this afternoon that he telephoned the Queen on the yacht.

I spent a heavy and not agreeable evening alone in the Tivoli Gardens and next morning felt oversmoked and headachy. Prince Axel appeared with Bentley and Alsatian at 10.30 sharp, much bowing from the hotel porter. 'Well and how are you?' he said in the familiar bored royal voice which always makes my heart sink. I exaggerated my condition and this caught his fancy at once. He looked at me narrowly: 'And you forgot to eat anything, I expect?' 'I'm afraid I did, Sir'. 'Now *this* was your mistake. You shall have a good lunch at a little hotel at Fredensborg, where the food is *excellent*. And now you must not smoke for two hours.'

---

* HRH Princess Marie Thérèse of Württemberg (b. 1934), fourth daughter of Duke Philipp, had married HRH Prince Henri, Count of Clermont (b. 1933), at Dreux, the church where the Orléans family is buried, on 5 July 1957. She was divorced in 1984.

† In the Second World War, Prince and Princess René had been obliged to flee from France to Spain, then to Portugal, and finally to the United States.

It was again a sunlit morning as we drove to the Amalienborg, past the little house in which Queen Alexandra was born. The Amalienborg Palais is in fact four pavilions, 18th century, set cornerwise round a little tidy square, with a fine equestrian bronze of some Danish King in the centre. The one I wished to see, the Christian VII Palais, was opened by the concierge and we went all over it. It was here that visiting Royalties always put up, and here that Princess May was bored to death by the *cercle* and early dinners. It is a fine baroque house, with Gobelins, intricate marquetry patterns on the floor, good French and Danish furniture – this latter an exaggerated version of Louis Quinze – tremendously bombé (to bursting point), and with huge pale ormulu ornamentation encrusted on it anywhere and everywhere.

From the Amalienborg we set out for Fredensborg, some 50 or 40 kms outside the city. We again stopped off at Bernstorff for some bumpers of sherry and to go to the loo. On our way thence we drove through the town of Hillerde, which has a medieval moated castle; we drove into the courtyard ('it's forbidden of course but they know me') – know him they did, children waving, people bowing in the villages as our Bentley sped by.

Fredensborg stands on a far bigger lake than I had supposed (the one into which Prince Eddy was pushed) – a really large sheet of water. It is a huge white palace, with a formal garden which the present Queen (clearly a woman of taste and knowledge) has restored to its seventeenth-century aspect – with royal initials made of flower-beds – alleys cut through to the lake – all based on old engravings and pictures of the place. Inside there is a gigantic hall running the height of the palace, indeed above it for the roof is a protruding dome. This is paved with black and white marble, one stone being marked as the site of the signing of the Peace after the (? Thirty Years) War to celebrate which Fredensborg (Peaceburg) was built and named. Round this hall runs a gallery from which in old days the public could watch the King and his court eating. The present Queen has restored the furniture, taken away ugly chandeliers, stripped the walls down to their original colours; she has not yet touched Queen Alexandra's apartments, which are pure Maples, white and blue. She has to do it without telling the King who is very conservative but often doesn't notice a change once it's done. She removed four Victorian chandeliers from a salon which had eight and he still thinks there are eight there (vide Q. Mary and K. George V). We went over many suites of rooms, all very light and airy and gemütlich. All very civilised. In one of the drawing rooms, lined with green silk, there is a tear in the fabric – above this is a little AA

1863 cut with a pen-knife – 'Uncle Sacha – the Tsar Alexander* – did that, you see; and the rubbed place comes from people touching it.'

After inspecting a hundred rooms or so we retired to a little hotel near the gates for lunch. This was luxuriously furnished with Knole chairs and settees, and standard lamps from perhaps Liberty's. We slumped at a table in the hall. 'And now you shall have a cigarette,' said Prince Axel kindly, taking out his silver cigarette case: 'I consider you have been very good this morning. And two dry martinis' he added to the obsequious waiter: 'driest of dry, please'. These, too, were served up in goblets. We began to talk about the sea. 'I realised you had been in the Navy the moment I saw Your Royal Highness. The sea does something to a face, one sees it in the eyes.' 'All that is very true, very true. And now I am an Admiral' Prince Axel replied with modest pride. He told me all about his work with the East Asiatic Company and much else. 'Two more dry martinis, please.' 'But, Sir, I shall get tight.' 'Oh no you won't. I shall look after you, put yourself in my hands. Just do what I say. We shall begin lunch with sardines – always remember this for the rest of your life – EAT SARDINES – the oil, you see. I get through every cocktail party from New York to Saigon ON SARDINES. I tell this always to the new boys in the East Asiatic Company – they ALL EAT SARDINES.'

In fact we began lunch with a bowl of fresh Russian caviar, presented by the manager, Mr Christenson, who asked me to go to see his son in the SAS bureau in London on my return home. This was accompanied by masses of schnapps, followed by champagne, and a chicken soufflé. There was a certain amount of fuss about getting Gin some water and food in the garden. We re-discussed the Day that Bertie Died – 'oh all you said yesterday about May has given us both such pleasure, for we think your book will be really good' Prince Axel at one moment declared. At neighbouring tables American tourists, tipped off by Mr Christenson or a waiter, gazed at Prince Axel and his guest in noisy rapture.

On the way back to Bernstorff (after coffee and of course cognac) we discussed Life and the Law of Coincidence, about all of which Prince Axel was very sound and interesting. At Bernstorff we settled down (3.15 p.m.) to 'a little whiskey and soda, what?' He told me his submarine stories from the war. I had left my cigarettes in the car and stepped out to get them. As I opened the front door I found myself nose to nose with a tall lady in black. She was wearing a nifty little hat with

---

*   HIM Tsar Alexander III of Russia (1845–94), married 1866, HRH Princess Dagmar of Denmark (1847–1928).

a short veil and carrying a parcel in her gloved hands. I stepped back. 'It is *you* who has been lunching my husband?' 'Yes Ma'am.' 'At the inn at Fredensborg? Was the food good?' 'Delicious Ma'am, the manager gave us a tin of caviar.' 'Now that I call really chic of Mr Christenson!'

She went upstairs and I returned to the terrace, Prince Axel and the whiskey flagon. Princess Axel ('Margarette', a Princess of Swedish origin) soon joined us. This was a singularly charmless woman who reacted strongly against one in a suspicious, Royal way. 'And who told you to come and see my husband, Mr Hennessy?' 'Wheeler-Bennett, Ma'am, who has just written King George VI's life*. He met His Royal Highness on the Queen Elizabeth.' 'Offergotseck yes I remember now – I have no memory for names, no memory for names at all' shouted Prince Axel. 'And why are you liffing in Shermany, Mr Hennessy' 'Offergotseck Margarette why shouldnteee,' 'And have you seen The Queen Mr Hennessy?' I was getting fed up so I annoyingly answered '*Your* Queen, Ma'am, or *ours?*' 'The Queen of England.' 'Offergotseck, Margarette, Lilibet commanded his book!' And so on. I think that Princess Margarette felt either that we were being too unroyally matey (her husband and I) or it was just natural reaction of someone who has been shopping in Copenhagen and comes home hot and tired to find a rollicking bucolic scene in progress with anecdotes of her revered cousin Queen Mary being flung and tossed about the terrace. 'As May used to say to me …' etc. I re-made my point, at Prince Axel's request, about Queen Mary being unstiff and that I wished to show this. 'With this I do not agree at all – Queen Mary was *not* stiff at all.' 'Offergotseck, Margarette, this is what he has just been telling you!' Princess Axel also had a fidgety royal habit of getting up and going out of the room (or off the terrace) for no reason at all, and suddenly returning, keeping me on my legs perpetually.

Prince Axel again mentioned his nap and telephoned for a taxi and I bowed my way out into the sunshine, leaving Princess Margarette seated primly on the terrace sofa, lost in thought. I fancy her husband is full of volatile fancies and enthusiasms and she tries to damp him down. She certainly left *me* ringing wet.

---

* Sir John Wheeler-Bennett's official biography, *King George VI: His Life and Reign* was published by Macmillan in 1958.

TWENTY-EIGHT

THE DUC DE BAENA

The Spanish Embassy, The Hague

November

The next recorded interview was with the Duc de Baena, whose Spanish style was José Maria, 16th Duque de Baena, 16th Duque Sanlúcar la Mayor, 10th Conde de Sevilla la Nueva, 4th Vizconde de Mamblas, and 14th Marqués de Villamanrique (1893–1985). His parents, who were aristocratic and Jewish, were friends of King Alfonso and Queen Ena of Spain. He was educated in England and became a chamberlain to the King before joining the Spanish Diplomatic Service.

As 'Pepe' Mamblas, he was well known in social and diplomatic circles in London and Paris in the 1920s and 1930s. He served as Spanish Chargé d'Affaires in London before the Second World War, wore exquisite clothes, and gave 'beautiful' dinner parties. He loved the Ballets Russes, was part of the circle of the Princesse Edmond de Polignac, and was passionate about aristocratic French novelists. He was a supporter of Franco and spent much of his time in the late 1930s making forays into the Pays Basque, trying to help his beleaguered countrymen.

During the summer and winter of 1937, he became the lover of the Australian novelist Patrick White, when the latter visited St Jean de Luz. Mamblas introduced him to the smart homosexual world in London, including figures such as Malcolm Bullock. Mamblas was the inspiration for the un-named Spanish Chargé d'Affaires in White's play, Return to Abyssinia.

He became a friend of Queen Mary, or as he put it, 'The Dowager Queen Mary of England ... honoured me with her friendship.'[122] Later Queen Mary asked him about the play and told him that she thought the Attaché character had been based on him. 'I learned later, in fact, it was I, incognito.'[123]

Lady Lascelles knew him and suggested to Pope-Hennessy that he might be a good source. She told him that Queen Mary used to send for him once a week at 2.45 pm, though he was never invited for a meal. They would then talk for an hour. This was often an awkward time for him, but somehow he managed to make time for a visit.

It was to the Duc de Baena that Queen Mary addressed her last letter. He had sent her the catalogue of the Goya Exhibition in Basle. She addressed him as 'My dear Friend …'*

Later he became Spanish Ambassador in Switzerland and Turkey and to the Netherlands. He succeeded his father as Duc de Baena. He was the author of The Dutch Puzzle *(1975).*

He was, said Lady Lascelles, 'a charming, civilised man, unmarried'.[124]

The Duc de Baena stressed Queen Mary's humanity, wisdom, sense of detail.

('One could flirt with her. I used to love to make her blush.')

Duke 'If Your Majesty was of my sex and my religion I should like to make you my father confessor.'

Q.M. (blushing deeply) 'Remember I was the mother of five sons.'

$\sim$

Queen Mary and the bombing of European cities – 'They will bomb Vienna, they will destroy it, they *want* everything to be destroyed.'

$\sim$

Train specially stopped at Badminton. Affection of the old station-master for Queen Mary.

$\sim$

Queen Mary's views on Queen Isabella of Spain[†]. Her visit to her in Paris in 1883.

$\sim$

---

* See *Queen Mary* (1959), p. 621. The letter was written on 18 March 1953 and Queen Mary died on 24 March.

† HM Queen Isabel II of Spain (1830–1904), Queen of Spain in her own right from 1833 to 1868, when she was deposed. She was the mother of King Alfonso XII (1857–85).

Queen Mary on the bench in Kew Gardens. The woman eating biscuits out of a bag. Enquiries and sampling of a biscuit (Lady Carisbrooke's* story).

~

When the Duke left London. Farewell at Marlborough House. 'And what about your staff?' 'They didn't do this?' (putting her knuckles to her eyes) 'They did? Then you mustn't let them do it. It is not good for them and *not* good for you.'

~

Queen Mary and Don Juan†, after he had expected to go to Balmoral.

~

When Queen Wilhelmina‡ abdicated, Queen Mary remarked: 'She is only 68, and *that is no age to give up your job.*'

~

Queen Mary's shock at realising she was eighty. The old lady from Cornwall who went shrimping on the rocks at 92.

~

'Write to me – *but not through my ladies!*'

~

---

* Lady Irene Denison (1890–1956), married 1917, 'Drino', 1st Marquess of Carisbrooke (1886–1960), elder son of Princess Beatrice.

† HRH Infante Don Juan, Count of Barcelona (1913–93), fourth son of King Alfonso XIII and Queen Victoria Eugénie of Spain.

‡ HM Queen Wilhelmina of the Netherlands (1880–1962), Queen from 1890 until her Abdication in favour of Queen Juliana in 1948.

'Anyone who is in the Line of Succession *should remember it*.'

~

Queen Mary and the Goya portrait of the painter's son in a grey top hat: 'You can see it was painted with love.'*

~

Queen Mary and Catholicism: her interest in the Duke's centenary-of-the-re-establishment-of-the-hierarchy luncheon party in 1950. Queen Mary wanted to hear every detail of it.

~

Queen Mary at Badminton, wearing velvet and pearls.

~

'You see, I am no longer properly informed.'

---

* This refers to the Goya exhibition in Basel, and Queen Mary's letter to the Duke on 18 March 1953.

TWENTY-NINE

THE DUKE AND DUCHESS OF WINDSOR

The King over the Millstream *or* Gracious Living

2 – 3 November

Pope-Hennessy went to interview the man perhaps most directly involved in the story: Queen Mary's eldest son, HRH The Duke of Windsor (1894–1972), who had reigned briefly as Edward VIII; and his wife, the former Wallis Warfield Simpson, for whom he had abdicated the throne in 1936 – then the Duchess of Windsor (1896–1986).

At this stage of their lives, they were living in voluntary exile in France, where they had finally put down roots, buying a house in the Bois de Boulogne, 4 Route du Champ d'Entrainement, and also the Moulin de la Tuilerie, not far from Paris. It was to 'the Mill' that Pope-Hennessy went.

There may have been two visits, one between 2 and 3 November, and another one from 29 November to 1 December; in which case Pope-Hennessy compressed the two visits in his notes.

During the first visit, he wrote to his brother, John:

> *... he immensely friendly and comical, looking like Ernest Thesiger as the Dauphin in St Joan, if you remember that – she an amiable Southerner, large-jawed, funny and like her book, naive, basically – sort of still surprised to be here, so to speak – they are like people after a cataclysm or a revolution, valiantly making the best of infinite luxury. I am delighted by them. The house – or rather houses, in the Sissinghurst style – are full of very pretty colours and ideas and objects – there is a general perfectionism that is very American and very restful. I must end, as I have to be ready to talk to the Duke when he has finished erecting a sundial with a Hilaire Belloc tag on it. He is wearing a scarlet felt baseball cap & brown gumboots, and has*

told me to write letters at his desk till he is ready. I am much taken by both of them as it happens.[125]

Following his first visit, he was sleeping in a drugged state one night, following hypnotism from his doctor, when the telephone rang at midnight and the Duchess of Windsor suggested that perhaps he could help the Duke with some articles on the changes in male fashions, illustrated from his own albums, 'and with himself as pioneer of these alterations of the Mode'.[126] *This idea was pursued for a while, but eventually the scheme came to nothing, Pope-Hennessy backing away from the project.*

It would appear that the second visit to the Mill was partly to discuss that project.

'I'm Not the Miller's Daughter, but I've Been Through the Mill.'
(Device frescoed in *trompe l'œil* – ribbon running through a mill wheel – in the Duchess of Windsor's drawing room at Le Moulin-des-Tuileries, Gif-sur-Yvette, Seine-et-Oise, France.)
'*Trompe l'œil*' is one of the few French expressions often in the Duchess's mouth, e.g.
Duchess to J.P.-H. 'And whaddya think of *my trompe l'œil* in the drawing room?'
J.P.-H. 'I was wondering who thought it up.'
Duchess 'Why, *Ah* did, *Ah* thought it up!!'

I awoke in a hotel *garni* in a suburb of Cologne at six a.m. to catch the fast diesel train to Paris. It was a bitterly cold dark morning; I had got to bed late. The train was swift, elegant and comfortable; and at twelve-thirty I was at the Gare du Nord, where the long blue station wagon (Cadillac) of the Duke and Duchess of Windsor was waiting, with a plump pigeon-shaped English chauffeur, dressed in discreet black with a black rosette in his cap. We drove out through jammed streets to Gif-sur-Yvette, which is near Orsay and off the Rambouillet road.

Le Moulin des Tuileries, which the Duchess has converted into her Petit Trianon, was once the home of the painter Drian* in its simple, earlier days. Like Sissinghurst, it consists of four or five houses, in this case of grey stone with tiled

---

* Étienne Drian (1885–1961), French artist.

roofs and white shutters; some of them converted barns. A wall surrounds the property, which is overlooked from the hillsides by small new villas and bungalows. Inside the wall is an elaborate water-garden, where the Duke works with five gardeners; he has made a series of waterfalls and cataracts by means of electric but concealed pumps. The car hooted at the wooden door in the gatehouse, and this was opened. We drove downhill into the court, and to the front door where the liveried butler (French) and an English footman were waiting. Divested of my coat and scarf and gloves, I was directed to walk across the sunny courtyard to the French windows of the Duke's study, a colossal room made from a barn, with great log fires smouldering either end, French windows in the middle, maps of his world-tours on the walls, souvenirs and uniform buckles everywhere: 'This room', the Duchess told me, 'represents the Dook's life.' Framed addresses, silver statuette of Queen Victoria etc. etc. The floor is covered with a curious tufted carpet in three shades of green, very fresh and pretty: '*What* a pretty carpet, Duchess; I've never seen one like it before': 'Ah call it mah lawn.' I walked through the French window, where the Duke was, wearing leather gardening trousers, a sweat-shirt and a tweed jacket.

The Duke of Windsor is, on first sight, much less small than I had been led to believe; he is not at all a manikin, but a well-proportioned human being. Just then his hair was blown out in tufts on either side of his head, and he was looking crumple-faced and wild, like Shaw's Dauphin. The hair is nicotine-coloured; but when he emerges from his shower and his valet's hands he looks very silken and natty and well-arranged; he has his father's eyes, and some, I fancy, of his mannerisms. He was drinking milk; for what the Duchess calls 'that lil' old ulcer'. I was soon startled to find that, except for occasionally repeating a complete story (which the Duchess stops when she can), he is not only the one member of the Royal Family for whom one needs to make *no* allowances whatever, but that he is exceedingly intelligent, original, liberal-minded and quite capable of either leading a conversation or taking a constructive part in one. He is also one of the most considerate men I have ever met of his generation. Like the Duchess, he is perhaps too open and trusting towards others; or else he was determined to be specially helpful to me.

On one of the sofas at the end of the room was seated the Duchess of Windsor, and opposite her a heavy-sitting, glandular woman in black, with a skull cap of cropped grey hair and a big soft face and body; I misjudged this woman, I later realised, chiefly because she had such a very whining voice and the most exasperating kind of French z-ish accent in English.

'Do you know Mrs Rogers?'* said the Duchess after I had shaken hands with her. 'Well, didya have a good journey? You got our wyah?' A few enquiries about Cologne and the train. The whole atmosphere was intensely unstrained and un-shy, owing, I should say, to the Duchess and the job she has done on the Duke. It is all very merry and very happy; life is quite blazingly a romp and must be kept that way. Every conceivable luxury and creature-comfort is brought, called on, conscripted, to produce a perfection of sybaritic living. It is, of course, intensely American, but I would think consciously aimed. The Queen Mother at Clarence House is leading a lodging-house existence compared to this.

THE DUCHESS OF WINDSOR

This is one of the very oddest women I have ever seen. It is impossible to assess what makes her function or why. I should say she was on the whole a stupid woman, with a small petty brain, immense goodwill (*une femme de bonne vo-lonté*) and a stern power of concentration. Like her house, she is tremendously American, and specifically Southern – it was like being back in Montgomery, Alabama, without the tree moss. I should therefore be tempted to classify her simply as An American Woman *par excellence*, were it not for the suspicion that she is not a woman at all. She is, to look at, phenomenal. She is flat and angular, and could have been designed for a medieval playing-card. The shoulders are small and high; the head very, very large, almost monumental; the expression is either anticipatory (signalling to one, 'I know this is going to be loads of fun, don't yew?') or appreciative – the great giglamp smile, the wide, wide open eyes, which are so very large and pale and veined, the painted lips and the cannibal teeth. There is one further facial contortion, reserved for speaking of the Queen Mother, which is very unpleasant to behold, and seemed to *me* akin to frenzy; I only got this one completely on the last evening. She is wildly good-natured and friendly; but with both of them one somehow feels that so much enthusiasm might suddenly gell up and one would be in the limbo reserved for the many,

---

* Lucy Wann, Alsatian widow of Air Commodore Archibald Wann (d. 1948). She married in 1950: second wife to Herman Rogers (1892–1957). It was with Herman Rogers and his first wife, Katherine (d. 1949), that the Duchess of Windsor had stayed at their villa, Lou Viei, in Cannes after her flight from England in advance of the Abdication. Lucy later lived in Monte Carlo, and tabloid biographers suggested a rift with the Duchess.

THE DUCHESS OF WINDSOR

many people who have treated them badly or turned out a disappointment. I like having my jokes laughed at; but there's no need to make the mill-beams rock with appreciation of them.

Her high smooth flat forehead is cloven by a deep singly vertical line of concentration. Her neck makes her age (sixty-one[*]) apparent, a tendency to wattles. Her jawbone is alarming, and from the back you can plainly see it jutting beyond the neck on each side.

I had two Bloody Marys and the Duchess two dry martinis, during which she told me about Elsa Maxwell's[†] self-invited arrival the next morning. I asked her about Miss Maxwell, and she said, 'Just you wait and see.' She told me about how Elsa had 'taken me apart' on the TV network. There is a very strong New York side to the Windsors' lives; and names like CBS keep cropping up in the conversation.

We walked across to the main house for lunch, during which we talked of Bridget Paget, Daisy Fellowes,[‡] Downside etc. The food was spectacularly good – *finesses* of which I had never thought like a purée of celery roots, instead of potatoes, for example. After lunch we went up to the drawing room which is over the hall and servants' part of the main house, and on a level at the back with the hillside. The Duchess took me to see my room, showing me the one in which my things weren't laid out (a mistake later rectified: 'David, go tell Sidney[§] to put Mr Pope-Hennessy's things in the black and white room. I want him to have that room, not the green one'). The room in the stables ('Les Saylibataires we call it, but we never do have bachelors') was very pretty and convenient, and once more prepared or planned by a perfectionist; there was nothing on earth that you might conceivably want that wasn't there – every kind of writing paper, nail-file, brush,

---

[*]   Official age [J.P.-H]. The Duchess was sixty-two.

[†]   Elsa Maxwell (1883–1963), an enormously fat American woman, who wrote books and social columns and was ingenious at making the rich have a good time. The Duchess and she were variously on excellent terms or engaged in bitter feuds.

[‡]   Daisy Decazes (1887–1962). Her second marriage in 1919 was to Hon Reginald Fellowes (1884–1964). She was a well-known figure in society, with a villa in the South of France and a yacht, *Sister Anne*.

[§]   Sidney Johnson (1923–90), the Duke's Afro-Bahamian valet from Andros, in the Bahamas. He joined their staff at Government House, Nassau in 1940, and they took him to Paris with them in 1945. He left the Duchess's service shortly after the Duke's death in 1972. He was later re-employed at the house, when Mohammed al Fayed took over the lease.

fruit, ice-water; the bathroom loaded with scent-bottles like a counter at a bazaar – a delicious sense of self-indulgence. She told me how to ring Paris, and how to ring London on the white instrument by the bed; there was a complete telephone book for the household, in which she is referred to as S.A.R.[*] la Duchesse (she is a Royal Highness to all the valets, as well as to Elsa Maxwell; I did a middling thing of head-inclination on arriving and leaving).

The Duke was superintending the installation of a new sundial, a Queen Anne brass or bronze dial found at Miami, and a base made by Jansen of crumbling 'antiqued' stone. After pottering in my bedroom, I wandered along the garden, up the hill past the millstream, attracted by a yelping noise (which I later identified as the Duke's theme when he is excited) and a stream of German oaths. Round the corner of the house I found the Duke, wearing a cerise felt baseball cap. He was jumping about rather wildly, and shouting 'Ja wohl, Ja wohl' and other military German expressions to a troop of French gardeners who were lugging the stone base of the sundial on to its mount, the ropes slipping and chipping the stone as it went. The Duchess, flat against the inside of the drawing room window, was looking on in a disinterested angular way, one hand on the window pane, with Mrs Rogers beside her.

'Oh, it's you? Hello,' said the Duke. 'Now this is a very big moment for us. We've been waiting for this bloody thing for months. Just take a look at it' – throwing me the brass sundial top as though it were a discus – 'Got it in Miami. It's Queen Anne, too. And here's what I've had cut in the stone: «I am a sundial and I make a botch of what is better done by any watch»: Belloc. I found it in one of his books[†] and I thought well we *must* have that. Good, isn't it?'

'I've never seen that by Belloc before, Sir.'

'Nor've I. But good, isn't it?'

'Isn't the stone chipping rather?'

'Bloody soft stuff. We'll have to turn it again.' He began shouting at the gardeners, again in German, while we all discussed the merits of cement or secotine to stick the bits on with. The Duchess edged out of the window, and I approached her

'Well, and what is the mat-ter naow?' she asked.

'The stone is chipping as they move it.'

---

[*] Son Altesse Royale. One of the Duke of Windsor's lasting concerns was that his brother had denied his wife the title of Royal Highness at the time of their wedding in 1937.

[†] Hilaire Belloc, an epigram in *Sonnets and Verse* (1923): 'I am a sundial, and I make a botch/Of what is done far (much?) better by a watch.'

'Now isn't that too bad? I must ring Jansen*.'

'I didn't know Jansen did sundials?'

'Why Jansen do just every-thing. I must say it's well antiqued.'

'Are the gardeners German?' I enquired.

'Well no, one is Alsatian, and one is Spanish, and that lil' boy is only four-teen. But, as the Dook's German is sort of better than his French, he likes to talk German with them.'

'Now I hope you'll get in your talk with the Dook this afternoon,' she continued. 'He's very excited about his *cadran* just now; but, when that's finished, you must catch him; But you'll find the Dook is kind of a slow starter,' with a great wide smile. The Duke shouted to me that I should go to his room and use his desk if I wanted to work or write letters, and he would be in later. Earlier, just after lunch, he had offered to show me his mother's letters; and; after some discussion, they arranged for his filing cabinet to be brought down that evening from Paris, in the station wagon bringing a young man named Walter Leese[†], for long the organiser of our Embassy and now working for Niarchos[‡].

I went and wrote some letters, and then sat reading *Middlemarch* until the Duke stuck his enquiring head through the door about three-thirty and came in, sitting on the sofa opposite my chair to talk. This talk, interrupted by tea in the drawing room, was exceedingly interesting and encouraging, and went on till seven. The pugs gambolled about during it – Disraeli, Trooper and Davey Crockett ('We did have a fourth, called Peter Townsend,'[§] the Duchess explained with her least nice grin; 'but we gave the Group Captain away').

---

* Maison Jansen, famous interior decorating house in Paris, represented by Stéphane Boudin (1888–1967) from 1936 to 1961. Jansen had created regal drawing rooms and galleries at 24 Boulevard Suchet, the first Paris home of the Windsors. He was also responsible for the decoration of Château La Croë in the South of France, and their last home in the Bois de Boulogne.

† Walter Lees (1916–2010), social homosexual figure, attached to the British Embassy in Paris, who later retired to London. Nancy Mitford based the character of Philip in her novel *Don't Tell Alfred* on him.

‡ Stavros Niarchos (1909–96), Greek shipping millionaire, who was the first to build oil tankers large enough to transport oil in substantial quantities.

§ Group-Captain Peter Townsend (1914–95), famed Battle of Britain pilot, and later Equerry to King George VI. In 1953 and 1955 there was press interest in the possibility that he might marry Princess Margaret.

'Now,' said the Duke with his cockneyfied vowels, 'expect you've got some questions to ask me, haven't you?'

'Well, not exactly questions, Sir. I think I had better tell Your Royal Highness just what material I have worked at and where in Queen Mary's life I am.' (This to make clear that I had seen everything.) He then talked with complete freedom, even of the delicate subject to which he obliquely refers as '1936', and made various points:

'My mother *loathed* the country. She was a Londoner. She was born – where was she born?'

'Kensington Palace, Sir.'

'That's it. She used to say to me, 'I was born in Kensington and I am a *Londoner.*' She hated Sandringham, Balmoral was a bit better; but we were always there too long. Sandringham was dreadful' (then usual description of squash in the cottage, absurd position for a monarch, Queen Alexandra etc.). Other points:

1. On my bringing up Queen Mary's superior accomplishments and education as compared to her in-law family, he completely agreed. 'Of my aunts, my father's sisters, well, you might say they could just read and write, period. That was all.' Princess Victoria* a bitch of the first order. After an illness, the King [George V] was told to go South and they all went to Genoa by train, and then the yacht met them (King, Queen, Princess Victoria). When Queen Mary came back she told her eldest son that every minute had been ruined for her by the King and Princess Victoria – whenever *she* organised visits to Pompeii, etc., *they* spoiled it all by silly jokes and laughter. 'I had been so much looking forward to going to Italy again, and we never do go away anywhere now; and now your father has asked Aunt Toria, and I would rather not go at all.'

2. 'Off the record, since you've seen everything, I'd better tell you how things were; but not for the book. My father had a most horrible temper. He was foully rude to my mother. Why, I've often seen her leave the table because he was so rude to her, and we children would all follow her out; not when the staff were present, of course, but when we were alone.'

---

* Princess Victoria, George V's second sister, who used to report the misdemeanours of his sons to him.

3. Extreme reticence of Queen Mary. Never mentioned the Duke of Clarence to them in their lives. Never told them anything about her upbringing or her father and mother. Duke just remembers a great looming shape – his grandmother, Duchess of Teck.

4. Had spent the morning wondering whom I should see. Made various extremely good suggestions, including Lady Eva Dugdale's daughter*. I ought to see Alec Hardinge[†] – 'I don't care for him as you may imagine. I just managed not to put my hand behind my back at my mother's funeral when I saw him.'

5. Queen Mary's spasms of improvidence. An *antiquaire* in Delhi, a Hungarian Jew named Imre Schreiber, would send her Jaipur enamels and jade elephants with jewelled howdahs on approval. 'Bought 'em all.'

6. Her greatest pleasure was Windsor, where there was always work to be done. 'Nobody had ever done anything about Windsor, d'you see. I don't believe Queen Victoria knew a damn thing about anything of that sort; and, when one of the children got married, they'd say 'Oh Mamma, may I have that chair that's always been in my bedroom?' and away it would go, leaving eleven in a set. Well, my mother corrected all that; she brought things back and bought them back too with her own money.'

7. His mother's passion for India. It caught her fancy as nothing else ever did.

8. I remarked I was puzzled by the shutting-down of Princess May's high spirits after marriage. 'Well, you're right there, I think. My father was a very repressive influence. I well remember when he used to go banging away for a week or two at some shoot in the Midlands and my mother never would go to those things; we used to have the most lovely time with her alone – always laughing and joking, down at Frogmore or wherever we might be – she was a different human being away from him. For instance, d'you remember in my book that story about giving M. Hua[‡] tadpoles on

---

* Lady Eva Greville (1860–1940), only daughter of 4th Earl of Warwick, married 1895, Colonel Frank Dugdale (1857–1924). She was Woman of the Bedchamber 1893–1940. Her daughter was Victoria (Vera) (1896–1973), by then married to Philip Frere.

† The Duke blamed Hardinge for warning him that press silence over Mrs Simpson was about to be broken.

‡ Gabriel Hua (1849–1909), tutor (along with Canon Dalton) to the Duke of Clarence and the Duke of York in their young days. Later his librarian. He also taught French at Eton.

toast for dessert? Well, she thought that was highly amusing; my father would have been furious. She liked anything of that sort when she was on her own with us.'

9. Lady Bertha Dawkins* was one of the nicest of women: 'We all loved her, we children'; but one of the ugliest. The King loathed sitting next to her because she was so ugly, and used to try to avoid it.

He said suddenly: 'You realise there are only three completely royal persons alive now? My sister, my brother and myself.' He remarked that almost everyone he could think of for me to see was dead. 'We're finding the same thing now too,' he continued wistfully. 'This year we've lost a number of great friends, real friends. It's because we're getting older, I suppose.'

Tea was another serious, perfectionist meal, with the Duchess struggling manfully with the teapot (she evidently hates tea, and looks very out of place pouring it out; but the Duke drinks, she assured, cup after cup all day; 'He leaves haff the cup, too, so it gets cold,' she added. After it we returned to the big room and went on talking. About seven the pugs became restless; and the Duke, who had been sipping milk brought him by the Bahamian house-boy (coloured), suggested a drink in the bar. When we got to the drawing room again, we found that Walter Lees had arrived – a youngish man who seems much cherished by the Duke and Duchess.

BAR SCENE 7.00 P.M.

J.P.-H. and the Duchess, who is pouring him out a dollop of whiskey. Duke in the drawing room talking to Mrs Rogers and Lees. The bar is small and low, attached to the drawing room and entered by a door beside the fireplace. Round two walls a gouache illustrated map of the Bahamas, from their beach hut there; soon to be replaced by two *trompe l'œil* someone gave the Duchess for Christmas.

Duchess of Windsor (lowering her voice dramatically and grimacing) '*That* is Her-man Rog-ers' wid-ow!'

J. P.-H. 'So I gathered. But surely she's not the Mrs Rogers in your book?'†

---

*   Queen Mary's Lady-in-Waiting.

†   The Duchess of Windsor, *The Heart has its Reasons* (Michael Joseph, 1956).

Duchess 'Why heavens no! She was Herman's second wife. And she kept him away from all his old friends; in fact, the Dook did say he'd never speak to her again. But she just wrote and proposed herself; said she sort of felt Herman was sending her towards us. You see you're having a pretty mixed-up visit, what with Elsa tomorrow and all.'

J. P.-H. 'She seems rather strange, Mrs. Rogers.'

Duchess 'She certainly is that. And she talks all the time, did you notice that? I couldn't shut her up at all.'

The Duchess settling herself on a low wide day-bed by the wall, her legs tucked up; she does not curl up; but somehow dismantles herself, so that she looks like a puppet lying in the wings of a toy theatre. J. P.-H. on a low stool.

Duchess 'We-e-ell, and has the Dook been much help?'

J. P.-H. 'Oh, a tremendous help, Duchess; I can't tell you.'

Duchess 'He was pretty close to his mother, you know.'

J. P.-H. 'Yes, I realised that.'

Duchess 'I suppose you've had to see *everybody* about yah book?'

J.P.-H. 'Oh yes, I have had a lot of interviews. The Duke's sister has been very helpful, and the Queen Mother.'

Duchess 'I don't think *she* was very close though.'

J.P.-H. 'The Queen Mother?'

Duchess (in a slightly steely tone) 'Why yes, I don't think the Queen Mother would know about Queen Mary.'

J.P.-H. 'Well, of course, she doesn't remember as far back as the Duke would.'

Duchess 'Y'know there are only three real royalties in the world today. The Dook, his brother Gloucester and his sister.'

J.P.-H. 'So the Duke was saying just now.'

Duchess (with seeming irrelevance) 'Just everything happens to me. When I was over in England last, I wanted a new maid; so I intervood one who'd been with [name omitted in manuscript] a year and a half. And I said, "And where were you before that?" Well, she told me she had been five years with the Queen Mother! Well, I brought her over here; but she was used to palaces. She thought the house in town was all right; but; when she came down here and I said to her "Isn't this a funny little place, Irene," she just pursed up her lips and said "It's very quaint", and I could see she thought it just wasn't the place for a former King of

England to live in. But I had to get rid of her: I had a Balenciaga* dress with a crinoline. Well, Irene ironed that crinoline so that you couldn't see what it was by the time she'd finished. I took it back, but even Mr Balenciaga himself couldn't decide just *what* she had done to that crinoline. And she just *burned up* five more of my dresses. Well, that surprised me, because I thought that, after all those years with the Queen Mother, if she hadn't learnt to iron a crinoline, what *had* she learned? And, you know, whenever I see pictures of those poor girls, with their suits all screwed up under the arms, I think of Irene. I'd like to take those girls' clothes apart and loosen them up.'

J.P.-H. 'Oh, Duchess, now *you* can tell me all about this young Saint Laurent at Dior's†. I do so much want to know.'

The Duchess became very intelligently informative about Dior's gifts, Balenciaga, the way their clothes are made and worn, her conversations with them – 'Well, I'll *buy* that dress; but I won't *wear* it' – how, with some very grand dresses, garnets go better than rubies – and so on. Controversial topics were evaded, and the conversation became imperceptibly flirtatious and slightly intimate.

Subsequent return to royal topics:

Duchess 'Isn't this a very difficult book to write?'

J.P.-H. 'Yes, it is, both because of Queen Mary's reticence, and because royal psychology is hard to grasp, if you know what I mean.'

Duchess 'I certainly do know. Why, when I first married the Dook I was very confused. Becoming a public figure in almost middle age was no joke. If I went out shopping to buy a length of scarlet rib-bon, people would collect to watch me, and I got, well, just so confused I'd buy green rib-bon instead and go running out of the shop. But the Dook now doesn't notice. If we went to a shop together, he'd just go right on choosing as if there was no-one there at all.'

J.P.-H. 'You must have a bad time in that way.'

Duchess 'Well, it *was* difficult.'

J.P.-H. 'But you've got over it now?'

Duchess 'Why, for Heaven's *sakes*, I've been married *twenty years*! Nobody's interested any more; they are interested in younger people than us. Though I

---

* Cristóbal Balenciaga (1885–1972) ran his fashion house in Paris 1937–68.

† Yves Saint Laurent (1936–2008), fashion designer. In 1957, when he was twenty-two, he took over running Dior after Christian Dior's sudden death in unsalubrious circumstances while taking a cure at Montecatini.

must say when we went to Lay Trwas Kartiers at Christmas*, it happened to be Children's Day. Well, how could I know it was Children's Day? A'd there was one mother pointed me out to her lil boy and began telling him the *whole* story of the Abdication. Noo York was bad, too, in the past; but there they jest don't notice any more. There's younger people they're interested in.'

Before dinner, having had my bath and changed, I was standing by the fire-place in the hall, when the front door flew open and the Duke scampered in, making his yelping noise on seeing me; he was wearing red trousers, a fur coat, and a peaked flying cap with fur ear-flaps. He was followed by the valet carrying some clothes.

'You were quick, weren't you?' he said as he dashed upstairs. When he came down again, very spick and span in a Balmoral tartan kilt, he smiled with great charm: 'I say, you saw a pretty quaint apparition just now? Whatever did you think, I wonder? My shower's broken, do you see, so I use another in one of the other rooms. Why they put me into red pants I can't imagine.'

We stood about talking, and presently a tapping of high heels and the creak of stiff silk announced the Duchess, who wound her way down the staircase sheathed in a red-orange very tight, almost hobbled, dress. We had vodka and *pâté de foie gras*, and then dinner. After dinner, the Duke lugged me off (most willingly on my part) for a preliminary look at his papers, which had arrived from Paris and were placed in a spare bedroom. A tall white tin filing-cabinet, with five or six drawers, stood on a ground sheet at the foot of a green chintz bed. He unlocked it, tossed me the keys, and we sat down side by side on the bed.

'There's a lot of valuable stuff here, you know,' he said. 'Unlike the Duchess, I am very well-documented. But I keep them all under years, not under people. Let's take a look now at 1936.' He seized one of the two 1936 files and showed me various letters – until we reached one from Queen Mary, begging him not to broadcast. 'Surely you might spare yourself this strain and emotion' etc. A look of real disgust crossed over his face. 'She even tried that! Well, I ask you … If I hadn't done that …'

We began to talk about the Abdication. 'People can say what they like for it or against it, I don't care; but one thing is certain: I *acted in good faith*. And I was treated bloody shabbily.' A random example of this treatment, with which I strong-ly sympathised, was the fact (attested by receipted bills) that he had produced

---

* Les Trois Quartiers, 23 Boulevard de la Madeleine in Paris.

£4,000 of the £8,000 for the St George's Chapel monument for his father, Queen Mary paying the other half, and he had not even been invited to the dedication of it; nor had it ever been published anywhere that he had contributed.*

He spoke of Queen Mary's coldness. 'Yes, Sir, I think one of her chief difficulties in understanding your dilemma was the fact that she had never been in love herself.'

'No, I don't think she had. You're right. My mother was a cold woman, a cold woman. And I, you see, I suppose I had never really been in love before. No, I hadn't. I thought I had, but I hadn't ever been in love.'

We spent some more time looking through letters in a random fashion, and then went back to the drawing room. Before we went, he spoke up, sitting wearily on the bed, with extraordinarily moving tired charm: 'Well, I did my best, you know. I tried to bring the Monarchy into touch.'

'But King George and Queen Mary started that, with their industrial tours in 1913 and so on.'

'In a way they did, but not really. And think of my grandfather.'† His face lit up mischievously and boyishly: 'Why, look at my grandfather. He'd just sit in an open landau, receive an address, snip a ribbon and declare something open, returning to Knowsley‡ to dine with his girl friends. Didn't even leave that landau. I did my best to change all that.'

When we returned to the drawing room, the record-player was booming; it lives in a concealed cupboard outside the drawing room door, and sound comes from God knows where.

'Now listen,' said the Duchess, stepping out of the bar, 'I've been thinking. It will *never do for Elsa* to know you're writing about Queen Mary. Why, I can jest see that Toosday column – here I am staying with the Windsors, and here is Mr Pope-Hennessy who is picking every hair off the Duke's head about his mother.'

'You're correct, sweetheart,' said the Duke.

'It's exactly what I don't want, publicity,' I added.

---

* This was the cause of a major row between them. The Duke was furious and attacked his mother, as a result of which he did not communicate with her again until the death of the Duke of Kent in 1942. During this phase, she never failed to remember his birthday, but he never acknowledged hers. The incident of the tomb row is not mentioned in *Queen Mary*.

† Edward VII.

‡ Knowsley Hall, seat of the Earl of Derby, near Liverpool. Designed by Capability Brown.

THE DUKE OF WINDSOR

'Not yet, you mean,' said the Duke.

'Well, altogether. Not that sort.'

'It'd get yew in-to every kind of complication, you know,' added the Duchess. 'It wouldn't go down well at *all*.' She spoke, I am sure, in perfect good faith.

'What do we tell Elsa he's doing, then?'

'Now let's think. What *are* you doing?'

'Couldn't I just be putting the Duke's papers in order?'

'She'll want to know *what* papers and why. No. Now let me see – couldn't you be listing my fai-ence?'

'Couldn't he be a doctor?' asked Mr Lees.

'Naow, he looks too grand to be a doctor,' corrected the Duke. 'I think you're right, darling. Faience.'

'And if she takes a check by long-distance, why she'll find the brother's at the Victoria and Albert Muse-um*, don't you see?' the Duchess interposed. She went off to change a record, walking with difficulty in her sheath of orange satin. I went with her. 'Have you heard "Love, Love, Love"?'†

'Yes. I mean no. I'm not sure.'

'The record about *us*?'

'Oh no.'

'Well, I'm going to put it on for you. The Dook hasn't heard it. I only heard it two nights ago after dinner in Paris. They put it on as a kind of sur-prise, and it certainly sur-prised me, I can tell you.'

She then put on the record, a calypso: 'It was love love love and love alone that caused King Edward to leave his throne' – 'that lady from Baltimore' etc.

'I'm going to call our lawyers Monday about it. *I* think it's libellous.'

We played it twice, the Duke jigging vaguely to it. 'I don't quite see where the libel would reside, Duchess,' I volunteered. 'Shouldn't you ignore it? You can't *now* say it *wasn't* love, so to speak.'

---

*   John Pope-Hennessy (1913–94) joined the Victoria and Albert Museum in 1938. He was Keeper of the Department of Architecture and Sculpture from 1954 to 1966, and Director from 1967 to 1973. See Introduction.

†   '*It was love, love, love alone – Caused King Edward to leave his throne …*' by Harry Belafonte (b. 1927). It contained lines such as, '*I don't know what Mrs Simpson got in her bone that caused the King to leave his throne …*'

'You're right there. But I think it just so undignified. *And so offensive to the Monarchy,*' with dark emphasis.

'But you must expect to pass into folklore, Duchess. I don't see what you can do about it.'

'I jest think it is un-dig-ni-fied,' with a squaring of the angular shoulders and a slight, stiff flounce. 'I'm going to call our lawyers all the same.'

The rest of the evening, quite a lot of it, passed in general conversation, wit, jokes, laughter, whiskey; till it was suddenly (as it was left to me to point out) twelve forty-five. The servants were still up, the breakfast times and foods were fixed. 'Now, don't you begin working too early on all that stuff,' admonished the Duke of Windsor. 'I'll come in and see how you're getting on around eleven.'

The next morning, after breakfast, I repaired with my key to the filing-cabinet in the spare room. I sampled some of the files for various years, and then settled down to 1936. I soon found it irresistible to read letters other than Queen Mary's for this period; and indeed the totality of the letters, and the way they are kept, make absorbing reading. If ever published, many years hence, these documents give a complete picture of the Abdication chaos: grave letters from Ministers; earnest pleas from the Duke of Buccleuch[*]; helpful offers from the Duke of York; brilliant résumés from Churchill[†]; screeches to 'Darling Wallis' from Lady Oxford[‡]; notes from Diana Cooper[§]; messages of good cheer from Sibyl Colefax[¶]; one or two bleak letters from Queen Mary – all crowded together. Some of the most interesting to my mind are long letters from the secretary of Mrs Simpson to her ex-employer at Cannes – a mixture of gratitude, criticism, outspokenness and disapproval, ending with a £25 Christmas gift from Mrs Simpson.

---

[*] Walter, 8th Duke of Buccleuch (1894–1973). He and his wife stayed with Edward VIII at Balmoral in the summer of 1936.

[†] Sir Winston Churchill (1874–1965), a great champion of the King, who wanted him to hold his ground.

[‡] Margot Tennant, later Countess of Oxford and Asquith (1864–1945), widow of H.H. Asquith, the former Prime Minister.

[§] Lady Diana Cooper (1892–1986), an early friend, who had been on the *Nahlin* cruise.

[¶] Sybil Halsey (1874–1950), American hostess in London, married 1901, Sir Arthur Colefax (1866–1936).

After two hours, the Duke put a quizzical head round the door and said, 'Well?' rather as one might to a child one had left with a wonderful new electric train. I said how fascinating I found them.

'Oh, you're reading the lot, I see,' he said, quickly taking in the situation. 'Well, why shouldn't you, after all? Nobody else has ever seen 'em.'

'They do give a most authentic picture of the 1936 times,' I volunteered.

'Don't they though?' He sat down on the bed. 'I used 'em for my book,* some of them. But, do you know, Winston behaved most awfully badly to me, I think. He wouldn't let me quote any of his letters.'

'I was wondering, Sir, why Your Royal Highness hadn't included a very good long letter from him, I have just read.'

'Just so, just so. Well, it was at the time he was going to be Prime Minister again, an election, and he thought it might do him harm in the country. I couldn't see why. Still, I said to him I was so anxious to have a Conservative Government in England again I'd sacrifice that part of my book for it.'

Talking of Queen Mary's part in it all: 'No, I'm afraid my mother was a *moral coward*. She would never, NEVER, talk to me about it. Right up to the end, if I said anything to her, she'd just cough slightly, hm, hm, like that and that was all. She evaded all discussion.'

He asked me where I thought his letters to his mother were 'They're all at Windsor, Sir, in brown holland bags, in one of Queen Mary's tallboys or chiffonières, or whatever you call them, with marble on the top, from Marlborough House. I've been through some of them.'

'Oh. So *you've* read 'em all, have you?'

'Not all, Sir. Some.' I asked him about a letter of hers of 1938, to which I'd read his reply, and he immediately fished it out and showed it to me.

We went on talking, and then there was a dog scratching at the door, and in came the Duchess, this time in green corduroy, the same suit as the day before in a different colour. She was pulling a silk handkerchief backwards and forwards through her jewelled hands.

'Dai-sy has been on the horn,' said the Duchess. 'She says to tell you will you lunch with her tomorrow after all.' (Daisy Fellowes had already telephoned to me earlier.) The Duke told her that I had said I wanted to work at the papers for at least a week, and that he had suggested May, when they are back from New York

---

* The Duke's memoirs were *A King's Story* (Cassell, 1951).

and he can help me. 'Why yes,' said the Duchess, without, I thought, noticeable enthusiasm.

They pottered off together, looking happy and poised and matutinal. The Duchess said lunch was at one-thirty, ten in all. Would I come for drinks just before then? I went on with the files, both early and late: the last twenty years very pathetic, someone trained to work with nothing to do but answer with scrupulous politeness letters from the Pelly Bible Foundation, Inc., or notes about snipe shooting at Tallahassee, Florida. Theirs is a small pond, I fear, for all it's being café society, or maybe because of that very limiting factor.

Earlier, while we were still alone, I had spoken to the Duke seriously about his papers: 'If it's not an impertinent question Sir, what are you going to do about these papers ultimately – when we're all of us dead, in fifty years' time?'

'What do you think I should do? I haven't a clue. Do you think they should go to Windsor?'

'I think it is essential they should, Sir, as they are English history. You don't want them muddling about.'

'I suppose not. I think you're right.' It was at this point that the Duchess had stepped smartly through the door with the pugs.

At one-thirty a telephone message told me that Her Royal Highness was expecting me for a cocktail in the big room. Here I found Elsa Maxwell, a lumpy, ugly creature looking like James Boswell and wearing a blue serge coat and skirt and a white shirt, and two elderly American brothers, one of them with a wife, a Frenchman named Jacques Allez (I think; the widower of young Lady Bessborough's mother*). In my capacity as faience expert I got muddled up at once talking to Mrs Alleyn, who asked me what I *did* in London and I couldn't remember. I sat next to Miss Maxwell at lunch: trout stuffed with trout and almonds, a Virginia ham of total perfection, and so on. Maxwell took no notice of me at first, but was slowly mystified by the way the Duke and Duchess treated one, and later in the afternoon enquired of all and sundry what I was really doing in the house. She never found out.

After lunch I sat by Miss Maxwell in the drawing room for a bit, as her egomania had begun to fascinate me; she is clearly raving mad, and all about herself. I innocently asked her about her television successes: 'Thirty-one million

---

* Jacques Allez of Paris had married Mrs Charles A. Munn (d. 1950), the mother of Mary, wife of 10th Earl of Bessborough (1913–93).

people and that's quite a lot of people,' she hummed; 'and they *love* me, they *like* me, I'm their *friend*; they rely on me; they expect things from me. They love me; they like me.'

'Then I expect they also write to you?'

'Nine hundred letters a day. I have six secretaries to deal with my mail. We have no libel law; I just make them laugh and then I hit out – boom!' An expressive stunted gesture of one prehensile fist into the other accompanied this. 'I'm out gunning for every kind of filth in our public life. America's terrible now, just terrible. Ever hear of a swine called Presley? Elvis Presley*? Well, I've been after him for some months, and he's beginning to feel it right now. Got evidence. Mrs So-and-So of Seattle; her little daughter goes to hear Presley, teenager too; comes back with his autograph – he autographs, writes his signatures on young girls – well, on their breasts to be exact. They get a bit of sticky-tape and put it over the signature, so it won't rub off, see. Filthy beast, terrible man.' And so on and so on and so on.

I went back to work at the papers till a late tea. During this the subject of Mr Cleveland Amery[†] came up, the young writer the Duchess had commissioned to 'help' her with her book, and who had subsequently given unpleasant newspaper interviews. She and Elsa Maxwell both attacked him violently, unaware that he is one of Mrs Herman Rogers's greatest friends, and is indeed to complete his present book, *The End of Society*[‡], in her house in Cannes this spring. They went on and on and on about him, the Duke saying they had treated him with such candour and hospitality, and then he had let them down. The general drift seemed to be that he had offered his services or, indeed, forced them on the Duchess. So for the record I asked: 'But how did you get involved with this man, Duchess?'

'Because I'm a yes-girl.'

Before dinner I demonstrated the Indian wire toy and gave it to the Duchess to bring her luck, as I really thought her kindness merited some gesture. She says she will have it copied in gold and coral at Cartier's. She kept playing with it, treating

---

[*]   Elvis Presley (1935–77), iconic American singer, dubbed 'The King of Rock 'n Roll'.

[†]   Cleveland Amory (1917–1998), American author, who had been employed to ghost the Duchess's memoirs. He said of her: 'You can't make the Duchess of Windsor into Rebecca of Sunnybrook Farm.' This was the character in fiction with whom she chose to identify.

[‡]   Amory published *Who Killed Society?* (Harper & Bros, 1960).

it chiefly as an arm adornment. She was wearing a full short skirt embroidered or, rather, encrusted with gold thread.

The evening passed in gossip and talk. After dinner I was in a corner with the Duchess and we discussed Them and England, and it was then she looked so very fierce when saying how badly they had been treated and kept referring back to the Queen Mother. Later we went over to the cottage inhabited by Miss Maxwell to see her new mink coat, the only thing she had bought herself as a present for years, she said (I believe this to be true as she is apparently a most generous woman and makes tens of thousands of dollars but hardly ever has her plane fare as she gives it all away). The Duchess modelled this coat and some other garments of Miss Maxwell's, coming in and out of the room like a mannequin. Her final appearance was in my overcoat.

'Now this, David, is the sort of coat you should have.'

'My God, what a frightful coat, where did you get that?'

'It's not a frightful coat at all, Sir, it's my new coat and particularly nice and well-cut. I designed it partly myself.'

'It looks like it. Much too short,' etc. Etc.

In the morning, about ten, I found Miss Maxwell, very neat in a dark suit with white tippet and cuffs in fur, seated upright in the hall opposite Mrs Rogers. The Duke, who was not going to Paris, appeared and I gave him the key to his filing cabinet. The Duchess's vast car was panting at the door, laden with maids and luggage, and she soon pattered downstairs looking very fresh and vase-shaped, in a tight white or cream-coloured tweed costume with a vast pale fur collar. We said goodbye and she took Miss Maxwell off, while I followed later in the station wagon with Mrs Rogers.

Thus ended a not uninteresting visit, during which I had been treated with very great kindness.

THIRTY

THE DUKE AND DUCHESS OF BEAUFORT

Badminton *or* 'So that's what hay looks like?'

22 November

Sir Owen Morshead only just recommended a visit to the Duke and Duchess of Beaufort at Badminton: 'The only point in your visiting the place would be to gain local colour and to talk to the Duchess. I am in two minds as to whether it is worth your while.'[127] Fortunately Pope-Hennessy was not deterred.

Queen Mary had spent the war years at Badminton, the home of the 10th Duke of Beaufort (1900–84), Master of the Horse, and his wife, Lady Mary Cambridge (1897–1987), who was the daughter of 1st Marquess of Cambridge, Queen Mary's brother. The Beauforts were known for their love of hunting. The Duke was known as 'Master' and in his book of memoirs, which he neither wrote nor read, appears the memorable line: 'Obviously the hunting of the fox has been my chief concern.' After the war they founded the Badminton Horse Trials, and it was traditional for the Queen and many members of the Royal Family to stay at Badminton for the event.

The Beauforts had no children. In fact the Duchess was not able to bear children. The Duke, however (a true countryman in that he liked to pursue any living creature, be they on four legs or two), was known as something of a ladies man.

I arrived at Badminton at eight p.m. on Saturday 22 November 1958 after a very crowded dirty journey in the Red Dragon, the express to Wales which stops there because of an old concession to the Beauforts when the railway was first put through their land. It was dark and misty and I climbed into the Land Rover. Ted, the nice chatty little chauffeur told me that Queen Mary used 'to call all of us by our Christian names, always.'

In the darkness one could not see the splendid park, and we drove through the village – sandstone 17th century cottages flanking the road – under the stable arch and into the courtyard. I was taken through a long back passage, across an octagonal hall, and into a high room panelled in black oak lozenges (this room I later learned does not belong in the house and came from Raglan Castle; it is the only unpretty room in the house). Here, in front of a big fire in the high Jacobean fireplace, stood the Duke of Beaufort, and, to my relief, David and Caroline Somerset* who were staying in the house but had to go out to dinner. After they left I had some desultory conversation with the Duke, who was immensely courteous and agreeable, a tall well-proportioned man, good-looking in a high-coloured slightly Roman Consulate way. He said Queen Mary had 'taken over the whole house leaving us two bedrooms' when she arrived in 1939 with fifty or more servants. He also told me that Lady Violet Vernon[†] was coming to dinner and that she had just had a hunting accident some weeks before and 'wasn't quite herself, she talks a lot'. Lady Violet appeared: a woman of about 48, with eyes set close together in her long face, silly, kindly, dressed in a white brocade dress with an immensely long stole of emerald green wool which she wound and unwound round her neck, or just trailed yard upon yard along the floor with one hand. Quite some time later the Duchess of Beaufort (who has inherited all her grandmother's[‡] lack of punctuality) came briskly into the room, looking like a wonderful white newt and dressed in scarlet velvet – a sort of house-coat bound tightly round her plump figure with a belt like a dressing gown. She advanced eagerly upon me and stood inside the fireplace to warm herself. Her hands were like cold stone.

The Duchess of Beaufort is an interesting throw-back, as well as a perfectly delightful human being. The first white newt-like impression wears off: for her face in fact is rosier by daylight than by night. She is short, plump, appears to have no eyebrows; her forehead slopes sharply back, her head is thrust a little forward giving her shoulders the appearance of being permanently hunched. Her hair is short, sparse and very very white – a lighter, thinner texture than wool, but without the sheen of silk. Her eyes are light blue and immensely merry. She adores laughter, and gesticulates as she tells stories – at which she is prime. She always

---

* David Somerset (1928–2017), eventual heir to the 10th Duke of Beaufort. He succeeded him as 11th Duke in 1984. He married 1950, Lady Caroline Thynne (1928–95), only daughter of 6th Marquess of Bath.

† Lady Violet Baring (1911–78), younger daughter of 2nd Earl of Cromer (a former Lord Chamberlain). She married 1937, Major Mervyn Vernon (1912–91), of Bowldown Farm, Tetbury.

‡ The Duchess was a granddaughter of the Duchess of Teck.

looks as if she wants to know what's going on or to hear something amusing, and darts about the house like a happy lizard, or rushes through the rainy garden in a mackintosh hood like an extinguisher.

'We're all standing, you see, because the dogs have the seats' she remarked; a fact I had only vaguely noticed before; and indeed the four armchairs and the sofa each had a small dog – terriers, pekinese etc. – lying firmly on it, a white linen cloth covering the chintz. These dogs are always at her heels, or else resting up; they are well behaved, obedient and genial and not, like the Windsors' pugs, spoiled or sophisticated. In fact no greater contrast could be imagined than between the Mill at Gif-sur-Yvette and Badminton House. (The Duchess was later much interested in what I could tell her of the Mill and its atmosphere. '*I* always think that Mrs Simpson should have a public monument put up to her in this country' she remarked; and: 'He could be *perfectly charming* but he could be *perfectly beastly*. He was two people really – he had frizzy-what's-name schizophrenia? That's what I mean. I always saw him as two people.' She, too, speaks of the Duke of Windsor in the past tense.)

We dined in the next room, which under Queen Mary's reign at Badminton had been the drawing room, the 'Oak Room' in which we had first met being her dining room; they would eat with her, being given at most half a snipe for dinner after a long hungry day out hunting or on the farm. The dinner-table could easily seat twelve or sixteen persons: 'We're very spread out, you see, but we're too lazy to shut the table up.'

During dinner the Duchess regaled me with anecdotes of the Queen at Badminton. 'When I saw her arrive I was scared *stiff* – more than fifty of them descended on me one afternoon and I was all alone, Master was away. You've never seen anything like that arrival in your life.' Queen Mary speedily took over the whole house, and arranged her own life and theirs. During the first air-raid a message was sent to the Duchess that the Queen was in the reinforced shelter and wished her to come down. 'It was a mistake, of course, she hadn't sent for me at all. Well there I was in the middle of the night, with my hair all anyhow and in a filthy old dressing gown; and there in the shelter sat Queen Mary, perfectly dressed with her pearls, doing a crossword puzzle. On one side of her was her Lady*, who had taken a sleeping pill and kept sagging over to

---

* Lady Constance ('Pussy') Milnes-Gaskell (1885–1964), Woman of the Bedchamber to Queen Mary 1937–53.

one side whenever the Queen said "High life in six letters beginning with a T, Constance" – she'd just grunt "huh-huh-huh" and flop over again; on the other side of the Queen was her maid gripping two jewel cases grimly. I never did that again, I just couldn't compete.'

During and after dinner the Duchess told me many things and roared with laughter at what I told her. She said the Duchess of Teck, leaving White Lodge two hours late, would always put her head out of the brougham and egg Kitchener on: 'Fly Kitchener! Fly!' she would cry. The Duke of Teck's room was re-done after Tel-el-Kebir and became a tent – the one he had used in that short campaign. 'He was *raving* of course' – 'where does all the madness come from? Look at the Duke of Windsor, then there was Prince John, then I'm mad in my own way.' She had been brought up on the word Rumpenheim; and felt that she resembled Princess Claudine of Teck. She was very proud of her great-grandmother Countess Rhedey – 'think of being trampled to death *by a squadron of cavalry*' – rather fine, that'. King George V's sisters were also idiots. There was a lot of madness about.

She had always wondered why Baroness Burdett-Coutts, a carefully chosen godmother, had 'never left her a bean' but fancies it was because the Baroness had done so much for her grandparents.

Her own mother 'adored' the Duchess of Teck.

Princess May was very proud of her legs and ankles. As a girl she would jump on to a sofa at games so that people could see them.

She was always told that the Duke of Clarence was 'an idiot'. Lord Claud Hamilton is 'abominable' and Alec Hardinge[†] a fool. Far from being cold, as they all thought, Queen Mary was full of heart. The Duchess had had a heavenly time when she replaced Princess Mary after the latter's marriage[‡]; she particularly loved the King and didn't mind the shouting.

She asked me which Strelitz it was who had had a baby by the footman? Queen Mary told her that the girl's mother[§] behaved very badly over it. In the war Aunt

---

[*] The Countess was killed when her horse ran away with her in Vienna in 1841.

[†] Alec Hardinge, 2nd Viscount Hardinge of Penshurst (1894–1960), Private Secretary to Edward VIII at the time of the Abdication, and to George VI 1937–43.

[‡] As a young girl, the Duchess was used as a companion to Queen Mary after Princess Mary married Viscount Lascelles in February 1922, and until she herself married in June 1923.

[§] Duchess Marie von Strelitz and her mother, Elisabeth.

Augusta turned very pro-German and wrote the Queen such dreadful letters that the Queen gave up answering them in the end.

As children they absolutely *hated* Princess Victoria.

Queen Mary was incredibly diffident. 'So you think they would *really* like to see me?' she would say; she consistently underrated herself and was touched at any sign of appreciation.

Once Queen Mary got an idea in her head she never got it out again 'for several days'. She was fundamentally very very German – the two things she liked most were *destruction* and *order*. When left to herself for the day she would have trees cut down right and left in the garden until the Beauforts diverted her into the woods. On leaving for hunting one day the Duchess said: 'Now, Aunt May, remember that those shrubs outside the stable wall are not to be touched'; the next day Queen Mary took her out and every shrub was gone, revealing a naked wall which then had to be cemented and painted. Before the Duchess could say anything Queen Mary, 'like a naughty child' said quickly: 'I'm so glad to see you like my yesterday's work'. She was determined that the great cedar tree outside the window, one of the beauties of the garden, should be felled, but they fought tooth and nail and saved it. When she got the idea of salvage into her head she would return home with the car laden with field-harrows and other implements left in the fields in the normal course of agriculture and they all had to be taken back again. When the wooding started, the Queen didn't want to use her petrol and with great difficulty a farm cart pulled by two horses was produced. In this were two basket chairs for the Queen and Cynthia Colville. 'You look as if you were in a tumbril, Aunt May.' 'Well, it may come to that yet, one never knows' she replied. Later she would set out in her green Daimler, bolt upright, with saws and other utensils strapped on to the back. The ivy-mania was more destructive than preservative in intention, the Duchess thought. She would go out in all weathers, from two till five; the Ladies loathed it, Cynthia lost her wedding-ring, Major Wickham* broke his wrist, they all would dodge behind the undergrowth to rest and smoke until she caught them. On days when they picked up roots in the open fields there was no chance of dodging.

---

*   Major John Wickham (1886–1962), Private Secretary to Queen Mary 1937–53. He was said by then to be senile and did not respond to Pope-Hennessy's requests for help with his book. The Duke of Windsor tried to stir him into life without success.

The Duke who had been hunting went to bed after Lady Violet left. The Duchess asked was I tired, she was enjoyin' it so? I said not at all. We sat up till 12.15. 'I'm like all of us, we are never tired, we're *monsters*, none of our family have *ever* felt tired or *ever* want to go to bed – is it the Cambridge blood, do you think?'

She was delighted to hear that I thought the Queen had enjoyed Badminton. 'I never quite knew, such ghastly things happened like the Duke of Kent's death*, and then these things alternated with such comedies, such as when the Queen, who hated dogs, gave the Bishop of Gloucester† a Spratts shape and said 'give this to that little dog' and he bein' deaf thought it was for him and munched it up.'

She thought the Queen liked Jack Coke‡ best of her entourage, because he was always like a bad schoolboy and always(?) getting into trouble which delighted her. 'Maggie Wyndham used to complain of the intellectual level of our conversation – she wanted to talk about Italy or Trollope and there were we all just talking about haymaking and hunting. But Queen Mary soon picked it all up. When she came here she didn't even know what hay was – when I pointed to a hayfield and said look at our hay she replied, studying it: "Oh *that's* what hay looks like, is it, I never knew that". She was totally urban but got used to the country.'

Queen Mary was very much interested in some unexploded bombs which fell behind the post-office.

Queen Mary had strong views on divorced people, but she always managed to find some excuse for seeing those who owned some house she wished to go over. They began to run out of houses before she left Badminton, as she never liked seeing the same house twice.

'*Why* was Queen Alexandra so beastly to her? She was, you know, too beastly. Jealous, do you think?'

'She felt the Abdication more than anything that happened to her in the whole of her life.'

---

*   The Duke of Kent died in a flying accident on 25 August 1942.

†   Rt Rev Arthur Headlam (1862–1947), 33rd Bishop of Gloucester 1923–45). A man described as 'brusque and insensitive, even hard and unsympathetic ... Deafness had long troubled him, but until near the end of his life he was a man of strong and massive frame.' [DNB, 1941–50 (OUP, 1959), pp.370–1].

‡   Major Hon Sir John Coke (1880–1957), fifth son of 2ⁿᵈ Earl of Leicester. Equerry to Queen Mary 1938–53.

The Duchess, five dogs flowing about her skirts, showed me upstairs to my bedroom; it was the first time I had got any impression of the house, other than that gained from the two Canaletto paintings of it on easels in the Oak Room. 'How perfectly lovely they are,' I had said to the Duke: 'I don't know about their being lovely, but they're very like the house' he answered. The staircase was highly polished, with somewhat shallow treads and darker balustrading; a further stair-case twisted to the wing in which I was sleeping. Next morning I was woken by the stable clock striking the hour and then after that by the man with morning tea. Looking out of the window, one could see the opposite wing of the house, all of the same Cotswold coloured stone, but saturated in mist and light November rain. When I got down at five past nine I found the Duke and Duchess seated at the breakfast table, she wearing a strawberry coloured tweed coat and skirt, and busy giving the dogs their porridge out of plastic saucers coloured pink or pale green. We had got on so well and so fast the night before that I felt that slight shyness inevitable on such occasions – i.e. those of seeing the person again the next morning; however this was soon dispelled and we discussed plans and the Sunday papers and how Lord Digby* staying for the Three Day Event had eaten the dogs' porridge by mistake each morning, and none of them had known how to explain it to him so he went on doing it. After breakfast the Duke said to his wife: 'Have you got any time before church?' 'Of course. What do you want me to do?' 'To come up to the Worcester Lodge and we'll take in Chapell on the way'. She looked steadily at him and then almost secretively: 'I think I'll take the dogs for a walk. You go with David.' This turned out to be a plan to show me the park and Queen Mary's Plantation; I only later realised or twigged that taking the dogs for a walk meant going to see the Duchess's newest possession-obsession, a Pyrenean sheepdog standing five feet high or so – I never got to see it, it was a secret pleasure of her own it seemed.

At ten David Somerset and I set off with the Duke in the Land Rover, skirting first the wall of the estate, off which Queen Mary had hacked all the ivy so that it looked still clean and new, and past many pheasants strutting aimlessly and tamely about in the stubble. We stopped at a gate by a tiny Gothic folly to pick up a stout bucolic man with grey hair and a red-wax face, dressed in an old raincoat with a scarlet shirt and holding staff in his hand. This was Charlie Chapell the head forester who had been in charge of Queen Mary's party and had deputed

---

* 11th Lord Digby (1894–1964), father of Pamela Harriman (later US Ambassador to Paris).

one of the undermen to keep with them 'to see they didn't cut their hands off or anything'. We drove to a plantation of new firs – Queen Mary's Plantation', 16½ acres and very impressive. He described, much as the Duke and Duchess had done, how organised she had been about it, and that in rain she would continue working beneath an umbrella. Places were chosen for her where the brambles had been cut away, but on the whole she went into any part of the woods however thick. He also described, as Ted Hallett had done, the *cigaretten pause* in the mid-afternoon; also how she would grunt when he said 'It's five o'clock Your Majesty' – 'TTTT-t-t-t-t is it five already?' He regarded it all as very entertaining, but said the work was useful and thorough; it also provided the company of soldiers with firewood all through the winter. We went on to see the Worcester Lodge, by Kent, an ornamental gateway with a fine small banqueting room with good stucco above it, and Swangrove House, a house built in 1703 on the edge of Swangrove wood and now inhabited by a farmer; here also there is a panelled room used for shooting luncheons. Queen Mary had cleared the brambles in front of Worcester Lodge and would also pop into Swangrove House, as well as into the houses in the village when so minded.

On the way back through the garden, one got a clearer impression of this very beautiful house, which was re-faced by Kent and, although a large house, does not give the feel of being one – partly perhaps because the library, the vast drawing room, the yellow drawing room and so on are shut up. All these rooms the Duchess showed me, as well as the famous [Eworth?]* portraits of the Elizabethan Somersets and a little back room [upper servants' hall?] where hang the portraits of Pss. Claudine of Teck, Duke Alexr. of Württemberg and so on. The great drawing room, designed by Wyatt, has magnificent yellowing Reynolds full-lengths as well as some charming little Houdon heads of Somerset children of that day. Upstairs she showed me Queen Mary's bedroom – unchanged and just as one wd. imagine it, with a silk-upholstered four-poster – her sitting room (whither she retired after dinner and the news), and her bathroom. She also showed me on the west front the state bedrooms, occupied by the Duchess of Teck and Princess May in the 1880s, the one a fine Chinese room, the other with an alcove, a tiny warm sitting room separating the two. She told me Queen Mary was constantly fussed about the rations, and cut herself and them down to a minimum, whereas

---

*   Hans Eworth (ca 1520–74)

her servants guzzled. It was a fear of being criticised publicly, she thought: 'people will say I am having special treatment' was the line.

Queen Mary would receive any special guest in the then drawing room (now dining room) and after dinner anyone she wished to see would be taken upstairs to her sitting room. Here she would often sit or lie on her chaise-longue, polishing her nails (of which she was proud) as she talked.

While at Badminton, Pope-Hennessy also had conversations with Abbott, the butler ; Perks, the gardener ; and Woodclarke, the bailiff.

MR PERKS

Mr Perks, the head gardener at Badminton, a small, thinnish man with dark eyes and going rather bald, an amused expression. He told me :

1. Queen Mary liked gardens very much, but not gardening. She was always coming round the garden, and he was warned that if he saw her coming he was never to try to slip off but to speak with her. She was always poking the ground or the beds with her stick and parasol. In the rain she wore short rubber boots, half way up her calf.
2. Whenever she found him doing anything she wanted to do it too. 'Now, I'm sure I can do that. Would it be a help?' She tried pollinating peach-blossom with a rabbit's foot on a stick which he had been using; one of the open blossoms fell off and she stopped. 'You see I'm knocking all the flowers off.'
3. She adored flowers 'from the orchid to the geranium, yes even the geranium.' She would have quantities of orchids and other flowers sent for her rooms from neighbouring nursery gardens as Badminton could not produce enough.
4. She would go out in all weathers.
5. One day she was wheeling one of her grandchildren (? a Gloucester infant*) in the village in a pram. 'Not even a curtain twitched, it was too disappointing. I had nobody to show Baby to' she told him afterwards.

---

* Prince William of Gloucester was born in 1941; Prince Michael of Kent in 1942; and Prince Richard of Gloucester in 1944.

6. On leaving, she saw the nine 'heads of department ; in the hall, and gave them each a present. Tears were streaming down her face. She said to Mr Perks: 'Oh, I *have* been happy here. Here I'm anybody to everybody and back in London I shall have to be Queen Mary all over again.'

Note on Q.M. & flowers from the Dss of Beaufort's talks: 'She was mad about flowers. She would be delighted at seeing *the* most hideous villa garden if it had a laburnum for instance in it. 'Isn't that *lovely*, too lovely ?' she would say as we drove by some ghastly house with a flower in the garden.'

After his visit, Pope-Hennessy recalled to his brother another line from the Duchess of Beaufort, which differs slightly to that recorded above:

I have also done Badminton, infinitely rewarding and I love the Duchess of Beaufort: 'Tell me why we are all so mad?' she said. 'My grandfather was raving, then there's the Duke of Windsor, Prince John, the Duke of Gloucester, and then I'm mad too.' I gleaned so much to enliven that chapter.[128]

THIRTY-ONE

Through a Box Darkly

December

This was Pope-Hennessy's second visit to the Windsors at the Mill, following the Duchess's late-night telephone call, in which she invited him to help the Duke with some fashion articles.

(SCENE: Inside the Duchess of Windsor's Cadillac; Beyond the limousine glass, which is up, the windscreen, which is dark blue, increases the sense of being in a glass box. The windows are closed, the world outside this scented enclosure shows as white mist. Warm air purrs through a small silver contraption which the Duchess, evidently rattled for some reason, switches on and off with a finger weighted with a heavy pearl. The Duchess, wearing a sleeveless coat of mink over a blue suit, is sunk back in one corner of the Cadillac, J.P.-H. in the other. It is eleven a.m. on the morning of Monday 1 December 1958 and the car is leaving the Mill. A small oncoming car heads straight for us.)

Duchess (shrinking back still further) 'Oah! Oah! That was *Boyer's* fault. He's on the wrong side of the road.'

J.P.-H. 'It's very misty this morning.'

Duchess 'It cert'nly is. Jaymes, do yew hate Munn-days the way I hate Munn-days?'

J.P.-H. 'I don't think anybody likes Monday much, Duchess.'

Duchess (vaguely) 'Well, I suppose it's if one's got worries.'

J.P.-H. 'Have you got worries, Duchess?'

Duchess 'Why, yes. It's all these people of ours, this army really. Well, you know Robert is going to live in Nice with his wife, and Alan is taking over at the Mill? Well, Alan's kind of a jumpy type and I don't know if he can handle a gun (Robert being in the Coldstream could of course). Oh yes, we always keep a gun down on the Mill, the Dook insists on it. We-ell, then I just hear that the under-chauffeur is going to marry one of the gurrls in the Lingerie.'

J.P.-H. 'Doesn't that sort of knit things up? Alan's marrying one of the maids, too, isn't he?'

Duchess 'Well, it does and it doesn't. Because today I hear that Sid-ney, the coloured boy y'know, who is taking Reginald's[*] place as the Dook's valet when *Reginald* goes, has gotten himself engaged to a white girl. I've just had to tell him that it's going to make it *very* awkward when we get to the States, it's different over hea-yah, but they-ah I can't arrive with a coloured valet married to a white girl. How can I?'

J.P.-H. 'I see it's complicated.'

Duchess 'It *is* complicated. And then my ex-husband died yesterday.'[†]

J.P.-H. '?!? Mr Simpson?'

Duchess (with a certain decisiveness) 'Er-nest Simpson. He'd had a throat operation.'

J.P.-H. 'Cancer?'

Duchess 'Yes.' (Looking suddenly at J.P.-H.) 'Naowh Jaymes what would *yew* do? The press'll be ringing all day. Should I say it's just a personal matter?'

J.P.-H. 'That would seem to me to be correct, Duchess. It *is* a personal matter.'

Duchess 'And would *yew* send flowers or a cable? That'd get out everywhere.'

J.P.-H. 'I should write a nice private note to the widow and leave it at that.'

Duchess 'That's what the Dook thinks. I think I'll do just that.'

J.P.-H. 'Did you ever see the wife, Duchess?'

Duchess 'Why, no. I saw *him* sometimes. He helped me with certain parts of my book.[‡] I wanted him to bring her to see me, but somehow he never would.'

J.P.-H. 'In one way, Duchess; this clears things up.'

---

[*] Reginald Willcock (1934–2000), the Duke's valet 1957–59. In 1960 he joined the Queen Mother's Household, in which he served alongside his friend, William Tallon (1935–2007), as page, until his death in August 2000, a week after the Queen Mother's 100th birthday.

[†] Ernest Simpson (1895–1958), to whom the Duchess was married between 1928 and 1936, died of throat cancer in London on 30 November 1958.

[‡] There was some correspondence between Ernest Simpson and the Duchess about her book. He disapproved of her attempt to justify her position, stating that he had been accused of every possible thing, but that the truth lay at the bottom of a well, and so far as he was concerned, anyone who wished to dig for it was welcome to do so.

Duchess 'It does, in one way.'

J.P.-H. 'The objection in 1936, as I have always understood it, was to two divorces.'

Duchess (purring reminiscently and sinking back into the mink) '"Two husbands living", that's what Queen Mary always said. "Two husbands living". Do yew think' (with a laugh) 'that we can all become Catholics and get married again?'

J.P.-H. 'Why not, Duchess?'

[END OF SCENE]

(and *verbatim*)

ACKNOWLEDGEMENTS

I am grateful to Michael Mallon for making the Pope-Hennessy interviews available to me, for his support and encouragement over a period of years (and therefore his patience), and for his meticulous checking of the text.

For permission to quote, I am grateful to Her Majesty The Queen for the letters of Sir Owen Morshead, Librarian at Windsor; HRH The Duke of Gloucester for an extract from a letter from his mother, HRH Princess Alice, Duchess of Gloucester; Mrs Lavinia Hankinson and the Hon Mrs Caroline Erskine for the letters of their father, Rt Hon Sir Alan Lascelles; Mr Ian Liddell-Granger for extracts from the letters of his great-grandmother, HRH Princess Alice, Countess of Athlone; the Lord Egremont for a letter from his great-aunt, Miss Margaret Wyndham; Juliet Nicolson for extacts from the letters and diaries of Hon Sir Harold Nicolson; and Mrs Joan Wheeler-Bennett for an extract from a letter of Sir John Wheeler-Bennett. Extracts from the letters of HRH The Princess Royal are the copyright of her grandson, the Earl of Harewood.

The staff at the Getty Institute in California were unfailingly helpful when I visited in 2008.

I am grateful to the late Lady John Cholmondeley for her perceptive insights into the life and work of James Pope-Hennessy, to whom she was a kind and generous friend for many years. I am also indebted to the late Kenneth Rose, Lady Antonia Fraser, Princess Josephine Loewenstein, the Hon Mrs Andrew Monson, Charlotte Mosley, Baroness Maria Teresa Ricasoli Firidolfi, Claudia Renton, Robert Golden and Lady Angela Oswald.

Richard Jay Hutto and Thibault de Bray helped track elusive images and Joanna Ling at Sotheby's kindly gave permission for the reproduction of the photograph of James Pope-Hennessy by the late Sir Cecil Beaton. Elizabeth Vickers reproduced many of the photographs in the book.

In respect of other material Ian Shapiro was as ever kind.

Marlene Eilers Koenig helped with the complicated titles of German and Russian Royalty, for which I am very grateful.

Finally I salute the meticulous care and support of Tom Perrin and Louise Naudé at Zuleika in bringing this book to publication.

Hugo Vickers
December 2017

SOURCE NOTES

1   *Dictionary of National Biography, 1971-80,* p. 679.
2   Sir John Pope-Hennessy, *Learning to Look* (Heinemann, 1991), pp. 81-2.
3   Sir John Pope-Hennessy, *Learning to Look* (Heinemann, 1991), pp. 82-3.
4   Sir Owen Morshead to James Pope-Hennessy, Windsor Castle, 13 June 1955 [Getty].
5   James Pope-Hennessy to Sir Owen Morshead, draft letter, 14 June 1955 [Getty].
6   Sir John Pope-Hennessy, *Learning to Look* (Heinemann, 1991), p. 83.
7   *The Times,* 8 July 1955.
8   Sir John Wheeler-Bennett to Hon Sir Harold Nicolson, 29 July 1955 [Getty].
9   Hon Sir Harold Nicolson to James Pope-Hennessy, 2 August 1955 [Getty].
10 Sir Alan Lascelles to James Pope-Hennessy, 1 August 1960 [Getty].
11 HRH The Princess Royal to Sir Alan Lascelles, 23 March 1959 [Getty].
12 James Pope-Hennessy to John Pope-Hennessy, 10 August [1949] [Getty].
13 Sir John Pope-Hennessy, *Learning to Look* (Heinemann, 1991), pp. 148-9.
14 HRH The Princess Royal to James Pope-Hennessy, 22 April 1957 [Getty].
15 James Pope-Hennessy note of conversation with Sir Alan Lascelles, Beefsteak Club, 25 July 1957 [Getty].
16 Sir Alan Lascelles to James Pope-Hennessy, Venice, 5 October 1958 [Getty].
17 Sir Alan Lascelles to James Pope-Hennessy, Venice, 5 October 1958 [Getty].
18 James Pope-Hennessy to John Pope-Hennessy, Hagnau, 24 April 1958 [Getty].
19 James Pope-Hennessy to John Pope-Hennessy, Hagnau, Whit Saturday – [24 May] 1958 [Getty].
20 James Pope-Hennessy to John Pope-Hennessy, Hagnau, 27 May 1958 [Getty].
21 James Pope-Hennessy to John Pope-Hennessy, Hagnau, Whitsunday – 24 April 1958 [Getty].
22 James Pope-Hennessy to John Pope-Hennessy, Hagnau, 8 August 1958 [Getty].

23   Hon Lady Lascelles to James Pope-Hennessy, 26 January 1959 [Getty].
24   James Pope-Hennessy to John Pope-Hennessy, Venice, 4 January [1959] [Getty].
25   James Pope-Hennessy to John Pope-Hennessy, 21 January 1959 [Getty].
26   Sir Alan Lascelles to Sir Owen Morshead, 12 September 1958 [Getty].
27   HRH The Duke of Windsor to James Pope-Hennessy, Waldorf Towers, New York, 1 May 1959 [Getty].
28   James Pope-Hennessy to John Pope-Hennessy, 16 August 1959 [Getty].
29   Sir Alan Lascelles to Sir Michael Adeane, as from Kensington Palace, W8, 23 March 1959 [Getty].
30   *Queen Mary*, p. 15.
31   *The Sunday Times*, 14 June 1959.
32   *The Sunday Times*, 14 June 1959.
33   *The Sunday Times*, 14 June 1959.
34   *The Times*, 26 January 1974.
35   *The Times*, 26 January 1974.
36   Nigel Nicolson (ed), *Harold Nicolson – Diaries and Letters 1945-62* (Collins, 1968), pp. 349-50.
37   Hon Sir Harold Nicolson to James Pope-Hennessy, Sissinghurst, 2 June 1958, quoted in *A Lonely Business*, p. xiii.
38   *Dictionary of National Biography 1971-80*, p. 679.
39   Sir Shane Leslie to *Sunday Times*, October 1959.
40   *Queen Mary*, p. 468.
41   Nancy Bradburne to *Sunday Times*, October 1959.
42   *Sunday Telegraph*, January 1961.
43   *The Times Literary Supplement*, 19 June 1981.
44   James Pope-Hennessy, foreword to the unpublished royal interviews [Getty].
45   Carlos Ruiz Zafón, *The Shadow of the Wind* (Weidenfeld & Nicolson, 2004), p. 5.
46   *Queen Mary*, p. 38.
47   *Queen Mary*, p. 77n.
48   *Queen Mary*, p. 23.
49   *Queen Mary*, p. 23.
50   *Queen Mary*, pp. 56-7.
51   *Queen Mary*, p. 100.
52   *Queen Mary*, p. 239.

53   *Queen Mary*, p. 104.

54   *Queen Mary*, p. 74.

55   *Queen Mary*, p. 186.

56   C. Kinloch Cooke, *A Memoir of Her Royal Highness Princess Mary Adelaide, Duchess of Teck* (John Murray, 1900), volume I, p. vii.

57   C. Kinloch Cooke, *A Memoir of Her Royal Highness Princess Mary Adelaide, Duchess of Teck* (John Murray, 1900), volume II, p. 316.

58   *Queen Mary*, p. 79.

59   *Queen Mary*, p. 110.

60   *Queen Mary*, p. 160.

61   *Queen Mary*, p. 217.

62   *Queen Mary*, p. 338.

63   *Queen Mary*, p. 65.

64   *Queen Mary*, p. 205.

65   *Queen Mary*, p. 220.

66   *Queen Mary*, p. 102.

67   *Queen Mary*, p. 189.

68   *Queen Mary*, p. 188.

69   *Queen Mary*, p. 188.

70   *Queen Mary*, p. 190.

71   *Queen Mary*, p. 194.

72   *Queen Mary*, p. 242.

73   *Queen Mary*, p. 339.

74   *The Times*, 5 July 1950.

75   *Queen Mary*, pp. 193; 196; & 203.

76   *Queen Mary*, p. 196.

77   *Queen Mary*, p. 400.

78   *Queen Mary*, p. 612.

79   *Queen Mary*, p. 238.

80   *Queen Mary*, p. 239.

81   *Queen Mary*, p. 310.

82   *Queen Mary*, pp. 391; & 392.

83   *Queen Mary*, p. 513.

84   *Queen Mary*, pp. 517; 537; & 180.

85   HRH Princess Alice, Countess of Athlone to Lady Cynthia Colville, 19 August 1955 [Getty].

86   Sarah Bradford, *George VI* (Weidenfeld & Nicolson, 1989), p. 460.

87 Maurice Michael, *Haakon, King of Norway* (George Allen & Unwin, 1958), pp. 191-2.

88 James Pope-Hennessy to John Pope-Hennessy, Sweden, 15 January 1956 [Getty].

89 James Pope-Hennessy to John Pope-Hennessy, Sweden, 16 January 1956 [Getty].

90 Andrew Devonshire, *Accidents of Fortune* (Michael Russell, 2004), p. 19.

91 John Pearson, *Stags and Serpents* (Macmillan, 1983), p. 188.

92 John Pearson, *Stags and Serpents* (Macmillan, 1983), p. 191.

93 Mark Girouard, *Hardwick Hall* (National Trust guidebook, 2002 revised edition), p. 46.

94 HRH The Princess Royal to James Pope-Hennessy, 22 April 1957 [Getty].

95 Earl of Pembroke to James Pope-Hennessy, 6 April 1956 [Getty].

96 Lady Estella Hope to James Pope-Hennessy, 12 July 1956 [Getty].

97 C. Kinloch Cooke, *A Memoir of HRH Princess Mary Adelaide, Duchess of Teck,* (John Murray, 1900), Volume II, p. 104.

98 HRH The Princess of Wied to James Pope-Hennessy, 17 June 1956 [Getty].

99 HRH Princess Alice, Countess of Athlone, *For my Grandchildren* (Evans Bros, 1966), p. 96.

100 James Pope-Hennessy to John Pope-Hennessy, Hagnau 24 April [19588] [Getty].

101 HRH Princess Alice, Countess of Athlone to James Pope-Hennessy, 1 May 1957 [Getty].

102 James Pope-Hennessy to John Pope-Hennessy, 13 August 1956. [Getty].

103 *The Times*, 2 March 1908.

104 *The Times*, 2 March 1908.

105 John Glendevon, *The Viceroy at Bay* (Collins, 1971), p. 10.

106 *The Times*, 25 March 1953.

107 Margaret Wyndham to James Pope-Hennessy, 7 November 1956 [Getty].

108 Michaela Reid, *Ask Sir James* (Hodder & Stoughton, 1987), p. 179.

109 Francis Martin, undated press cutting, 1954.

110 Sir Owen Morshead to James Pope-Hennessy, 22 May 1957 [Getty].

111 HRH The Duchess of Gloucester to James Pope-Hennessy, Barnwell Manor, 12 May 1957 [Getty].

112 Noble Frankland, *Prince Henry, Duke of Gloucester* (Weidenfled & Nicolson, 1980), p. 229.

113 James Pope-Hennessy to John Pope-Hennessy, Ladbroke Grove, 29 July

1957 [Getty].

114   Sir Alan Lascelles to James Pope-Hennessy, 11 April 1958 [Getty].

115   HIM Empress Frederick to HRH Princess Friedrich-Carl of Hesse, Windsor 8 March 1897. [Kronberg Archives]

116   The Marquess of Cambridge to James Pope-Hennessy, 9 July 1958 [Getty].

117   L.L. Laughlin, Memorandum for Mr D.M. Ladd, Federal Bureau of Investigation confidential report, Washington, 29 September 1941 (declassified).

118   Dom Odo of Württemberg, OSB, to James Pope-Hennessy, 14b Alsthausen, Krs. Saulgau, 22 May 1958 [Getty].

119   James Pope-Hennessy to John Pope-Hennessy, 27 May 1958 [Getty].

120   James Pope-Hennessy to John Pope-Hennessy, Schloss Altshausen, 12.20am, 27 May 1958 [Getty].

121   Peter Quennell (ed), *A Lonely Business* (Weidenfeld & Nicolson, 1980), p. 98.

122   David Marr, *Patrick White – A Life* (Random House, Australia, 1991), p. 249.

123   David Marr, *Patrick White – A Life* (Random House, Australia, 1991), p. 249.

124   Hon Lady Lascelles to James Pope-Hennessy, 11 May 1958 [Getty].

125   James Pope-Hennessy to John Pope-Hennessy, written at the Moulin de la Tuilerie, letter dated 28 December [in fact November] 1958 [Getty].

126   James Pope-Hennessy to John Pope-Hennessy, 26 November 1958 [Getty].

127   Sir Owen Morshead to James Pope-Hennessy, 26 January 1958 [Getty].

128   James Pope-Hennessy to John Pope-Hennessy, 26 November 1958 [Getty].

BIBLIOGRAPHY

All books consulted for this book are shown with publication details in the Source Notes. This bibliography is therefore more for recommended reading should the reader wish to find out more about the different characters who appear in the text.

Queen Mary

Obviously the first recommendation is James Pope-Hennessy, *Queen Mary* (Allen & Unwin, 1959). A work of pure genius.

King George V

There are three biographies. The most recent is:
Kenneth Rose, *King George V* (Weidenfeld & Nicolson, 1983), of which it has been said 'Not a dull word about an essentially dull monarch.' Then there are the two authorised biographies:
Harold Nicolson, *King George V – His Life & Reign* (Constable, 1952), covering the political life, &
John Gore, *King George V – A Personal Memoir* (John Murray, 1941), covering the more personal life.

The Duke of Windsor

The best biographies are:
Frances Donaldson, *Edward VIII* (Weidenfeld & Nicolson, 1974), beautifully, if unsentimentally written, &
Philip Ziegler, *King Edward VIII* (Collins, 1990), with full use of the Royal Archives.
The Duke's memoirs were: HRH The Duke of Windsor, *A King's Story* (Cassell, 1951), engagingly told, albeit ghosted.

King George VI

Sarah Bradford, *George VI* (Weidenfeld & Nicolson, 1989), with extensive research in numerous archives, & the official biography:
John W. Wheeler-Bennett, *King George VI – His Life & Reign* (Macmillan, 1958), with full use of the Royal Archives.

The Duke of Gloucester

For more on the Gloucesters:
Noble Frankland, *Prince Henry, Duke of Gloucester* (Weidenfeld & Nicolson, 1980), the authorised life, &
The Memoirs of Princess Alice, Duchess of Gloucester (Collins, 1983), very dry & highly entertaining.

Princess Mary Adelaide, Duchess of Teck

There is the official biography in two volumes:
C. Kinloch Cooke, *A Memoir of Her Royal Highness Princess Mary Adelaide, Duchess of Teck, Volumes 1 & 2* (John Murray, 1900), &
S.W. Jackman, *The People's Princess* (The Kensal Press, 1984).

Princess Alice, Countess of Athlone

HRH Princess Alice, Countess of Athlone, *For My Grandchildren* (Evans, 1966), a spirited autobiography, &
Theo Aronson, *Princess Alice, Countess of Athlone* (Cassell, 1981), a good authorised biography.

Princess Arthur of Connaught

There are two privately printed volumes:
Alexandra, *A Nurse's Story* (John & Edward Bumpus Ltd, 1955), &
Alexandra, *Egypt & Khartoum* (John & Edward Bumpus Ltd, 1956).

The Princess of Wied

A classic volume in German (hard to find):
Fürstin zu Wied, *Vom Leben Gelernt* (Ludwigsburg, 1953)

Grand Duchess Xenia of Russia

John van der Kiste & Coryne Hall, *Once a Grand Duchess* (Sutton Publishing, 2002).

Sir Alan Lascelles

There are three volumes of diaries:
Duff Hart-Davis (editor), *The End of an Era* (Hamish Hamilton, 1986)
Duff Hart-Davis (editor), *In Royal Service* (Hamish Hamilton, 1989)
Duff Hart-Davis (editor), *King's Counsellor* (Weidenfeld & Nicolson, 2002)

James Pope-Hennessy

Some of the interviews in this book appear with a biographical note and letters:
Peter Quennell (editor), *A Lonely Business – A Self-Portrait of James Pope-Hennessy* (Weidenfeld & Nicolson, 1980).

Books by the editor on this period:

Hugo Vickers, *Elizabeth The Queen Mother* (Hutchinson, 2005), &
Hugo Vickers, *Behind Closed Doors – The Tragic, Untold Story of the Duchess of Windsor* (Hutchinson, 2011).

A NOTE ON IMAGES

All images reproduced in this book are from private collections or in the public domain. There are, however, two exceptions. The photographic portrait of James Pope-Hennessy, on the picture insert, is reproduced by kind permission of the Cecil Beaton Studio Archive at Sotheby's. The photograph of Mother Marfa (page 158) is the copyright of Historic Royal Palaces.

INDEX